Private Anarchy

Private Anarchy

Impossible Community and the Outsider's Monologue in German Experimental Fiction

Paul Buchholz

NORTHWESTERN UNIVERSITY PRESS

EVANSTON, ILLINOIS

the
modern language
initiative

THIS BOOK IS MADE POSSIBLE BY A COLLABORATIVE GRANT
FROM THE ANDREW W. MELLON FOUNDATION.

Northwestern University Press
www.nupress.northwestern.edu

Printed in the United States of America

10 9 8 7 6 5 4 3 2 1

ISBN 978-0-8101-3662-5 (paper)
ISBN 978-0-8101-3663-2 (cloth)
ISBN 978-0-8101-3664-9 (e-book)

Cataloging-in-Publication Data are available from the Library of Congress.

for Adriana

CONTENTS

ACKNOWLEDGMENTS

This book about "impossible community" was made possible by a very real community, extended across many years and many miles. During the past decade of writing, I never needed to feel as alone as the fictional characters I discuss.

The encouragement and rigorous critical commentary of the German Studies faculty at Cornell helped me through the earliest stages of this project. Anette Schwarz has been indispensable mentor, from our theoretical discussions of the literary construction of kinship ties, to her tireless proofreading of my writing. Patrizia McBride has provided essential guidance in framing my project both in terms of method and historical context and has always helped give me a clearer picture of where I am going. I thank Peter Gilgen for training me in the art of argumentation and for showing me how to reconcile an energetic love of literature with a commitment to logic and a sober awareness of intellectual tradition. Diana Reese's seminar on Kafka and Kleist at Cornell in 2007 was the actual starting point for this entire undertaking, and Leslie Adelson provided core insights during and after my colloquium at the Institute for German Cultural Studies in 2009. My graduate colleagues and friends from Cornell, Johannes Wankhammer and Sam Frederick, have always been helpful with free intellectual consultations. After Cornell, the German Department of New York University provided my first temporary intellectual home after graduate school, during my postdoctoral position there in 2010 and 2011. Thanks are due to Eckart Goebel for helping me brainstorm on walks through Lower Manhattan, and to Paul Fleming for generously showing me the ropes of the profession. During those years, I benefited from feedback I received at invited lectures at Rutgers University, where Fatima Naqvi shared helpful insights into Thomas Bernhard's works, and at Indiana University, where questions and comments of Fritz Breithaupt, Benjamin Robinson, Claudia Breger, and William Rasch helped me to rethink the direction of my project.

Though it is hardly "sunny," *Private Anarchy* is very much a Californian book, and the arc of its argument was developed during my years of teaching at Scripps College in Claremont and living in Los Angeles. I thank Mark Golub for our continuing friendship, for helping me place my work in dialogue with political theory, and for cheering me on with text messages in the most stressful of times. I thank Marc Katz for his almost daily mentorship and encouragement, and David Roselli, who helped me further explore ideas in hallway banter and carpool conversations, as did Sabrina Ovan and Aaron Matz. I thank Friederike Schwerin-High and Hans Rindisbacher at Pomona College for their collegiality and mentoring in my early years on the job. The students who participated in my seminar "Critiques of Community" at Scripps in spring 2014 engaged in lively discussions of theory that underscored the stakes of defining community in the twenty-first century. Farther north, my year at the University of California-Berkeley was crucial in seeing this manuscript to its completion, and I am very grateful for the support provided by my colleagues Niklaus Largier, Karen Feldman, Tony Kaes, Deniz Göktürk, and Chenxi Tang. Their comments and questions following an invited lecture in 2015 helped me understand how and why the project could speak to a broader humanities audience. As an aside on California: I thank the staff of Stories Books and Café, particularly the poet John Tottenham, for maintaining a terrific literary space in an ever-changing corner of Los Angeles, which gave me faith that old books could have a future.

Now in Atlanta, I would like to thank my colleagues in the German Studies department at Emory. Hiram Maxim, Caroline Schaumann, Miriam Udel, and Peter Höyng have given me the warmest welcome possible in my new intellectual home (and have taught me to appreciate the finer points of Viennese life!). My first months at Emory were also my last months of writing, and I am grateful for their encouragement and advice during the final stage of preparation and submission.

The research for this book was made possible by grants and material support from several organizations and institutions. I am grateful for the financial support provided by the German Academic Exchange Service (DAAD), the Cornell University Graduate School, and the College of Arts and Science at New York University. Special thanks are due to the Office of the Dean of Faculty at Scripps College for their years of generous research support. Funds from the Division of Arts and Sciences at UC Berkeley and Emory College of Arts & Sciences made it possible to complete the manuscript, and I am very grateful for their support. I had the privilege to conduct research at the Thomas Bernhard Archive while it was located in a charming lakeside villa in Gmunden, Austria, and I thank the archivist, Bernhard Judex, and director, Martin Huber, for their indispensable assistance there. Tremendous thanks to Dr. Peter Fabjan, Thomas Bernhard's half brother and his literary executor, for his hospitality during my stay in Gmunden and for granting quotation permission for the unpublished drafts of *Leichtlebig.* The German Department at the University of Michigan generously hosted me both as a Visiting Research Student in 2009–10, and again as a Visiting Scholar in 2015, and I am grateful to the faculty and staff there for helping me access the incredible resources of the Hatcher Library. Many thanks to Henry Carrigan, Trevor Perri, Maggie Grossman, and J. D. Wilson at

Northwestern University Press for their hard work and enthusiastic support. I also would like to thank the anonymous reviewers, whose rigorous feedback was key to my final revisions. I am very grateful to Tim Roberts, of the Modern Language Initiative, and freelance copy editor Susan Murray for their essential work in the final stages of manuscript preparation.

These pages are imprinted with the voices of the interlocutors and critical readers who engaged with drafts of the manuscript and helped me to develop its core theoretical claims. Adriana Chira provided essential guidance through the history and debates of social theory and helped to lay the foundations for the book's argument. Jack Davis provided essential input on my analysis of Bernhard and Kafka. His nearly continuous feedback was crucial to the fourth chapter, introduction, and to the book as a whole, as were his world-class jokes and song recommendations. I am very grateful to Ari Linden for his meticulous comments on the first chapter, and to Carl Gelderloos for indispensable advice for revising the second chapter. Thanks also to Peter Staudenmeier for our conversation about Landauer in Kreuzberg, which finally convinced me that I could try to connect these authors in the way I do.

Without my stellar undergraduate professors at the University of Wisconsin, this book would not exist, nor would I be a German professor. My mentor at Madison, Gerhard Richter, first taught me the art of close reading. Speaking of Wisconsin, I thank my longtime friends Clay Kolbinger, Joe Bolstad, Ethan Schowalter-Hay, and Eugene Wasserman for transcontinental conversations about books, music, and art that helped shed light on the strange and sobering realities of the creative process.

From the earliest days of my studies, my loving parents in Milwaukee encouraged and supported my choice to study literature and taught me to embrace learning for its own sake. I still have the copy of Kafka's *Trial* that my mother gave me as a present when I was sixteen, before I knew the author's name—that sure sealed my fate! I still have the copy of *Flatland* that my father gave me at age seven, which opened the door to the strange universes of reading. My brother John, from the beginning, taught me how to live with a sense of humor. I thank my parents-in-law in Baia Mare for their endless warmth, and for the shared language that emerged through our encounters, without a stable system of signification to start from.

For teaching me to swim upstream, for ruthless criticism, and for our animated conversations every morning over oats and coffee, I thank Adriana Chira.

Private Anarchy

Introduction

The problem of alienation, so central to theories and critiques of modern society, often becomes legible in literature in the form of monologue. Modern prose monologue, as an embedded form, can highlight a lack of communication and community, an imprisonment within the self, or sequestration within some segment of a social hierarchy. While it is technically true, as Mieke Bal writes, that "the content of a monologue can . . . be practically anything," authors of the nineteenth and twentieth centuries have frequently utilized this embedded form as a showcase for extreme and unwanted solitude.[1] Taking a general inventory of modern Western literature in 1959, literary scholar Victor Erlich wrote that "in narrative fiction of the last hundred years or so monologue, whether of the written or of the oral variety, has often served as a verbal epitome of loneliness and isolation."[2] According to Erlich, this model of monologue as the nadir of alienation was foreign to the "formative period of the European novel," when "written monologue-forms had pointed up the distinctiveness of the 'self'" and emphasized "the personal, the private, the idiosyncratic."[3] In the nineteenth century, however, monologue frequently fails to initiate that productive "self-inspection" that Shaftesbury (writing in 1710) saw as the purpose of the writer's "home-dialect" of soliloquy.[4] Monologue becomes, Erlich suggests, a genre of negative speech that indicates absence rather than inner abundance: it is language without a listener, without a respondent, without a set social function, spoken for nobody. Already in the late eighteenth century, as Jürgen Wertheimer points out, literary monologue became associated with a "withdrawal from social relations into the vacuum of absolute dialogue," that is to say, it was already a *dialogue with nobody*.[5] Even if the Enlightenment monologuist Jean-Jacques Rousseau could praise the pure enjoyment of solitary selfhood, he could do so only after establishing a chain of painful absences, confirming that he had "no brother, neighbor, or friend, and no company but my own."[6] In the wake of the Enlightenment, prose fiction increasingly tends to stage and record the monologue of an outsider, caught in a "*preposterous* social situation," who expects and demands a degree of social recognition that is impossible to attain, and so speaks to nobody, or talks at a stranger who is not listening.[7] Dina Al-Kassim has more recently argued that the *rant* is a privileged genre for the articulation of personhood in modernist literature: "The rant materialized a speaking subject whose resistant speech emerges, or more aptly, irrupts to contest the public space that abjects it."[8] What Erlich calls the preposterous monologue, and what Al-Kassim calls the rant, is the anguished or angry verbalization of failed socialization.

A recurrent theme of modern prose monologue is, then, the paradox of the "lonely crowd" of modern society, where mass social integration coincides with abjection and alienation.[9] The idea of the "lonely crowd" pinpoints the familiar irony of life in mass society: the more we are connected through our institutions and infrastructures, the more alone we feel. One could say that the emergence of the social *mass* corresponds to the opening of a *vacuum* between its constituents; density and vacuity go hand in hand. This commonly felt paradox shaped the development of classical social theory, and it survives today in critiques of Internet culture that point out that the more densely interconnected we are, the less we really know one another. The impression of a lonely crowd is not restricted to leftist critiques of capitalism or to conservative dismissals of socialism's mass collectivity. Rather, the diagnosis of universal anonymity is a modern, transnational tradition that has accompanied other familiar grand narratives of industrialization, secularization, rationalization, disenchantment, and mechanization.

No national literary tradition has monopolized alienated monologue, but the Russian novelist Fyodor Dostoevsky's figure of the Underground Man helped to legitimate and popularize this subgenre. Having completely withdrawn from human community, the Underground Man rants against any and all ideas and values that underwrite modern visions of human unity in the wake of the Western Enlightenment: civilization, reason, idealism, even consciousness itself. Faced with the leveling forces of secular mass society, Dostoevsky's misanthropic Underground Man embraces and amplifies his own feelings of isolation and relentlessly "projects" his voice into a "total vacuum."[10] He takes a bad situation and deliberately (even artfully!) makes it worse. As such, the Underground Man appears as the proper subject of modernity's "lonely crowd," obsessed with multitudes of other people yet utterly estranged from them. The Underground Man's rant, which appeared in print in the 1864 novel *Notes from Underground*, coincided with the general shift in the function of soliloquy in European and American literature described by Victor Erlich. As Erlich has shown, the history of prose monologue is also a history of literature as a medium of social thought. Literature becomes a privileged site for the verbalization of alienation. This shift encourages the cultivation of a subgenre in which alien or "underground" voices can be stylized, analyzed, celebrated, or critiqued.[11] For simplicity's sake, my shorthand term for this emergent subgenre will be *the outsider's monologue*. The outsider's monologue is the literary form that tackles the modern paradox of the lonely crowd, as it tends to verbalize a collective and unwanted solitude. From Dostoevsky's *Notes* to Ralph Ellison's *Invisible Man*, the alienation intrinsic to such fictional speech is, if not universal, then at least definitely collective.[12] With the help of the literary text, a single instance of alienation (one character's monologue) can be grasped as a shared problem. The "I" in such speech is usually implicitly also a "we," a negative collectivity bound together by a shared alienation. Solitude is never entirely solitary. This is what the Marxist philosopher of language Valentin Volosinov meant when he wrote that "solitary self-experience" of European intellectuals is also a "we-experience."[13] The philosopher Martin Heidegger, writing in an entirely different theoretical framework, also noted that being alone is simply another way of being together.[14] The outsider's monologue, at least since its canonization in nineteenth-century literature by way of the Underground Man, has provided readers with a concrete way of imagining the reality of such philosophical insights. The outsider's monologue makes it possible to open the page of a private discourse and declare, "That's us!"

The eccentric tradition that I will examine in this book, however, takes the idea of collective solitude to an even further extreme than the "outsider" literature outlined above. The twentieth century saw the emergence of a series of experimental German-language writers who amplify alienation to other unexpected and productive ends. These writers, whom I have gathered under the heading of *Private Anarchy*, do not only employ the outsider's monologue as a way of symptomatizing some version of modern alienation. They also identify monologue as *the* medium for the imagination and creation of new community beyond the practical options available in current, concrete reality. Their literary experiments, then, attempt to redeem the frightening prospect of collective alienation, turning it into a starting point for an affectionate and anarchic form of togetherness. This group of experimental writers is scattered across the long twentieth century, so even my chronological study in this book will require some significant jumps forward in time, across major cultural periods. Beginning with the anarchist and philosopher Gustav Landauer (1870–1919), I will then study the early modernist prose of Franz Kafka (1883–1924), before turning to two self-stylized outsiders of the mid- to late postwar era, the Austrian Thomas Bernhard (1931–1989) and the East German émigré Wolfgang Hilbig (1941–2007). What unites these authors—despite considerable distances between their historical moments and social milieus—is a strong sense of alienation pervading their prose, which is bound up with a shared interest in the three interrelated discourses of pessimism, nihilism, and anarchism. These discourses become a resource for rethinking accepted notions of community in modernity.

Community (in German, *Gemeinschaft*), as conventionally defined around the turn of the twentieth century, is a form of coexistence grounded in blood ties, spatial and geographical proximity, and shared, unchanging values. The experimental authors under consideration in *Private Anarchy* polemicize against this "grounded" vision of community, playing instead with the idea that the *voiding* of such common ground—the onset of alienation—is actually a precondition for a form of community. Each author posits a set of antisocial and anticommunicative characters, for whom any conventional form of coexistence is strictly impossible: characters who talk only to themselves, who live in their own hallucinations, and who either openly or implicitly abhor the company of anyone. In short, they posit characters who not only *inhabit* but also *exceed* the alienated condition of modern anonymous society. These fictional characters are, in both the literal and slang sense of the phrase, "insanely alone": they go beyond any "normal" notion of solitude and discover its opposite. Radically antisocial, these outsiders produce an excessive language that first epitomizes absolute solitude, but then reimagines community in stringently anarchic terms. Their ways of *talking to nobody* actually prefigure an alternative vision of human relationships, in which the boundaries of individual selves are dynamic and unstable ("in-process," as Julia Kristeva would say).[15] Each author provides an image of what the historian Nayan Shah has recently termed "stranger intimacy."[16]

Today, from our vantage point in the twenty-first century, the ideas of anarchic and antisocial community developed by these experimental authors might look less strange than they would have when first conjured by Landauer, Kafka, Bernhard, or Hilbig. This is not only because of the proliferation of virtual communities online that constantly connect us when nobody is around. It is also an outcome of contemporary literary and critical theory: since the 1980s, poststructuralist thinkers have produced a range of theories of "negative community," notions of togetherness that are based not on shared identity or value systems but on a *lack* thereof.[17] Examples include Jean-Luc Nancy's "inoperative community," Giorgio Agamben's "coming community," and Roberto Esposito's "community of those who do not have community."[18] Each of these thinkers conceives of community as a togetherness that is impossible to fix or finalize and for this very reason becomes desirable and necessary. Jean-Luc Nancy's idea of literary community, or "literary communism," provides a particularly useful point of comparison with the authors examined in *Private Anarchy*. For Nancy, literature is a community of solitudes that distills and clarifies the truth of community as a perpetual state of lack and incompletion. Literary voices are singular and solitary, but they can only be singular and solitary by emerging alongside (or "compearing" with) other singular and solitary voices. Literature offers an antimythological, anti-essentialist, and therefore antifascist model of community because it mounts an "infinite resistance to everything that would bring it to completion."[19] For Nancy, as for the other contemporary critical theorists, community is a necessary impossibility, an ever-present horizon that is never reached. The postmodern idea of "negative community" can provide a helpful, descriptive language that sheds light on the desires and ideas that motivate the experimental fiction of Landauer, Kafka, Bernhard, and Hilbig. However, instead of entirely folding the history of experimental literature into this paradigm of postmodern philosophy, in *Private Anarchy* I will show that these literary authors developed their own distinct ideas of negative community prior to, or apart from, the discourses of poststructuralism. Responding to a distinct set of literary, philosophical, and political traditions linked to the idea of "nihilism," these authors make the idea of solitary community manifest on the level of narrative form, through creative constructions of monologue. As such, wherever possible, I will work to develop a descriptive vocabulary that emerges out of the texts being studied (by Landauer, Kafka, Bernhard, and Hilbig), as well as out of the texts that influenced them (such as the writings of Arthur Schopenhauer and Fyodor Dostoevsky).

Such is the case with the title phrase of this book, *private anarchy*, which captures the surprising juxtaposition of solitude and spontaneous sociality that characterizes the experimental works in question. I derive this phrase from Gustav Landauer's playful 1903 coinage of the term "weltabgewandter Anarchismus," which I will translate as "unworldly anarchism" and literally means "anarchism turned away from the world."[20] Landauer openly acknowledged the absurdity of this celebratory term, pairing it with the equally baffling phrase "menschenfeindlicher Sozialismus" (misanthropic socialism), which also presents a contradiction in terms.[21] Taken together, these two terms capture an unorthodox attitude toward community, which runs counter to practical politics: Landauer's unworldly anarchism consists precisely in the cultivation of anarchy in the isolated mind, which he believes will allow us to rediscover hidden conditions of community in ourselves. The isolated hermit, speaking only to himself, is preparing the conditions for community. Absurd as Landauer (deliberately) makes this idea sound, he is not alone in entertaining this thought. A similar pattern repeats itself in all the experimental prose works under study in *Private Anarchy*. In each case, an instance of extreme alienation from others, which has already been incurred by the structure of "anonymous society," is intensified until it turns into its opposite.[22] The bottom falls out of solitude, opening a portal into a new world. Within the experimental literature of private anarchy, the outsider's monologue is no longer simply a symptom of shared alienation but a glimpse of otherworldly community.

Here, an explanation of my use of the words "private" and "anarchy" is in order. By *private*, I mean the condition of isolation that emerges through soliloquy, where the speaker's voice remains unheard and unacknowledged by others. As private language, monologue points both to the emancipatory and oppressive dimensions of modern privacy. The private is positive, insofar as it carves out an autonomous realm separated from the coercions of social life, enabling a kind of freedom away from others. At the same time, when the private dominates as a supreme value, it can constrain and oppress, insofar as it enforces an ideology of self-interest that forecloses possibilities of sharing and creative cooperation, while minimizing possibilities of spontaneous encounter. By *anarchy*, I mean the emergence of an alternative reality of spontaneous and dynamic relations, which is first imagined within the bounds of monologue as private discourse, and which finally explodes these boundaries. Afterimages of politics are inevitable whenever we write either of these words. The locution "private" connotes a capitalist model of property and a bourgeois form of domestic containment. Anarchy consistently connotes revolt, resistance, rebellion, creative destruction, and a vacuum of authority that is either radically liberating (à la the pacifist anarchist Pyotr Kropotkin), or nightmarishly violent (à la Thomas Hobbes's state of nature, or the wrath of Fyodor Dostoevsky's "possessed" nihilists). Private anarchy can be thought of as an imagined third way, carved out through the creative possibilities of fiction, which cannot be reduced to a bourgeois notion of privacy or to an activist conception of alliance and mobilization.

Private anarchy, then, should be understood as a fictional moment of de-alienation that arises within a paradigm of privacy and subverts it. The private anarchy presented in the works of Landauer, Kafka, Bernhard, and Hilbig is a narrative explosion that reroutes a story about solitude in a drastic and unexpected new direction.[23] In the wake of this explosion, the boundaries between different subject-positions are dissolved and fluidly renegotiated: the speaking "I" might become indistinguishable from the authorial "I" of a disembodied narrator, and this "I" might also merge into the identities of characters who were initially distant and distinct from the speaker. What results is a stream of language in which fluid relations prevail and identity is never fixed, and that forms the basis for imagining a new community of strangers. Formally speaking, this explosion of anarchy can be described as a drastic form of *metalepsis*, a moment where the discursive layers of a narrative text are transgressed in a way that would normally be considered impossible. The reader can no longer make a methodical distinction between the framing narrative discourse of the text and the subjective raving of a formerly alienated speaker. A blending occurs that is arguably more destabilizing than cases of free indirect discourse, where the voices of narrator and narrated character are blended into a single voice. In the fiction of private anarchy, such "blending" is a decisive and irreversible plot-event with irreversible consequences for all characters: alienation is overcome through an experience of depersonalization that makes way for an anarchic model of community. The determining voice (the narrator's) becomes inseparable from the determined voice (the characters'); the frame vanishes into the story that it frames, and the outermost frame separating fiction and reality is called into question. These are the moments at which the text becomes unreadable from the vantage point of narrative coherence, but they are also the moments when the social and political themes of the work become suddenly coherent: the text overturns and transforms the alienation that defines a given sociopolitical world and that is initially taken for granted as the natural setting of each narrative (the German empire for Landauer, Prague around 1900 for Kafka, postwar Upper Austria for Bernhard, the industrial margins of the GDR for Hilbig). The counterimage of community, which is offered up by these anarchic experimental works, is the negation of this or that given, historical world. The private anarchy of these texts prefigures another possible world, which would be otherwise impossible for the characters to realize. To summarize: the literature of private anarchy embraces what would otherwise be dismissed as impossible, preserving the promise that prose fiction can de-narrate our world and imagine another. An act of verbal nihilism, such as an incessantly negative outsider's monologue, which might otherwise evoke despair and depression, is actually the starting point for a productive imaginative process that leads, in Landauer's words, "through separation to community."[24]

My description above should not sound too celebratory. The subversions of private anarchy have their ethical and political limits. As the authors studied in *Private Anarchy* experiment with this arc from solitude to solidarity, gender remains an omnipresent and unsolved problem. The monologue that initiates the verbal voiding of the world is, from Landauer and Kafka to Bernhard and Hilbig, always delivered by a male speaker. Initially, the masculine voice performs a familiar "heroic" posture of authority and absolute self-reliance; such a posture was properly canonized in German literature, for instance, by Goethe's *Sturm und Drang* hymn "Prometheus," in which the rebellious titan claims to invent humanity out of himself with his own voice.[25] In the works considered in *Private Anarchy*, such masculine voice can become deformed in surprising and productive ways. By verbally voiding the world, the outsider replicates masculine authority and autonomy to such an extreme that they collapse in on themselves. Particularly in the texts by Kafka, Bernhard, and Hilbig, there no longer is any heroic, stable self behind the monologue, which instead conjures an anarchic "we," bound together by kinships and affinities improvised in the play of language. However, this anarchic and experimental language of the "we" is not infinitely subversive, because it remains the domain of an exclusively masculine voice, which becomes homosocial rather than heroically individual. The masculine monologue introjects aspects of feminine social and sexual reproduction, for instance by playing the role of community mediator, and by maternally "birthing" new selves and communities. Moreover, these introjections of the feminine and the maternal turn out, in practice, to be a way for experimental fiction to "do without" feminine subjects. They offer anarchic countervisions of male homosociality but do so by perpetuating an enduring myth of European literary culture: namely, that it is the male thinker (à la the masculine tortured genius) who experiences alienation most acutely and voices it most astutely. Within the long and enduring European traditions of intellectual masculinity, these experimental texts represent an extreme case of how masculinity can work against masculinity and produce radically different visions of how the world could be, without, however, ceasing to privilege masculinity. The outsider's act of verbal voiding—for all its radical disruptions and departures from conventional ideas of community—remains embedded within a literary tradition committed to the construction and performance of masculine voice.

Monologue and Metalepsis as Devices of Isolation and Community

Private Anarchy is, then, a story of creative recycling. Because this fiction is so clearly embedded in longer literary traditions, it is possible to define it formally, in terms of how it recycles, combines, and transforms preexisting literary devices. Two complementary narrative devices define all the works studied in this book: *monologue* and *metalepsis*. Monologue, in each work, locates its speaker at the "epitome of loneliness and isolation," in an utterly alienated world devoid of meaningful relations.[26] The disruptive device of metalepsis—known commonly as the "breaking of the fourth wall"—represents the transgression of isolation, performing a linguistic maneuver that reframes emptiness and alienation and transforms them into the basis for togetherness. Monologue conjures a void; metalepsis *steps out* into this void, transfiguring and transporting the speaker into another world. Monologue is isolation; metalepsis is relation. In what follows, I will outline the function these devices, which are common to all the texts studied in this book.

Monologue is a special subgenre within prose fiction in part because of its tendency to produce absence. When Victor Erlich calls the modern monologue of alienation "preposterous," he means it is speech that is *absurdly dislocated*, situated in an inappropriate place where it does not function and should not be. The preposterous monologue is not characterized simply by the length of an utterance but by orienting gestures that establish an utterly negative relation to the social and discursive situation of its delivery. Such speech is not delivered "on" an appropriate occasion but rather effaces its occasion of delivery: "the point of departure is soon forgotten."[27] Within prose fiction, such alienated monologue can have the effect of rendering its surrounding narrative frame a "mere contrivance," eclipsing the narrator's work of describing and orchestrating the scene of delivery.[28] In the most preposterous cases of the outsider's monologue, the speaker effects a drastic digression that makes the established discursive context appear to be an inessential fiction. The fictional world appears to melt away upon the utterance of one speaker's words. Such preposterous speech involves a negative pointing-gesture, or deixis, that stipulates the absence of the speaker from a common context. This is what distinguishes the most extreme forms of monologue from dialogue, which according to Jan Mukařovský must reference the "actual situation in which the discourse takes place," for instance through "spatial and temporal deixis represented by demonstrative pronouns."[29] Dialogue contains markers acknowledging coexistence. Preposterous monologue, as described by Erlich, employs antideixis in order to *deny* coexistence, demonstrating that the speaker does not inhabit the same space as any potential listener or reader. It says, in effect: "I am not here," for instance by referring to things that no other character can perceive or aggressively denying what other characters do perceive. Through gestures of self-absenting, the outsider's monologue voids the surrounding social world and tends "to reduce the 'other' to the status of a mere shadow."[30] The speaker turns the other characters presented in the narrative into inactive and insubstantial projections. This can be achieved, for instance, through a disruption of the conventional use of pronouns. Whereas dialogue, according to Mukařovský, necessitates a clear semantic opposition of the personal pronouns "I" and "you," the preposterous monologue levels the distinction between these different positions and thus between other-directed and self-addressed speech.[31]

As Erlich shows, a paradigmatic example of this sort of shadow-conjuring is found in Fyodor Dostoevsky's *Notes from Underground*. Here, the pseudo-oral transcribed monologue of a misanthrope continually makes "futile use of 'you,'" sparring with absent characters who are in no position to respond to his polemics and rejoinders; the Underground monologue is full of inappropriate pronouns. This misuse of pronouns in a monologue "underscores the total vacuum into which the monologue of the 'underground man' projects itself."[32] Here, Erlich's explanation borrows from the vocabulary of stagecraft and public speaking. Vocal projection is the amplification of the human voice for the sake of an audience, which actors practice in order to make their lines "audible and understandable" within a particular space (and as such, it was particularly important prior to the invention of electric amplification).[33] The transcribed monologue of the Underground Man accomplishes the inverse of such professional voice projection: it clarifies its own *unlistenability*. Erlich imports the vocabulary of the theater, where there is a clear context of enunciation, in order to describe a kind of enunciation that nullifies context. This operation is, of course, not sonic but semantic. The Underground monologue projects a vacuum onto the surrounding world by referring to social relations that *could* exist but do not, addressing listeners who might hear but do not, conjuring corporeal presences that might fill the surrounding space but do not. Monologue, in this case, can be defined formally as a kind of *verbal nihilism* that actively eclipses and erases context. "Verbal nihilism," then, will be my consistent term for the type of negative monologue studied throughout this book.

Verbal nihilism is, in the fiction of private anarchy, only the first step in a longer creative process. The voiding performed by the outsider's monologue *matters* because of what it ultimately triggers: the collapse of discursive hierarchies and the emergence of a strange new form of community. The formal device by which this is accomplished has been known, since Gérard Genette, as "metalepsis," which in turn is an instance of what Brian Richardson calls "unnatural narrative."[34] Broadly defined, metalepsis is a violation of a text's hierarchy of narrative levels, as when a fictional character accedes to the level of an extrafictional authorial narrator, or when an authorial narrator claims to enter the world of fictional characters. From Landauer and Kafka, to Bernhard and Hilbig, the fiction of private anarchy is unified through a common reliance on metalepsis as a transgressive and productive narrative device. Metalepsis dislocates preexisting narrative positions, throws voices into relations that should be impossible, and breaks down taken-for-granted boundaries. For Landauer, Kafka, Bernhard, and Hilbig, metalepsis enables the singular and strange instance where extreme isolation can turn into a condition of community, where a subjective sense of emptiness turns into a new common ground. Their characters and narrators are dislocated and relocated within new and unexpected relations.

In the fiction of private anarchy, metalepsis becomes a way of making relations that should have been impossible into an instrument of community. The idea that metalepsis could have this function was only faintly implicit in its initial articulations within the field of classical rhetoric, and in its introduction, nearly two thousand years later, into the method of narrative analysis. Quintilian, in his *Institutes of Oratory* from the year AD 95, explained metalepsis as a fairly marginal rhetorical device, which "is very rarely used, and is extremely liable to objection."[35] Quintilian's explanation is so dismissive that he hardly takes time to explain how it works: "For the nature of metalepsis is that it is an intermediate step, as it were, to that which is metaphorically expressed, signifying nothing in itself, but affording a passage to something."[36] This "passage to something" works through a transposition (or "smuggling") of a metaphor from one utterance into the next utterance, so as to smooth out the transition between the two. Here, for instance, would be a way of using metalepsis as a transition between utterances: "Tensions in the country boiled over. But the heat was not enough to avoid undercooked political ideas." The passage from the first to the second statement works through a repetition of related metaphors (boiling, cooking), easing the change in focus from one topic to the next. Classical metalepsis works by building on the linguistic reality conjured by an initial metaphoric statement and expanding this reality into a second statement. A form of contact is permitted between themes that would otherwise remain unrelated. This contact is attended by a slight sense of the preposterous or inappropriate, because metaphors here are treated as if they were factual circumstances (the "boiling water" of a political crisis becomes visible, usable, accessible in another situation). Rhetorical metalepsis is, then, something like a metaphor that wears out its welcome and wanders into other statements.

The modern definition of metalepsis as a disruptive narrative device involves an analogous form of "passage" or "transit" of elements across distinct areas of a text. However, whereas *rhetorical* metalepsis permits the "passage" from one utterance to another, the transit permitted by *narrative* metalepsis involves downright impossible forms of contact, communication, and relation. Gérard Genette first described metalepsis in his 1972 *Narrative Discourse* as a transgressive "form of transit" between different textual layers, which for the sake of storytelling must remain strictly separated.[37] For instance, the delusional monologue of a fictional madman ranting on the street should remain distinct from the authoritative discourse of a narrator, who first told us about that ranting character.[38] A narrator who is reporting on events in the past should not be able to wake up his character with his voice, as does the authorial narrator of Robert Walser's novel *The Robber*: "The Robber had been lying there, so to speak, innocently, as if in a bed, asleep. Wouldn't I, for my part, sooner let a child like that sleep than pour into his ear remarks like one mentioned above and give him an energetic nudge so as to call out to him in the best intellectual manner: 'Get up now, it's time'? And so then, of course, the Robber had to get up, and here he stands."[39] Metalepsis, as exemplified in Walser's audacious passage, enables impossible transit between situations separated by time and space, and textual boundaries. The authorial narrator telling the story of the Robber steps back—with his voice—into a past time (which he is creating through his narrative discourse), in order to modify the course of events. Such baffling scenarios have motivated subsequent scholars to speak of metalepsis as a kind of imaginary "time travel," or as a passage between parallel universes.[40] Narrative metalepsis is far more cognitively challenging than Quintilian's metalepsis, with its trick of relating unrelated themes. It sets up a coexistence of that which does not coexist, or a relation between unrelated speakers.

We know that metalepsis is happening because it is accompanied by the sense that it *should not* be happening. Metaleptic transit is, properly speaking, a kind of trespassing within a narrative text, which might for instance cut through the discursive fences that separate a fictional world from the authorial voice that conjures it, or jump across the unsurpassable chasm that separates the narrated past from the present moment in which a storyteller is telling a story.[41] This transgression may not always involve the enactment of a real impossibility; an authorial narrator can claim to be coexisting with a fictional character but at the same time make clear that this coexistence is primarily rhetorical, meant to underscore (for instance) the storyteller's emotional connection to the events. However, the most extreme forms of metalepsis are actually *ontological*, in that they purport to overcome (for instance) the distinction between fiction and reality, redefining what exists in the fictional world and "our" nonfictional world. As Genette shows, ontological metalepsis is by nature an absurd and unsettling device because it entails the "unacceptable and insistent hypothesis, that the extradiegetic is perhaps always diegetic, and that the narrator and his narratee—you and I—perhaps belong to some narrative."[42] This description perfectly captures both the transgressive and productive sides of metalepsis. Metalepsis is transgressive because it breaks the mimetic illusion of fictional narrative, destroying the self-sufficient world in which the events of a story play out. On the other hand, it is productive because it posits a new and surprising relationship. By setting up a bond between beings who inhabit different planes of reality, who would not otherwise coexist, metalepsis asserts an unforeseeable "we." This "we" might encompass a fictional character and an authorial narrator, as well as extrafictional readers. Here it is useful to extend the metaphors of fences and trespassing mentioned above: when I overstep a fence, I meet my neighbors and assert my unity with them, which is otherwise denied by the fence. Brian McHale used the term "metaleptic relation" to describe these impossible bonds that are so frequently asserted within works of postmodernist fiction.[43] McHale shows that metalepsis signifies a strange kind of "love" that oversteps assumed boundaries. With this, McHale shows that metalepsis indicates a *hope*, within postmodernist literature, for connection and community that would seem otherwise impossible. In other words, metalepsis *is* community. It is literature's way of declaring community against what may seem to be an inescapable isolation.

In this book, I will extend and modify McHale's speculation about metalepsis as a guiding figure of "love" in postmodernist fiction and describe another literary and intellectual history in which the device assumes a central position. I will show that (both modernist and postmodernist) experimental German prose, over the course of the long twentieth century, tends to employ metalepsis for the imagination of community in contexts where community has become otherwise unimaginable. The turn-of-the-twentieth-century authors Gustav Landauer and Franz Kafka, both of whom wrote under the influence of philosophical pessimism and nihilism, and who addressed new anxieties about mass society, deploy metalepsis as a technique of imagining togetherness. The postwar authors Thomas Bernhard and Wolfgang Hilbig, who share a profound pessimism regarding modern industrial society and its political institutions, both deploy metalepsis as a figure of communion that —in a thoroughly polemical manner—compensates for the disappointments of existing models of socialism and communism. All these authors, who see solitude as a passageway to alternative community, make the transgression of metalepsis into a centerpiece of their prose narratives. The breakdown of distinct discursive layers is not only a fluke or a joke but rather a narrative climax. Metalepsis takes the place of the traditional plot-event and functions as a consummation of new relationships between alienated characters, their narrators, and even their implied readers. Metalepsis is the anarchic mechanism that allows alienation to become community: an isolated self, speaking about nothing but its own loneliness and isolation, is allowed to "break into" a second reality, where new relations can be imagined. By narrating such "breaking points," Landauer, Kafka, Bernhard, and Hilbig stake out a model of de-alienation that is outside the social (because it takes place in profound solitude) but that also prefigures a drastically different configuration of social relations, in which cruelty, competition, suspicion, and prejudice might be supplanted by another condition marked by mutual aid, love, and "indiscriminate intimacy."[44] The fictional experiments of *Private Anarchy* entail a combination of devices: the monologue of alienation is paired with an explosive metalepsis, thereby creating hope at the nadir of hopelessness.

Voided Community in German Intellectual History

If such experimental fiction is political, it is through the subversion of a commonsensical narrative of "community" that prevailed within German, and broader European, social thought from the mid-nineteenth century onward. This dominant narrative, which circulated across the political spectrum, told of the disappearance of premodern community bound by tradition and kinship, followed by the rise of modern anonymity. A void, so the story goes, has opened up between everyone and everyone else, and the only ties that remain are ones of impersonal dependency and exploitation. To trace the development of this account, it helpful to turn to one of its early, sober formulations: Karl Marx's *Grundrisse*, the manuscript he worked on between 1857 and 1861. The *Grundrisse*, which served as the foundation for *Capital*, provided a basic template understanding the void of community in modernity—a *saturated* void, in which human relations still exist but in a monstrous and alien form. For Marx, the disappearance of community from the modern world can be traced back to the beginnings of monetary economy: "Monetary greed, or mania for wealth, necessarily brings with it the decline and fall of the ancient communities [*Gemeinwesen*]. Hence it is the antithesis to them. It itself is the community [*Gemeinwesen*], and can tolerate none other standing above it."[45] Community, for Marx as for Engels in *The Origin of the Family*, first means the collective holding of land and material resources, which preceded the advent of private property.[46] Here Marx partly recalls Rousseau's account of the emergence of society as a history of decline, in which "the first person who, having enclosed a plot of land, took it into his head to say *this is mine* . . . was the true founder of civil society."[47] Yet for Marx, unlike Rousseau, community was the primary state out of which ancient peoples emerged; isolation is modern. Marx does not imagine, as Rousseau does, that people were first "wandering in forests, without industry, without speech, without dwelling, without war, without relationships, with no need of his fellow man."[48] Marx does not rely on the conceit of a presocial human being that has fallen out of his natural state. Instead, Marx sees that, over the course of the history of civilization, an original community based on collective interests has been *destroyed and replaced* with the inhuman workings of money, which becomes the "general substance of survival for all."[49] For Marx, it is not that *every* kind of community vanishes with the appearance of money. Rather, the forms of community (*Gemeinwesen*) that emerge through the rise of capitalism are inherently negative, in that they consist in a common experience of exploitation rather than in consciously shared humanity. The proletariat is a collective of the dispossessed, who have in common the need to compete with one another on the labor market. There is, of course, a Marxist solution to this problem. Once the proletariat unites around the common cause of abolishing private property, it also puts an end to itself: "Both the proletariat and its conditioning opposite—private property—disappear with the victory of the proletariat."[50] Prior to this abolition, a true community, genuinely orientated toward the good of all, does not exist. It is in this sense that human beings under capitalism presently live in a vacuum: the world contains, for now, nothing but transactional and competitive social relations. Marx remains far removed from nihilism because the *nothing* that suffuses modern society is not an absolute nothing but a determinate negation of human community, a negation that prefigures its own negation. As modern social thought developed, this would change.

Ferdinand Tönnies adapted aspects of Marx's theory of capitalism in his book *Gemeinschaft und Gesellschaft* from 1887, foregrounding the absence of genuine community as the most salient characteristic of modern society. The binary opposition of premodern *Gemeinschaft* and modern *Gesellschaft* had a long, problematic career that extended into the twentieth century; the simplification of these categories into markers of an idyllic past (of "community") and a nightmarish present (of "society") cannot be blamed entirely on Tönnies. He conceived of "community" and "society" as a heuristic typology that would enable empirical social research. Tönnies was not exactly a conservative; he actually shared Marx's view of capitalist society as an untenable and temporary stage of human history, which would likely be followed by a violent revolution because of intolerable inequality. But what his book *Gemeinschaft und Gesellschaft* supplied, within the broader sphere of German intellectual culture, was a relatively static binary opposition between community (which is rooted in blood ties of family) and society (which works through the transactions between competitive individuals). A certain reading of Tönnies's book tells us that civil society has emerged because of a universal indifference and nihilism, which has allowed egoism to overtake any moral ways of life. The new world of *Gesellschaft* consists of a mass of self-interested individuals, where all concerns beyond the individual's needs and desires vanish. This, indeed, was Tönnies's view: "Nothing happens in *Gesellschaft* that is more important for the individual's wider group than it is for himself. On the contrary, everyone is out for himself alone and living in a state of tension against everyone else."[51] These sentences transmit a selective portion of Marx's insights, namely that the continual need to maximize profits has resulted in a growing mass of proletarians who are "recruited from all classes" and are forced to compete with one another for ever-lowering wages.[52] Unlike Marx, Tönnies does not describe "society" by first foregrounding the contradiction between exploiter and exploited. What brings about modern capitalism is, rather, the disappearance of a common will and the ascent of a calculative rationality that is always focused on individual gain: "Nobody wants to do anything for anyone else, nobody wants to yield or give anything unless he gets something in return that he regards at least as an *equal* trade-off."[53] One notices how these two central explanatory sentences, featured toward the beginning of his *Gesellschaft* chapter, evoke the vocabulary of nihilism. There is *nobody* looking out for us; there is *nothing* between any of us. Nobody cares. Unlike Marx, Tönnies establishes a link to the vocabulary of nineteenth-century nihilism, which stipulates (and even celebrates) the absence of all value and authority.

In the early twentieth century, it becomes increasingly common for social thinkers to point out the nihilistic implications of the modern economic and bureaucratic social order. Nihilist philosophy and social theory find different routes to reach similar conclusions: a moral vacuum has opened up in the middle of society, all collective will has vanished, and personal obligations of one person to another are null and void. Such pessimism is not restricted to German social thought. The foundational French sociologist Émile Durkheim, in his writings on professional ethics, discussed the risk of "anarchy" in modern society.[54] Durkheim cautioned that, as a rapidly expanding "economic order" becomes coextensive with all of society, there is an acute danger that a "moral anarchy" will take hold.[55] This is because the economic order, unlike other social systems, has no intrinsic ethics that regulate responsibilities of individuals toward others. If our only connection to one another is through our participation in the transactional system of the economy, all sense of mutual obligation among individuals vanishes.[56] A "moral vacuum" emerges as the "amoral character of economic life" seeps into all sectors of society.[57] Durkheim echoes his German contemporaries by making a *recognition of the void* into the basis for sociological inquiry. "Anarchy" is not the chaos brought about by particular radical leftists; it is another name for the de facto emptiness of modern life perceived by many social thinkers around 1900. No radicals are required to create the vacuum.

It was not until after the end of the First World War that a vocabulary of *voids* and *vacuums* became commonplace as descriptions of contemporary social life. Helmuth Lethen notes that intellectuals began to fetishize the term in the 1920s, using it both to describe the collapse of common values (which had already been prefigured by Nietzsche decades earlier) and to index the coldness and emptiness of a Europe that had been ravaged and significantly depopulated by the first modern war.[58] Within literary writing, the Austrian novelist Hermann Broch was probably the most significant voice to stipulate the "vacuum" of contemporary reality. The naming of the vacuum, in his novel trilogy *The Sleepwalkers* (*Die Schlafwandler*), coincides with the narration of the last days of World War I (and hence, the consequences of modern absolute rationality). The theme of the vacuum takes a central place in the final volume of Broch's trilogy, *Hugenau, or Objectivity* (*Hugenau oder die Sachlichkeit*). While the novel's narrative chapters focus on the downfall of a pacifist newspaper editor in Trier during the war, a sequence of interspersed essayistic chapters entitled "The Disintegration of Values" ("Der Zerfall der Werte") provides a theoretical gloss on how the spiritual-intellectual conditions of modernity have created a condition of moral anarchy, and by extension, ruthless warfare. Broch's narrator follows in the analytic footsteps of Max Weber (who in turn resonates with Durkheim and Tönnies), in arguing that modern rationality, prefigured by Protestantism, has produced an array of competing value-systems, and finally a total vacuum of values. Economic rationality has, for Broch as for Weber, created fundamentally isolated individuals who cannot take recourse to any guiding system of values. The image that Broch's narrator constructs to convey this modern, secular predicament is "the colorless vacuum of gray absoluteness" (das tonlose Vakuum einer grauen Absolutheit).[59] Color conveys the nature of modern nihilism: the gray vacuum is not a black void of sheer emptiness but rather a dark blur, a saturated space where discernment, differentiation, and valuation are nonetheless impossible. Distinctions between good and evil have been blurred; all experience has been homogenized. A reader of *The Sleepwalkers*, who has (in the novel's narrative chapters) seen the rampage of a German deserter toward the end of the war, is led to understand that this gray vacuum is the proper setting of the novel's narrative occurrences: the gray vacuum is the world. It is not possible for the characters to do good anymore because they dwell now in a monochrome world devoid of value, where individual characters have become isolated, interchangeable, and therefore disposable. The novel finishes by crushing any hope that a new peaceful community can take shape in this gray world, as the deserting soldier Hugenau murders the pacifist editor Esch and rapes his wife. This couple, who came together at the end of the novel's second volume, *Esch, or Anarchy* (translated in English as *The Anarchist*), had come to signify a resistance to the moral anarchy of urban life in the early twentieth century, where human life is regularly bought and sold through the apparatuses of mass industry, as well as through the exploitations of crude mass entertainment. With Esch's death, Broch's *Sleepwalkers* extinguishes the remaining hope for a humane future in the wake of the war's violence. The anguish conjured by the dramatic climax of the novelistic narrative is given its signature image with the narrator's original term "gray vacuum."[60]

Broch's novel appeared between 1930 and 1932, but such a vocabulary of "void" and "vacuum" was already commonplace in the period immediately following the First World War. In Siegfried Kracauer's 1922 essay "Those Who Wait," "vacuum" is treated as a commonsensical term that describes a universally recognizable social and spiritual condition, as epitomized by the educated inhabitants of major cities. In short, the "vacuum" is the empty, value-free space that surrounds the atomized individuals of the "age of materialism and capitalism," where there is no longer any common religious dogma or metaphysical certainty.[61] Isolated and individuated to the extreme, the modern self is "unattached and lonely in a spiritual/intellectual world dominated by the principle of *laissez-aller*, a world in which every major trans-individual agreement has long since been blown apart."[62] In short, human beings of the present now have nothing in common any longer *except* the vacuum, dwelling in a voided world from which all transcendental principles have vanished. The "people" that concern Kracauer cannot be conceived of as a unified group, except as an aggregate of "companions in misfortune" who collectively suffer from a fear of emptiness (*Horror vacui*).[63] Kracauer stipulates this emptiness as the most salient and recognizable feature of modern human existence. In this sense, Kracauer's essay is different from Marx's and Tönnies's accounts, which adopt a distanced, "zoomed-out" narrative perspective in order to draw a historical continuum from premodern community to modern society. Kracauer locates his account squarely in the present, and the ubiquity of the vacuum is a fait accompli, already recognized and accepted by the majority of his readers. It seems that the vacuum is now the primary fact of life and the underlying essence of society, and not simply an explanatory term that would describe the disappearance of some earlier system of relations. By establishing the vacuum as "our" only proper common ground, Kracauer is able to enumerate the entire spectrum of contemporary political and cultural movements as distinct *responses to the vacuum*. Political activism, literary and philosophical activity, and scientific discipline all become understandable as reactions to the same void.[64]

While Kracauer seems to take the vacuum for granted as the accepted common ground of modernity, he does not actually *endorse* use of the term. Instead, he points out that it is dangerously abstract and unreal. He invites his reader in by deploying "vacuum" as a commonsensical term, only to cancel its commonsensical validity at the last moment. At the end of his essay, Kracauer reframes the prevailing vocabulary of vacuum and void by invoking the "reality" that these terms obscure and that is not, in fact, empty at all. "Reality," rather, "is filled with incarnate things and people and therefore demands to be seen concretely."[65] After describing a whole spectrum of people who feel that there is *nothing* of significance left in the world, Kracauer makes the seemingly obvious point that the world, in fact, is far from being empty. The world is populated with humans and saturated with things, and as such is not really a vacuum after all. That Kracauer needs to point this out at all is a clear indication of the power and prominence of the imaginary of the vacuum around 1920. If it is necessary for a writer to remind his audience that the world still exists, then this suggests that nihilist ideas have become so ubiquitous as to obscure the most basic vision of embodied, material reality. It suggests that a language of nothingness has gotten in the way of any basic description and documentation of the world. An exaggerated nihilism has overtaken accounts of human life, which is dangerous, because it prompts exaggerated and violent reactions to a problem that may not actually exist as such.

The anthropologist Helmuth Plessner, a friend and interlocutor of Kracauer's, clarified the dangers of such nihilist description in his 1924 critical essay "The Limits of Community." Plessner cautioned against the authoritarian potential of the "ideal of a shimmering community overflowing through all of its supporters," which had emerged as a reaction to the "immeasurable chilling of human relations" in modernity.[66] From today's perspective, we can see the striking foresight of Plessner's critique, given that Nazism promised the "restoration" of a racial German "Volksgemeinschaft" (Community of the People), in response to the perceived emptiness of modernity. Plessner showed how something called "community"—which he argues is a tightly and violently integrated form of homogenous society, excluding freedom and autonomy—is called upon to by politicians and mobilized populations to fill a void, so that the alleged atomism of liberal society can be overcome.[67] Through Plessner's discussion, we can see the complicity of the discourse of "vanished community" with the rise of populism and fascism in German and Central Europe. Since the early postwar era, historians have noted that National Socialist ideology was indebted in part to conservative intellectuals of the late nineteenth and early twentieth centuries, who called for a "new community in which old ideas and institutions would once again command universal allegiance."[68] The emphatic description of modern emptiness, therefore, often had the insidious function of provoking the restoration of a vanished racial and/or national community. The political discourse of the modern "vacuum" prompted real, violent reaction.

In refuting any activist revival of old community, Kracauer and Plessner adopted de facto antifascist positions, which recognize the particular gaps and absences of modern existence without exaggerating them or pretending to fill them in. Kracauer's plea for a return to the incarnate things and persons of the world represents a sober and patient response to the perceived void of community. He concedes that there is no unifying set of universal values, no universally binding religious beliefs, stable metaphysical notions, family values, or national feeling, in society as it currently exists: there is no effective social glue, for now. Community, as perfect cohesion through one tradition or another, has indeed been lost, and it is not coming back. However, the world itself is still abundantly full of people and things that we do not yet understand, and so we should patiently return to examining these rather than trying to force the return of a lost community. Kracauer answers the commonplace narrative of vanished community by pointing to the concrete relations in which we are *presently* entangled, which are as yet opaque and cannot yet be clarified in terms of an immanently present community.[69] If we are patient, a qualitatively different kind of "community" may then emerge. Gerhard Richter shows how Kracauer's notion of "waiting" leaves open an alternative conception of community, where common ground is found in the absence of defined bonds: "Because the encounter with an authentic other is continuously deferred, this illegible waiting is the reality of the community, even as this community is not constituted by a readable meaning or sense ('konstituierenden Sinn'), much less a decodable existence ('Sein')."[70] Meaning qua value does not assert itself, yet this persistent absence qua deferral can be the basis for new community. Kracauer's theoretical intervention is to show that the modern emptiness that has been called "vacuum" by cultural pessimists is in fact an openness in which the fixed form of community is always yet to be determined. Kracauer disrupts the dominant narrative of vanished community by making a home, as it were, in the so-called vacuum.

Nihilism as the Art of Voiding

In the past section, I have told a (very brief and selective) history of social theory in terms of European thinkers' *images of emptiness*. I summarize: from the mid-nineteenth to the early twentieth century, social theory developed diverse ways of stipulating and explaining a vacuum or void at the heart of social life. The absence of community—and the presence of a vacuum—became a kind of common sense among intellectuals that laid the groundwork for critical analysis of contemporary society; meanwhile, talk of the vacuum, and of vanished community, circulated widely in the popular-political sphere. In this context, social thinkers developed different critical practices of narrating the disappearance of community and "naming the nothing" that defines modern society.[71] In this book, I will tell a parallel story. The experimental authors that I will study in *Private Anarchy* subvert the commonsensical narrative of vanished community by taking a polemical and unorthodox stance toward the modern "void." They experiment with the strange idea that the social "void" is in fact a *precondition* for community. Community *needs* the "nothing." If there is a one defining difference between the social thinkers above and the experimental writers whom I will discuss in *Private Anarchy*, it is in their approach to the *verbalization of the void*. For the above philosophers, sociologists, and cultural critics, the verbalization of the void (naming the nothing) is descriptive in nature. They point to "real existing" emptiness of the modern world. This emptiness is either (for Marx, Tönnies, Durkheim, and Broch) an oppressive and currently ineluctable feature of social life, or (for Plessner and Kracauer) a commonly accepted social fact worthy of interrogation. By contrast, the experimental authors I will study in *Private Anarchy* treat the verbalization of the void as a *creative act*, which conjures something new with unexpected meanings and consequences. In the literature of private anarchy, the *conjuring of the void* is an art.

As noted above, the story I will tell in *Private Anarchy* is one of recycling. In treating the practice of void-conjuring as a creative art, experimental writers were repeating the gestures of another defining discourse of the nineteenth century, which circulated across the boundaries of literature, philosophy, and politics: *nihilism*. Much more obviously than social theory, literary and philosophical nihilism is, by definition, the emphatic stipulation of one void or another. Defined as a linguistic practice, nihilism is a verbal act of "voiding" where someone asserts that there is *nothing* where most or all people are inclined to believe that there is *something* (whether it be "substance," "God," "value," or "meaning"). Compared to the scientific descriptions of modern social theory, the verbalization of voids within nihilist philosophy and literature is more obviously excessive and polemical, and as such, more obviously a creative act. It is not a matter of giving evidence for this or that absence but rather of finding the most powerful words for saying that there is *nothing*, *nobody*, *no* reason, and so on. The writers of *Private Anarchy* can, in turn, be seen as a bridge between nihilist literature and social theory: they redefine the problem of alienation and emptiness described by social theory, by playing with the verbal art of *void-conjuring* developed in the (often highly misanthropic) texts of nihilist literature and philosophy.

The nihilist art of voiding is somewhat older than modern social theory. Prior to the emergence of modern sociology and Marxist theory, polemical and excessive declarations of the void had already become a common practice of intellectual culture of the nineteenth century, transcending the boundaries between particular metaphysical frameworks and political ideologies. It was not always this way. Around 1800, discourse on "nothingness" and "nihilism" is usually accusatory, as for instance in Jean Paul's 1803 treatise *Preschool for Aesthetics* (*Vorschule der Ästhetik*), where he accuses romantic "nihilists" of having fashioned a void for themselves in order to make way for entirely free aesthetic play.[72] Not long thereafter, however, nihilism turned from an accusatory description into a voluntarily chosen position.[73] If the once-influential philosophy of Arthur Schopenhauer (1788–1860) has one enduring legacy that has outlived his (by most accounts obsolete) Platonic aesthetics, it is the *pleasure of revealing the void* that defines his writing. Schopenhauer's philosophy can impress (and even entertain) us today for the polemical gesture made in the final sentence of his book *The World as Will and Representation*, which writes off the entire universe in a few well-chosen words: "to those in whom the will has turned and denied itself" —that is, in those who have extinguished all desire to live—"this very real world of ours with its suns and galaxies, is—nothing."[74] The power of these sentences lies in their counterintuitive embrace of loneliness and alienation, their audacious embrace of perfect isolation over any bonds with the world and its inhabitants. The conjuring of this void is the quintessential performative act of Schopenhauer's writing, as it resolutely refutes the lofty ends of art and philosophy and beckons instead toward a state of perfect darkness.

Schopenhauer's gesture of universal negation was appropriated from Buddhist thought, and as such is hardly original. Nonetheless, it became a central channel for introducing a language of universal negation into German-language letters. Nietzsche, initially a follower of Schopenhauer, sought to conjure a form of "nothing" that would outdo Schopenhauer's in its polemical force. This is most evident in the explanation of "eternal recurrence" in the chapter "European Nihilism" from Nietzsche's posthumously published *Will to Power*. Here, he invents a particularly imposing image of "nothing." For Nietzsche, the most powerful "nothing" is not the ontological void that Schopenhauer superimposes on the stars and galaxies but "existence as it is, without meaning or aim, yet recurring inevitably without any finale of nothingness: *the eternal recurrence*."[75] What is striking and confusing about Nietzsche's phrase, which has become one of his signature slogans, is that it does not by itself tell us *what* eternally recurs (my experience as a student was that many academics use the phrase "eternal recurrence" as if it were self-explanatory, without stating the subject). Here, Nietzsche clarifies what recurs: "the nothing (the 'meaningless'), eternally!"[76] By design, Nietzsche has omitted the subject of eternal recurrence in order to stress its total negativity: what recurs is a lack of meaning that goes on and on but never results in the disappearance of the world "with its suns and galaxies," as promised by Schopenhauer.[77] It is a nothingness without relief or release. In this way, Nietzsche initiates a kind of competition with his predecessor, a race to coin the most arresting description of the void and thus to distill "the most extreme form of nihilism," so that he could then claim to overcome it before anyone else.[78]

The proto-anarchist Max Stirner can be counted as an honorary participant in this philosophical competition, without having directly engaged with either thinker. More clearly than Schopenhauer or Nietzsche, Stirner sought to claim the "nothing" (*Nichts*) all for himself, beginning his 1844 book *The Ego and Its Own* with a phrase taken from Goethe, "I have set my affair on nothing."[79] Stirner's polemical identification with nothingness goes even further than Nietzsche's, as he claims to *be* the nothing, when he writes, "I am the creative nothing, the nothing out of which I myself as creator create everything."[80] In their constructions of "nothing," all three thinkers are engaged in a performative conjuring of a void, an act that is supposed to cause a world-historical break, finally shattering the collective hallucination that others consider to be the world's reality. With Schopenhauer, Stirner, and Nietzsche, the conjuring of the void is an audacious demonstration by the master-philosopher that it is possible to disembark from the train of collective human history without ever embarking on any socially recognized path toward salvation or revolution (that is, without partaking in any existing forms of religion or politics). In other words, each of these thinkers strikes a muscular, heroic, and masculine posture, performing the ability to live *in*, *with*, or *as* a void, and consequently without community. Before it became commonplace for sociologists to stipulate the emptiness of modern existence, these thinkers of nihilism assured their audience that they had already made a home in the void.

The Political Engagements of Private Anarchy

The experimental fiction that I will study in *Private Anarchy* evokes both the sociological discourse on vanished community and the nihilist embrace of the void. Situated thus between social thought and philosophical nihilism, these writers subvert the premises of *both* of these discourses. The creative conjuring acts of nihilism result in community—something that they would seem to foreclose, especially if one is a doctrinaire Stirnerian or Schopenhauerian. The work of verbal voiding, in the fiction of private anarchy, becomes a necessary step in opening up space to imagine a togetherness that transcends ideas of the sovereign self as well as the bonds promised by traditional kinship ties. As such, the forms of verbal nihilism encountered in the fiction of Landauer, Kafka, Bernhard, and Hilbig are located at some distance from the mainstream of "cultural pessimism," or "cultural despair," that fueled the reactionary, fascist politics of the twentieth century, and that Plessner critiqued in *The Limits of Community*. Still, it should be kept in mind that many twentieth-century cultural historians have implicated the philosophies of pessimism and nihilism (as articulated in works by Arthur Schopenhauer, Max Stirner, Fyodor Dostoevsky, and Friedrich Nietzsche) in a broader intellectual history of cultural despair, antimodernism, antiliberalism. To put it in other, more pointed, words: the nihilist writing that appealed to Landauer, Kafka, Bernhard, and Hilbig became retroactively implicated in reactionary politics in the twentieth century. Postwar cultural critics who were seeking out the intellectual roots of National Socialism often gathered together the traditions of pessimism and nihilism under the umbrella term "irrationalism," which they saw as an intellectual blueprint for fascism. Examples include the American historian Fritz Stern's study *The Politics of Cultural Despair* from 1961, Georg Lukács's Marxist treatise *The Destruction of Reason* from 1954, and Hans Helms's 1966 study *Ideology of Anonymous Society*, which identified Stirner as a direct precursor to German fascism.[81] For instance, according to Stern, Nietzsche and Dostoevsky were the most significant voices of a "pervasive pessimism concerning the future of the West" and instigated a "movement against modernity," which, Stern showed, was subsequently vulgarized and popularized by twentieth-century conservatives and fascists in Germany.[82] At its worst, pessimism became a crude means of justifying reactionary and exclusionary politics: a renewed national community was the answer to the problem posed by cultural pessimism. Nihilist and pessimist discourse has been tainted by the history of reaction and violence that followed it. This is exemplified concretely by the case of the Romanian nihilist philosopher Emil Cioran, whose philosophical negativity made it possible for him to endorse Hitler.[83]

However, the fact that the experimental fiction of private anarchy has certain influences in common with reactionary thinkers does not mean that their experiments with verbal nihilism led in the same direction. One of the basic ideas underlying my analyses is that there is a range of *different* pessimisms and nihilisms and that the meaning of the voids and vacuums they posit are subject to contestation. This is an insight that has become fairly commonplace since the 1980s debates over the putative *Sonderweg* (special path) of German history that led toward National Socialism. In this debate, historians such as Geoff Eley and David Blackbourn questioned a straightforward causal link between nineteenth-century cultural despair and twentieth-century fascism, and problematized the idea that such despair was peculiarly German (late nineteenth-century German culture, for instance, was also marked by a "shallow optimism" regarding technological progress and was hardly entirely pessimist).[84] In light of these arguments, pessimism and "despair" need to be considered internally differentiated modes of thought, which could be deployed to a wide range of ideological ends. The cultural currency of pessimism in German and Austrian culture of the early to mid-twentieth century made it into an object of contestation. As soon as despair became an intellectual and political orthodoxy, niche subcultures and countercultures of unorthodox pessimism arose that resisted integration into nationalist projects of collective action and reaction. Writing in the early twentieth century, in societies that saw the rise of fascism, Gustav Landauer and Franz Kafka represent niche forms of nihilism-pessimism, which are perversely intermingled with peculiar and unexpected optimisms that do not correspond neatly to any political mainstream. Their prose perversely *embraces* the atomization and anarchy that were bemoaned by reactionaries as a symptom of modern massification. As I will show in chapter 5, Wolfgang Hilbig reprises Kafka's odd optimism regarding a "society of nobodies" in the context of the postwar era that followed the catastrophe of Nazism, innovating a pessimism that privileges spontaneous "stranger intimacy" over ideologies of preexisting, organic kinship.[85] If the dominant (and politically successful) form of German cultural pessimism bemoaned the decline of culture and the absence of community, the countercultural pessimism of these experimental writers embraces emptiness in the hope of finding in it a community that is antitraditional and utterly otherworldly. In particular, Kafka, Bernhard, and Hilbig take distance from commonsensical, reactionary conclusions of cultural pessimism and appropriate the language of nothingness to drastically different ends. Rather than seeing renewed community as the answer to pessimism, these authors imagine how the most extreme pessimism qua nihilism (following such postulates as, *there will be nothing*, or *we are nothing*) already contains within it conditions for alternative models of community, which subvert available definitions of community.

This is not to say that the implications of all these writers' experiments are all the same. For each of the authors studied in *Private Anarchy*, the anarchic imagination of community has distinct political stakes. Landauer, Kafka, Bernhard, and Hilbig were each attempting, in their own idiosyncratic ways, to work through particular impasses in available forms of collective identity. Existing scholarship on these writers has stressed the ways in which these writers are ambivalent commentators on ethnic and national identities who were concerned with the implication of these identities in twentieth-century histories of violence, war, and cultural survival. As German-Jewish writers, Gustav Landauer and Franz Kafka variously engaged with emergent forms of *völkisch* nationalism and rising anti-Semitism, responding implicitly and explicitly to processes of assimilation as well as projects of Jewish emancipation and Zionism around the turn of the twentieth century in Germany and Austria-Hungary. When their writings pose the question of community, it is frequently shaped by discourses on Jewish community in the fin de siècle period. Vivian Liska has recently shown how Kafka's literary work innovates creative conceptions of "uncommon community," as the author grappled with a question that he posed in his own diary in 1914: "What have I in common with the Jews?"[86] Recent scholarship on Gustav Landauer has likewise considered Landauer's dynamic, often ambivalent relationship with his own Jewish identity, which shifted from a stance of antipathy and denial prior to 1900, toward an open embrace of Jewish ethics and mysticism in later years, as Landauer became one of Martin Buber's major interlocutors, shaping his ideas of anti-authoritarian and pacifist Zionism.[87]

Whereas Landauer and Kafka were concerned with a collective identity that was violently marginalized in twentieth-century Europe, the postwar authors Thomas Bernhard and Wolfgang Hilbig turned their critical attention to myths of national identity that underwrote the foundation of postwar nation-states: for Bernhard, the Austrian Second Republic, and for Hilbig, the socialist German Democratic Republic (GDR). Their critical reflections are concerned with political boundaries and systems shaped by the geopolitical balance of power during the Cold War. Bernhard's narrative and dramatic works perform a multifaceted interrogation of Austrian identity: they contest narratives of Austrian "innocence" in the Nazi era, dismantle the façade of Austria as a provincial touristic idyll, and ironize the "identification with Hapsburg cultural achievement" that obscures more recent histories of fascism and violence.[88] Wolfgang Hilbig, as an outsider of GDR literature, critically engaged the myths of collective identity constructed in socialist East Germany, questioning (for instance) the foundational narrative of how the GDR was founded on an organized and widespread resistance to Nazism by German socialists. As Paul Cooke writes, Hilbig "strives to inscribe a less limited notion of identity than the one afforded him by the East German authorities."[89] For Bernhard and Hilbig, literature permits experimentation with alternative, anarchic models of collective identity that diverge from the state's history of national birth. In their verbal art, inherited national identities are relegated to the background as new forms of outsider community come to the forefront. The goal of *Private Anarchy* is to show how these authors assemble unique theories of the social through experimentation with form.

In this way, my approach is sympathetic to the method of political formalism recently developed by the literary scholar Caroline Levine.[90] Levine reads literature as an interplay between—and collision of—distinct social and aesthetic forms, such as hierarchies of importance and power, and fixed temporal routines or rhythms. These hierarchies, routines, and rhythms can be subverted or transformed through the formal experimentation of any given literary work. The historical and social context of a text's production cannot fully determine the outcome of such formal experimentation. If we turn our attention to the play of forms happening within a given text, we may reveal original theories of social interconnection that did not necessarily preexist that text. So it is with the works of Landauer, Kafka, Bernhard, and Hilbig: by melding verbal forms that represent separation (monologue) and boundary-crossing (metalepsis), an unexpected, anarchic form of community arises. These authors cull raw materials from their social environment and from the cultures of German and European letters. But these materials are dismantled and reassembled so as to produce the image of another possible social world. My point is not to ignore the proximity of these literary works to, for instance, histories of anti-Semitism, German fascism, and postwar amnesia regarding historical guilt. Rather, I hope to show how these authors respond to oppressive and alienating contexts through the imaginative pathways of antimimetic literature. "Antimimetic" is for narratologist Brian Richardson the defining feature of unnatural narrative, a form of fiction that plays with impossibilities and flaunts transgressions of reality as we know it. Following Richardson, it is possible to see the unnatural transgression of metalepsis as a unique "collectivist narrative technique" that experiments with new models of relations. For Landauer, Kafka, Bernhard, and Hilbig, metalepsis is an unnatural technique that sidesteps organicist and essentialist conceptions of group identity and moves toward a conception of collectivity that is anarchic, spontaneous, improvisational, always conjured performatively through a set of speech-acts.[91] This speech is influenced by nihilism, but it cannot simply be called by that name and so understood without further clarification. The project of *Private Anarchy* is to find out what we might call it instead.

Structure of the Book

The structure of *Private Anarchy* is for the most part chronological. The first two chapters examine the emergence and creative transformation of "verbal nihilism" in the nineteenth century, and the last three chapters examine the fictional experiments that built on those earlier expressions of nihilism, in order to innovate unfamiliar visions of community. The conclusion carries this story forward into the twenty-first century and places the (entirely male) tradition of private anarchy in dialogue with literary feminism.

Chapter 1 is a literary and intellectual history of a single form, examining the models of monologue developed in the nineteenth-century discourse of nihilism. I argue that the monologue emerges as a central verbal genre of nihilism, positioning the speaker in a communicative void where all social values and relations are nullified. This conception of monologue differs from positive models of soliloquy that defined literature of the mid- to late eighteenth century. If the soliloquies of Rousseau's solitary walker and Goethe's Werther, for instance, tended to celebrate the freedom and ingenuity of the individual subject, nineteenth-century nihilist discourse treats monologue as an instrument of disappearance, whereby the subject becomes "nobody" and the world becomes "nothing." The two primary authors considered in this context are the German philosopher Arthur Schopenhauer and the Russian novelist Fyodor Dostoevsky. In both of these authors' works, monologue is associated with the position of a social and ontological outsider, whose solitary voice conjures an *abyss* or *void* underneath commonly accepted social reality. The monologues of Schopenhauer's "madman" and "genius" and Dostoevsky's "underground type" refute the possibility of any existing human community and insist that the only thing we have in common is nothingness. At the end of the chapter, I show how Friedrich Nietzsche consolidated these very different writers into a single history of nihilism. Nietzsche located their writings within a development of "pessimism-nihilism-anarchism," which he saw as a necessary prelude to the creation of a new future. For Nietzsche, as for Schopenhauer and Dostoevsky, abject isolation is an indispensable aspect of such subversive nihilism. Through the works of all three writers, monologue emerges not as an expression of essential selfhood à la Rousseau but as a crucial strategy for voiding the given world—a strategy that will take on new dimensions in subsequent experimental texts.

The second chapter turns to works of the Gustav Landauer, who around the turn of the twentieth century composed a number of fictional texts that explicitly take up the nihilist and misanthropic comportments presented by Schopenhauer, Dostoevsky, and Nietzsche. As an anarchist, Landauer imagined ways in which the pessimist-nihilist mind-set could serve as a potential starting point for a new form of political community that is opposed to all forms of coercive and institutional authority. His early novel *The Death Preacher* from 1893 appropriates nihilist visions of solitude in order to narrate the emergence of an "unworldly anarchism" and a "misanthropic socialism" within the mind of the novel's withdrawn intellectual hero, Karl Starkblom. Starkblom envisions the founding of a revolutionary political community of outsiders who are bound together by a common, misanthropic rejection of social reality. Monologue, paradoxically, becomes a necessary medium for the representation of a future anarchic community without fixed authority, values, or institutions. In the peculiar narrative structure of *The Death Preacher*, the nihilist monologues of the protagonist interrupt and overtake the novel's initially realist mode. This structure of interruption reflects an anarchic desire for a "community without community" that emerges in the vocal voiding of a shared, stable social world. Although Landauer's novel is not well known, it prefigures the experimental fusion of misanthropy and community that recurred over the course of the twentieth century in works by Kafka, Bernhard, and Hilbig.

Chapter 3 shows how Franz Kafka's short story "Description of a Struggle" creatively adapts the tradition of verbal nihilism examined in chapter 1, in order to create distance from accepted formations of bourgeois sociality around the turn of the twentieth century. I show how Kafka constructs a strange vision of community that emerges out of a shared experience of nothingness. Beginning with the story of a solipsistic officer worker in Prague (who immediately and explicitly recalls the "annihilated" underground type

Goliadkin from Dostoevsky's *The Double*), Kafka's "Description of a Struggle" introduces a chain of embedded stories about different nihilistic outsiders. These characters are all connected by the unsettling premonition that they, along with the world around them, are on the verge of disappearing into nothingness. Haunted thus by their own insubstantiality and insignificance, these characters become caught up in extended, self-referential monologues about their life in the vacuum of modern society. But Kafka's text does not simply lament the emptiness of modern urban existence. Rather, the enunciation of this emptiness through monologue becomes a way of creating community in absence of any shared identity, against the backdrop of a vanishing world ("a space that no longer had a landscape," as Kafka's narrator describes it).[92] A virtual "community of the void" emerges in the volatile narrative structure of Kafka's prose. Structurally, "Description of a Struggle" is a monologue within a monologue within a monologue, ad infinitum; each solitary voice sustains itself by becoming embedded within another solitary voice. Kafka's first major story therefore experiments with the idea that literature could be a medium for fostering and preserving a community of solitude.

Chapter 4 focuses on the early fiction of the Austrian writer Thomas Bernhard, who like Kafka expands the figuration of Dostoevsky's "underground type" and places the misanthropic monologues of this alien figure at the center of the narrative text. I present a comprehensive study of Bernhard's early novel-project *Leichtlebig*, which was revised into his literary breakthrough *Frost* in 1963 and partially published in 2013 under the title *Arguments of a Winter Walker* (*Argumente eines Winterspaziergängers*). *Leichtlebig*, I argue, is unique for its anarchic experimentation with narrative levels and for its detailed thematization of socialist and communist politics in the early postwar era—concerns that would consistently shape Bernhard's later, better-known writings. In *Leichtlebig*, a young socialist railroad worker becomes acquainted with a misanthropic, morbid "Doctor," whose monologues overtake the text and eclipse the primary narrative. Whereas the railroad worker Leichtlebig inhabits a world that is tightly structured by class distinctions and the corporatist political-economic institutions of postwar Austria, the Doctor introduces an overwhelmingly nihilist perspective that voids this social reality and eclipses it with the linguistic "hypertrophies" of his monologues, in which the boundaries between individuals, as well as between distinct times and spaces, are dissolved. The Doctor's discourse appropriates and radicalizes models of solitude posited by Dostoevsky and Schopenhauer, in a chaotic attempt (which recalls Landauer) to conceive of an alternative, anti-institutional model of human togetherness, which both resembles and transcends socialist claims of solidarity.

Chapter 5 turns to the work of a late twentieth-century author, who (like Bernhard) responded to existing socialist vocabularies of solidarity and envisioned literature as the site for an unworldly, negative community bound together by a radically solitary, anticommunicative language. Wolfgang Hilbig's prose texts "Old Rendering Plant" ("Alte Abdeckerei," 1991) and "The Lore of the Trees" ("Die Kunde von den Bäumen," 1992) reiterate Kafka's early fascination with abysmal speech and the "society of nobodies" (which the text explicitly invokes), as part of a multilayered reckoning with German national history since National Socialism, while keeping in mind the industrial deformation and pollution of natural landscapes in socialist East Germany. Both texts by Hilbig present the monologues of an isolated, formerly proletarian protagonist, who throughout his life has taken to solitary walks into a polluted no-man's land on the periphery of his city, where he witnesses the grotesque alterations of the natural landscape. These solitary walks through a postnatural landscape turn out, unexpectedly, to be the starting point for the narrator's initiation into a subculture of outcasts and "nobodies," abject workers who are at home in the material refuse produced by state socialism. Hilbig's implied reader becomes privy to the noncommunicative, associative language of these "nobodies." By the end of each story, it is implied that Hilbig's *reader* (like the narrator) has acquired the ability to hear and understand this abject, abysmal language. Hilbig's texts thus stage the formation of a virtual community of outsiders, which emerges through the transgressive circulation of alien voices between the different levels of its narrative structure. I conclude that Hilbig's community of outsiders recapitulates the earlier, anarchic visions of Kafka and Bernhard but now explicitly relates this vision to the crisis of ecology at the end of the twentieth century. The slogan that Hilbig eventually created for his own work and voiced within his 2002 acceptance speech for the Georg Büchner Prize captures both the contours of his own work as well as of all the works studied in *Private Anarchy*: "Literature is Monologue." Yet what Hilbig means is that literature is a practice that allows the *sharing* of monologues, which circulate between anonymous readers and writers. Literary monologue, Hilbig argues, is the main ingredient for dissident community.

In my conclusion, I further consider the possibilities and limits of this idea of literary subversion as it has endured into the twenty-first century in the works of the Hungarian novelist László Krasznahorkai. I then place this ongoing tradition of private anarchy into dialogue with the countertradition of literary feminism represented by the Austrian writer Ingeborg Bachmann. I show that, although all of these writers share an approach to voice that fuses solitude (monologue) with community (metalepsis), the anarchic visions of inclusion innovated by Landauer, Kafka, Bernhard, and Hilbig remain limited by an attachment to masculine identity, which they efface but do not escape.

Chapter 1

✦

Voices of the Vacuum
Monologue in Schopenhauer, Dostoevsky, and Nietzsche

In European letters around 1800, the verbal form of monologue was associated with the creation of an empty space where the individual could exercise forms of freedom unavailable in social life. As literary scholar Jürgen Wertheimer has shown, this period saw numerous writers staging a "withdrawal of the individual out of the space of social relations into the vacuum of absolute dialogue."[1] Such absolute dialogue was actually a monologue, a solitary and unworldly discourse that has given up on all social communication but allows the self to discover new forms of emphatic and perhaps more authentic communication on its own. In such cases, to be authentically human also means to be an alien to humanity, at home in a private vacuum.

The most famous practitioner of monologue as "vacuum speech" may have been Jean-Jacques Rousseau. His *Reveries of a Solitary Walker*, written between 1776 and 1778, presents an authentic and free communion with his true inner self that begins with an experience of absolute alienation from humanity: "Being on this earth is like being on another planet onto which I have fallen from the one on which I used to live."[2] Casting himself as an extraterrestrial, Rousseau fashions an elegant language that expresses total social nonrelation, anticipating Immanuel Kant's innovative notion of "sublime" misanthropy from his 1790 work *Critique of Judgment*.[3] With Rousseau's monologues, the world in all its abundance and diversity vanishes into the self, which becomes an inexhaustible source for meaningful experience. Nothing outside the self matters. In the fifth chapter, or "walk," Rousseau praises at length a form of experience that concerns "Nothing external to the self, nothing but oneself and one's own existence: as long as this state lasts, one is self-sufficient like God."[4] The written monologue is a site where this freedom can be exercised without restraint, as evidenced in the solitary walker's attitude toward the natural environment around him: through his reveries he collects and assembles images of the lonely island around him into a pleasing tableau that is patently artificial. To live with *nothing but oneself* is a state of enjoyment where one avails oneself of the internal abundance of experience, memory, and imagination.

Rousseau's model of solitude resembles Kant's sublime misanthropy because it is, at its core, a form of solitary humanism that stops short of categorically hating humanity and refusing life itself. Such solitude upholds a positive notion of the human individual as an absolute good and so cannot be dismissed as pure nihilism. When he writes of engaging with "nothing but oneself," the word "oneself" carries all the emphasis, and the word "nothing" is a mere marker, pointing away from any human community and toward the interior realm of self-experience, which could be called a vacuum but is actually rich with interiority. It is not that he actually wants—as later nihilists would—sheer nothingness. Rousseau negates everything *but* the self, embracing a relative nothing but not complete nothingness. Monologue, in this context, is a form of speech that conserves value rather than negating it. It was not until the nineteenth century, with the rise of self-conscious discourses of nihilism, that the form of monologue became associated with a vacuum in which world *and* self are negated. This radicalized conception of monologue as "vacuum speech" emerges in the works of several key literary and philosophical figures of the nineteenth century, including those who sought to denounce or overcome nihilism.

Conjuring Voids through Monologue

As an intellectual tradition, nihilist thought is unified by the interrelated tropes of *vacuum, void,* and *nothingness*. These terms frequently work in a way that contradicts their expected invocation of a sheer emptiness undifferentiated by any determinations. As negative spaces, the voids and vacuums named by nihilist writers can become worlds in their own right.

Over the course of the nineteenth century, these tropes of empty space (voids, vacuums, and abysses) enabled the formation of nihilism as a kind of *verbal art*, which performs a complex act of vanishing and conjuring. From Schopenhauer's philosophy of the early nineteenth century, to Kafka's first writings around 1900, practice of this verbal art of nihilism involves a sort of storytelling that is also associated with postmodernist fiction: the nihilist writer *narrates* and *de-narrates*, saying something is "there but not there."[5] Such practice of the verbal art of nihilism is not restricted to those writers who unambiguously avowed nihilism; it also appears in the works of authors who sought to invert and subvert nihilism's tropes of the void, playing with and against nihilism's acts of conjuring and disappearance. As such, the literary tradition of verbal nihilism was enriched not only by the pessimistic Schopenhauer and the solipsistic Stirner but also by the Christian Dostoevsky and the life-loving Nietzsche. These authors contributed to the verbal art of nihilism not simply through their philosophical "ideas" but through the innovative verbal strategies of conjuring-vanishing performed in their works by a variety of philosophical figures and fictional speakers. By ventriloquizing nihilism, they enriched the "vacuums" and "voids" of the nineteenth century, helping to imagine how these voids might coexist with substantial and corporeal reality. As such, they achieved the inverse of the realist novel of the same century, which presented readers with vivid images of the increasingly populated, industrialized, and centrally governed societies emerging in Europe at the time.[6] Where Balzac and Zola imagined masses, these writers imagined voids.

In both literary fiction and philosophy, the conjuring-vanishing act of nihilism is performed through a monologue, by a speaker who addresses nobody, guards against any responses or retorts, and thereby preserves the vision of a void (rather than yielding to acknowledgment of an abundant material and social world). As such, the figure of the male misanthrope acquires a special status in the tradition of nihilist writing. The void is verbally conjured by a speaker for whom community and communication are impossible and who locates himself in a *nowhere* alongside *nobody*. The misanthrope inhabits a familiar posture of heroic lonerism, coded as masculine, which is carried out to such an excess that it forfeits any claims to moral or social authority. The misanthrope wants to perfect a noncommunicative posture, achieving and maintaining (to quote Victor Erlich) the "verbal epitome of loneliness and isolation."[7] This self-removal positions the speaker on a distinct ontological level, which is incommensurable with the inhabited, human world. Monologue, within the more intense currents of nineteenth-century nihilism, becomes the verbal form that invokes a primary emptiness that underlies all existence.

This chapter will examine how monologue, over the course of the nineteenth century, was theorized and employed by philosophers and fiction writers as a kind of *verbal nihilism*, which performatively conjures a void with monologue. I will show how Arthur Schopenhauer, Friedrich Nietzsche, and Fyodor Dostoevsky experimented with misanthropic characters who refuse all possibilities of communication and community in order to develop specifically nihilist verbal techniques. This is not to say that all of these writers *are* technically nihilist (Nietzsche and Dostoevsky in their own ways wanted to move beyond nihilism). Yet each of them was instrumental in creating an idea of how nihilism *works* and *sounds*, and in each case this work is accomplished by monologue. In both theory and in practice, these writers render monologue as a genre of speech that is distinct because of its special temporality that dissociates it from social discourse (it is incessant and unanswerable). This tendency toward antisocial separation is, in each writer's work, paired with particular spatial metaphors, such as *void*, *abyss*, and *underground*, which indicate the ontological separation of the monologic speaker from the social world. In this way, monologue becomes an art of erasure, actively aimed at *absenting* and *self-absenting*. In each case, this art of erasure works as an alternative to concrete social critique: a speaker aims to undo an oppressive social and material context through the sheer power of incessant speech. The unhappy, inhabited world vanishes under a flood of words. It is a conceit of pessimism that proved to be attractive to many experimental writers of the long twentieth century.

Monologue as the Annulment of "Context" in Schopenhauer

In the final pages of his 1819 work *The World as Will and Representation*, Arthur Schopenhauer presents his readers with a character who dwells in an *empty* universe that is accessed through our own, familiar shared universe, yet clearly separate from it. The "saint" who drops out of known existence locates himself within an empty space that is both *separate* from, yet also *embedded within*, the wider framework of "this very real world of ours with all its suns and galaxies."[8] Schopenhauer's ascetic, radically solitary saint is a black hole, *avant la lettre*: the universe vanishes into his mind, which is an anomalous node where the "will" that makes up the cosmos cancels itself out. What made this terminal state of transcendence possible? What techniques could be deployed, and by whom, to exit the universe in this way? One technique of note, which appears roughly in the midpoint of the book's long argumentative arc, is the monologue.

For Schopenhauer, monologue is a verbal practice performed by a special kind of ontological outsider that annuls both the self and the world around it. As anticommunicative speech, monologue helps to efface the outsider's particular placement within the world as a temporal, spatial, and causal nexus. One name that Schopenhauer gives to this nexus is "context" (Zusammenhang), elsewhere referred to as a "chain" (Kette).[9] To exist in context is to exist in chains because it is nothing more than a manifestation of the blind drive that Schopenhauer calls the "will," which in its insatiability is the cause of all suffering. To exist within this context, which arises out of the will, is to exist within a perpetual state of conflict, unfulfilled desire, and pain. Every individuated body located in time and space (from the planets to human beings) strives in accordance with the will, and so strives against the bodies around it. So, *any* existence in the temporal and spatial "chain" is at war, whether we are speaking of carnivorous insects or educated human beings. If Hobbes thought that "the war of all against all" characterized human life before the contractual founding of the State, Schopenhauer believed that the war of all against all rages on unabated into civilization. Thus Schopenhauer apodictically invokes Plautus's dictum that "man is a wolf to man," suggesting that no new social visions (such humanism, liberalism, republicanism, or socialism) will ever bring about peace (*WWR1*, 147). Insofar as social relations exist, they are conflicts. Insofar as any being is embedded within a context of any kind, it suffers. A "relationship" is identical to "striving, . . . longing and desire" (309). This is because every relationship is an attack of some kind: appropriation, competition, exploitation, or destruction. Community cannot disappear from Schopenhauer's world because it was never there in the first place.

To clarify the totality and inescapability of this "context" qua "chain," Schopenhauer speaks of nature as a book in which all our lives are written. "Nature," here, is synonymous with the "will": "Every individual, every human apparition and its course of life, is only one more short dream of the endless spirit of nature, of the persistent will-to-live, is only one more fleeting form, playfully sketched by it on its *infinite page, space and time*" (322, my italics). This infinite page is the context of all human life, the medium in which all individuated beings are located and related. Elsewhere, Schopenhauer speaks of this universal context in terms of a "storm" that moves endlessly along a horizontal axis. In each case, Schopenhauer imagines "context" as a gapless matrix bound together by the same terrible necessity. When Schopenhauer reveals that the context of each "human apparition" is an endless text, he underscores the immobility of life itself: a person is no more capable of running away from conflict and suffering than the word in a book is capable of jumping off the page. However, for a particular kind of ontological outsider—the "genius"—such a jump becomes possible.

In his book *Genius and Monologue*, Ken Frieden notes that monologue "swerves away from dialogic norms," deviating from the inherently social nature of language.[10] In Schopenhauer's system, this "swerve" has more radical consequences than it did in Rousseau's reveries, where avoidance of the social enabled the recovery of one's true self. For Schopenhauer, monologue swerves away from existence itself, deviating not only from the basic interactional nature of language in particular but also from the chains of "context" in general (that is: humanity, the universe, everything). How does this break occur? It seems to start with a farewell to conventional language. Language, for Schopenhauer, is an instrument of reason, which is important above all because it enables collective action. Any existing form of human community has been predicated on the use of a common concept, some universal term that had to be applied to a multiplicity of objects or situations. Speech has provided the medium of conceptual thought that made human civilization possible: "Speech is the first product and necessary instrument of [man's] faculty of reason. Therefore, in Greek and Italian speech and reason are expressed by the same word. . . . Only by aid of language does reason bring about its most important achievements, namely the harmonious and consistent action of several individuals, the planned cooperation of many thousands, civilization, the State" (*WWR1*, 37). Language creates and coordinates relationships on a mass scale. Once language is invented, collective action becomes compulsory. This, again, reflects the fatal necessity of

Schopenhauer's system, where one's use of the faculty of reason excludes the possibility of freedom and further enslaves the individual to the will. Consequently, to be a linguistic deviant, in Schopenhauer's system, is to be a social and ontological deviant, who simultaneously divorces himself from communication, community, reason, and "context" in general. Schopenhauer later devotes a portion of his discussion to the eccentric speakers whose speech disrupts context: the genius and the madman. Schopenhauer presents both these figures as anticontextual speakers, whose discourse interrupts and forecloses further collective or competitive action. Their speech annuls the chain of relations that characterize human life, disrupting the otherwise endless continuity of the "page" on which nature inscribes all human life. Such speech is unique because it is an instrument of escape from the world.

I will briefly explain the "method of genius" according to *The World as Will and Representation*. Aesthetic perception for Schopenhauer is synonymous with "genius." The "method" of genius is "the way of considering things independently of the principle of sufficient reason" (*WWR1*, 185). If suffering is always bound up with one's relational existence (one's temporal, spatial, and causal position on the "page" of nature), then only an alternate form of nonrelational cognition can interrupt suffering. Indeed, Schopenhauer suggests that genius arrives as if out of nowhere: genius "is like a silent sunbeam, cutting through the path of the storm, and quite unmoved by it" (185). But what makes this anticontextual condition possible? The first answer is simply: a special ability to see through things. The ability to employ the "method of genius" is extremely unequally distributed among humanity, so only very few people are capable of lingering in this state. Unlike the common person, geniuses are marked with a special ability to apprehend the most basic manifestations of the "will," which for Schopenhauer is the single substratum of all existence. This ability "must be inherent in all men in a lesser and different degree," but it is above all the providence of the genius (194). The genius can immerse himself in the cognition of timeless Ideas outside of the categories that would usually enable participation in practical life: time, space, and causality. Schopenhauer writes that "the objects of genius as such are the eternal Ideas, the persistent, essential forms of the world and of all its phenomena" (186). When one perceives things as timeless, unchanging Ideas, one begins to see that the apparent particularity and individuality of things is in fact the ephemeral manifestation (the "objectivation") of a more fundamental plain of existence. Geniuses can temporarily escape the all-encompassing context in which all human apparitions are permanently registered. Geniuses lose themselves in the perception of objects and so can be displaced from the painful relationships that, altogether, make up the field of practical life. They move closer to the terminal point (which is reached by the "saint" at the end of Schopenhauer's book) of seeing the entire universe as *nothing*. If we read this section of *The*

World as Will and Representation with an eye to the book's final chapter, we see that the figure of the "genius" has a proleptic function, providing a partial preview of the saintly figures who are able to "overcome the world," and achieve an "ocean-like calmness of the spirit" through "the free denial, the surrender, of the will" (410–11). The first taste of such calm is delivered in monologue.

In giving account of how an individual can become and remain a genius qua "pure knowing subject," Schopenhauer goes on to construct an anthropology that posits the genius as a particular class of persons (186). He sets the genius apart from the "two hundred and fifty millions who are always living in Europe and renew themselves every thirty years" (191). In a few broad strokes, Schopenhauer offers a picture of the inadvertently antisocial life of the genius. He does this by turning from a philosopher into a documentarian: instead of describing the genius's mode of aesthetic cognition in schematic terms, Schopenhauer begins to give concrete and anecdotal accounts of what geniuses are like as people. He enumerates the different forms of behavior that characterize the genius as a stranger to humanity, as a being who is often living "out of context."

The genius, as a speaker, is "inclined to monologues" (neigt . . . zu Monologen) (*WWV1,* 272).[11] This inclination is crucial in distinguishing the genius as an ontological outsider who is located at the outermost threshold of nature's "endless page" of time and space. Extending Schopenhauer's metaphor, one could say that the genius is the one capable of nontemporal, nonspatial, and noncausal perception, which locates him "nowhere" in the world as we know it (that is, in the "world as appearance"). The genius's voice, by extension, is a voice that announces departure from our world. When the genius follows his inborn inclinations, he steps toward a void beyond all context: an ontological vacuum where there are no individuals, no world, and no suffering. In other words, the monologue is the sound of incipient transcendence.

I say "incipient" transcendence because the escape from existence achieved by the genius is not equal to that achieved by the ascetic saint, the protagonist in the final section of Schopenhauer's book. The saint—who unlike the genius appears to be an entirely silent figure—experiences the world as *nothing*. The genius, by contrast, is a boundary-figure who participates in the context of practical life but also temporarily transcends it through aesthetic contemplation. Whereas saints are terminal figures, geniuses are caught in a kind of purgatory where they see past the world of appearances but continually return to and suffer through it. As such, geniuses undergo perpetual displacement. Because the "impression of the present moment on them is very strong," they are repeatedly "carried away" in two different senses of the phrase.[12] As subjects of pure knowledge, they are "carried away" into a timeless and space-less realm of Ideas where there is no suffering. But as embodied persons, the strong impression of the present "carries them away into thoughtless actions, into emotion and passion" (190). They get "carried away" doing awkward and absurd things in everyday life. Partially liberated from individuation, they suffer an exceptional kind of pain, which––from the pathetic tone of Schopenhauer's account––appears to be worse than a normal individual's mental suffering could ever be. For geniuses, emotion and passion are, counterintuitively, not the precipitates of individual desire or mood. The geniuses' outbursts of feeling feelings are, rather, part of the ongoing disembodiment and depersonalization that accompany their talents of perception. Living on the threshold between the visible world and its nullification, geniuses live halfway outside of social life. This affects their use of language, which they cannot (like common people) use instrumentally to accomplish practical tasks or to achieve superiority over other people. They are incapable of calculating how their conversations should play out to their own benefit (190). They can't plan social interactions in ways that serve their own interests, and they "will not conceal what it would be more prudent to keep concealed" (190). The genius's inclination to monologues is the crystallization of these various negative relations to the world. It is the speech that publicly demonstrates their virtual absence from the social world.

The genius's monologue absents the world by way of transcendental distraction. Such a speaker forgets the social context of utterance: "They will not in conversation think so much of the person with whom they are speaking as of the thing they are speaking about, which is vividly present in their minds" (190). Thus, monologue verbalizes timeless ideas existing outside of all known space, pointing to something that nobody else can see. As such, it is a form of speech that will always be inappropriate to any concrete communicative context. Geniuses neither participate in conversation nor address listeners but rather interrupt and ignore the other speakers. We might see this as a sign of vanity and self-absorption, but for Schopenhauer, such neglect of social context is not a sign of rudeness or tyranny. Geniuses do not try to dominate anyone with their interruptive monologues. Rather, for Schopenhauer it is a *virtue* to speak to nobody in particular, and into thin air. This act of speaking *to nobody* is different from soliloquy, also known as the "dialogue of the mind with itself."[13] The solitary speech of the genius is also not geared toward self-inspection or self-questioning. The genius's monologue would better be described as a language purified of any communicative function, which ventriloquizes underlying and invisible nature and so dispenses with distinct subject-positions (that is, the speaking "I," the listening "you"). Instead of conversing with another speaker about or within a particular context, monologic speech dissolves context and points to the Ideas that stand behind the visible world, tapping into a preworld stage before nature was nature. This is, of course, still a dialogue, but it is carried on neither with the self nor with another person. It is directed toward a nonhuman addressee that is impossible to locate in rational terms.

With this model of transcendence in mind, Schopenhauer turns commonsensical notions of social ethics on their head. The genius's ignorance of his speakers and his utter failure to acknowledge other people are not at all ethical failures. There is nothing insulting, rude, or egotistical about the genius's habit of talking past other people. For Schopenhauer, to forget the other (and to forget context) represents an admirable form of selflessness. In other words, the genius does not speak in monologue in order to declare social authority or to silence the perspectives of other speakers who live near him. The genius's habit of delivering monologues is, rather, the marker of a kind of metaphysical innocence, which by comparison makes all speakers with dialogic ambitions appear suspicious. The social ineptitude of the genius carries a moral promise. His hapless ignorance of social context is one of the crucial "preliminary stages to 'salvation'" in Schopenhauer's book.[14] Monologue demonstrates the possibility of dropping out of the competitive, violent continuum of practical life (*WWR1*, 77). But precisely because the genius is continually demonstrating his nonparticipation in social life, Schopenhauer sees him as the ultimate victim of social life. His condition could be called *antisociological* since he remains ignorant of how people actually pursue self-interest in social contexts. Such an antisociological bearing is suggested through Schopenhauer's remark about the poet, a subcategory of the genius, who in his poetry is concerned with the timeless Idea of "man." The poet "may know *man* profoundly and thoroughly, but *men* very badly" (*WWR1*, 194). This means that the poet understands the timeless essence of humans but not their everyday practices of trickery and duplicity. Likewise, he is unaware of how language might be used (as Schopenhauer notes earlier in the book) to facilitate collective action and to assure political or social authority. His language does not lead, coerce, or deceive anyone. Monologue, then, is a concrete, outward manifestation of the nonparticipatory nihilism that characterizes Schopenhauer's system. Although the genius is primarily important because of his ability to create timeless artworks, his monologues more clearly underscore his status as both a social and ontological outsider with an almost saintly innocence.

During his discussion of art, Schopenhauer presents the "madman" (der Irre) as a foil to the genius, who exhibits similar behavior but for very different reasons. If the genius is an authentically unworldly being who has access to the realm of Ideas behind the world-as-appearance, the madman is one who *claims* to exist in another world due to a pathological condition. The genius annuls context out of talent; the madman annuls context inauthentically due to a chronic affliction of the mind. As such, Schopenhauer produces parallel vocabularies that set the one figure apart from the other. The word that Schopenhauer uses to describe the solitary speech of madman is not the noun "Monolog" but the verb "irrereden" or "mad-talk" (*WWR1*, 277). Like the genius, the madman is also continually dislodged from their present location in time and space, but not because of an ability to be a subject of pure knowledge. Whereas genius-monologue negates context by verbalizing timelessness, the speeches of the madman are grounded in a defective memory. Schopenhauer dabbles with psychology here, claiming that the madman's *Irrereden* is a symptom of trauma: he falsifies the past because of an experience that is too painful to acknowledge or remember. Madmen, Schopenhauer explains, do not hallucinate. Rather, they extricate themselves from a common temporal and spatial context by inventing for themselves a false past: "There are gaps in their recollection that they fill up with fictions" (*WWR1*, 192). Madmen—and not artists—are the true producers of fiction and the creators of alternate universes. They are antisocial because their speech denies the possibility of inhabiting the same world as other people, asserting the existence of invisible circumstances that nobody else can see: "Their mad talk relates always to what is *absent* and *past*" (192). Mad talk addresses the present only through counterfactual nonevents and nonentities. Such talk is monologic in the sense that it is located in a world that exists for nobody else and must remain incomprehensible. Schopenhauer describes this ongoing work of falsification as a form of prosthesis. A traumatic moment in the past is replaced by the creative insertion of a new past: "just as a limb affected by mortification is cut off and replaced with a wooden one" (193). Speaking from an invented set of premises, the madman uses monologues to refute the possibility of a shared context, engineering fictions that nullify spatial, temporal, and social connections: "The mad person is wholly incapable of any reference to what is absent or past, but is determined solely by the whim of the moment in combination with fictions that in his head fill up the past" (192–93). Schopenhauer speaks of this nullification of *context* as a neglect of "connexions":

> We see that the madman correctly knows the individual present as well as many particulars of the past, but that he fails to recognize the connexion, the relations, and therefore goes astray and talks nonsense. Just this is his point of contact with the genius; for he too leaves out of sight knowledge of the connexion of things, as he neglects that knowledge of relations which is knowledge according to the principle of sufficient reason, in order to see in things only their Ideas. (*WWR1*, 194)

> Sehen wir nun angegebenermaßen den Wahnsinnigen das einzelne Gegenwärtige, auch manches einzelne Vergangene richtig erkennen, aber den Zusammenhang, die Relationen verkennen und daher irren und irrereden; so ist eben dieses der Punkt seiner Berührung mit

> dem genialen Individuum: denn auch dieses, da es die Erkenntnis der Relationen, welches die gemäß dem Satze des Grundes ist, verläßt, um in den Dingen nur ihre Ideen zu sehen und zu suchen. (*WWV1*, 277)

If human life is thought of, with Schopenhauer, as a story written on nature's "endless page," then both genius-monologue and mad speech would be two ways of disrupting the connective chain of this narrative. The external verbal activity of both the genius and the madman actively absent shared experiences (an idea of a common past, or of conventional conversation). In both cases, a speech addressed to nobody projects a void into the surrounding world: "the other links in the chain . . . retreat into darkness" (*WWV1*, 277).[15] Such speech *generates* darkness in the world. Genius-monologue and mad speech both produce the appearance of a speaker incapable of reproducing the discourses that enable social life, who lives with one foot in the void. As in other sections of *The World as Will and Representation*, there remains a sharp distinction between the authentic outsider-monologue of the genius and the inauthentic outsider-language of the madman. The genius really does escape into a timeless realm where individuation is unmasked as an illusion. He has access to truth; he really does approach the underlying nullity of visible reality. The madman's void is fake. He falsifies memory because of a personal experience of unbearable suffering, compulsively pronouncing self-serving fictions that are devoid of any truth. The madman's counterfactual rant may sound like a denial of the given world, and a transcendence of time and space, but he is in fact only fashioning a *new* world for himself, in order to compensate for a past trauma. Different mental operations are at work in these two modes of alien speech: the madman's memory artificially induces a disengagement from the world-as-appearance, whereas the genius's perceptive ability is already truly disengaged from it.

One overarching goal of Schopenhauer's discussion of madness is to set authentic transcendence apart from merely apparent transcendence, to sort the *real* voiding apart from counterfeit voiding. In insisting on a sharp distinction between these two ways of being an outsider, Schopenhauer repeats a general elitist tendency of *The World as Will and Representation*: he narrows down the count of people who might be capable of escaping the tyranny of the will. It is certainly fair to accuse Schopenhauer of an aristocratic worldview here. As Michael Allen Gillespie writes, the trajectory of transcendence traced in *The World as Will and Representation* is written down for a select few, that is, almost *nobody*: "Some few may be warmed by its lambent flame, but beyond their circle there is only a cold and uncaring night."[16] *The World as Will and Representation* ends by referring to a very narrow circle ("those in whom the will has turned against itself") and making that small circle into the true witnesses to *nothingness*. The frequently acknowledged misanthropy of Schopenhauer's philosophy is inscribed in the author's rhetorical strategies of eliminating false alternatives. Madness may resemble genius, but it is not a substitute for it. Even when madness annuls spatial, temporal, and causal context, this annulment is pathological and duplicitous rather than truthful and timeless. Schopenhauer wants to ensure that we do not mistake the inmates of asylums for artists. This elitism is grounded in Schopenhauer's pessimism: if transcendence were so commonplace (that is, as common as the mentally ill), the world would not appear to be as terrible and intractable as Schopenhauer describes it.

In order to defend the distinction between genius and madness, and therefore to keep the count of geniuses at a minimum, there must be criteria for telling the two apart. These two forms of character must be outwardly legible so that it becomes possible for the philosopher to identify one or the other. Just such a process of identification is recounted during Schopenhauer's discussion of genius and madness, as he adopts the first person and provides anecdotal evidence for his claims. He reports that he has often visited asylums, and by looking into the inmates' eyes he was able to detect traces of genius that had lost the battle for superiority within that individual. Here Schopenhauer employs a metaphor of "layers," describing genius and madness as conflicting parts of a single individual. In one madman whom Schopenhauer met, genius "glimpsed" through the thick surface-layer of madness, which had ultimately won the "upper hand" within that person (*WWV1*, 274). In describing a genius that he had met, Schopenhauer speaks of how the dominant layer of genius is lightly painted over by a "light" or "quiet coating" (leiser Anstrich) of madness (274).[17] In making these distinctions, based on the legibility of physiognomic features, Schopenhauer mixes metaphors of vision (glimpsing through) with sound (quiet coating). The philosopher assumes that he can authenticate one individual's status as "genius" and another's status as "madmen" through his own work of physiognomic analysis.

The stability of Schopenhauer's entire system is at stake in these discussions. If these character types (genius and madman) were only arbitrary labels applied within the course of social life, they would lose their exceptional, negative status. When Schopenhauer tells us that we will only count those people as geniuses who have delivered timeless works to humanity, he needs (for the coherence of his argument) to assume that the genius-artwork will remain one independent of any cultural factors (*WWR1*, 191). Schopenhauer forecloses the possibility that art originates through the collective workings of a broader culture, just as he dismisses the possibility of being a genius without producing art (we might think here of people who have every ability necessary to make great art but cannot do so because of censorship or poverty). The discussion of the geniuses' "monologues" and the madmen's "mad talk" are important moments in Schopenhauer's broader process of elimination. These modes of speech, like the eyes and faces of artists and asylum inmates, are distinguishing markers that are supposed to help us tell these two alien-figures apart from the rest of humanity, and to tell them apart from one another. As a whole, *The World as Will and Representation* assembles a delicate hierarchy, held in place by a series of authenticating gestures. These gestures continue right up to the end of the book; in describing the salvation experienced by the "saint," Schopenhauer grants that "to meet with [saints] is of course rarely granted to us in our own experience" but assures readers that the existence of real saints has been "vouched for with the stamp of truth by art" (*WWR1*, 411). I would speculate here that Schopenhauer's ceaseless work of authentication (and de-authentication) has the potential to create uncertainty (if not skepticism) in the reader. In reading *The World as Will and Representation*, we are led to think that the philosopher has provided us with the abstract criteria for distinguishing the voice of a solitary genius from the voice of a madman (and for distinguishing real saints from fakes). But once we have finished the book, we are also left with the anxiety that, without the authority of the philosopher who reads voices and faces, we might not be able to tell all these different hierarchized modes of denial apart from one another. We might get the different outsiders mixed up, and madmen, geniuses, and saints will bleed into one another. All the outsiders' monologues start to sound the same. How can we know if we belong to the "few" whom this book was meant to comfort?[18] These are the uncertainties that linger in the wake of *The World as Will and Representation.*

The Appropriation and Reception of Schopenhauer's Outsiders

It may be that these ambiguities actually helped Schopenhauer's mass appeal. It is possible that the position of uncertainty and ambivalence in which *The World as Will and Representation* leaves its readers also enabled the widespread appropriation of his philosophy in art and literature of the nineteenth and twentieth centuries. Because Schopenhauer so often authenticates his arguments with anecdotal evidence from lived experience, he virtually forces his readers to imaginatively bridge the gap between philosophy and life, supplementing his philosophical theorization with evidence of personal and vicarious aesthetic experiences. In other words, the text may encourage an antisystemic, identificatory mode of reading. Critic Heinz Gerd Ingenkamp has argued that *The World as Will and Representation*, despite its apparently rigid systematicity, can be read as a "convolute," which tries and often fails to impose order on a diverse array of intertexts.[19] As a convoluted text marked by argumentative and evidential gaps, *The World as Will and Representation* invites creative forms of reading and appropriation, whereby readers imaginatively transpose themselves into the different outsider-positions described in the book. Anyone can be a genius, from a certain angle.

This, I would argue, is what happened to Schopenhauer's nihilist model of monologue in the subsequent course of intellectual history: it was expanded into a general model of the outsider, which could be applied much more broadly than Schopenhauer's own terms. In this way, Schopenhauer helped facilitate secular fantasies of *unworldly speech* in the nineteenth and twentieth centuries. This unworldly speech did not depend on any outmoded notion of divine inspiration but on the idea of a fundamental vacuity: a void underlying the universe as it normally appears to us. In this way, Schopenhauer created a new vision of the outsider that allowed the classical vision of the "genius" to survive into the nineteenth century in an altered form. On the one hand, Schopenhauer reproduced the terms of the *Geniekult* of the eighteenth century, hypostatizing the genius as an absolutely autonomous mind. What Schopenhauer added to this already-canonized image of monologic genius was a new, negative metaphysical basis with no muses and no gods. In *The World as Will and Representation*, the genius debuts as a clairvoyant nihilist. Through both works and words, this nihilist genius de-realizes the worldly context in which all of us are trapped; he gestures toward a complete nullity that underlies all individuated existence. Schopenhauer thus lays the groundwork for a new privileging of the monologue: monologue is a voice from the void that nobody else can see. Truly solitary speech—insofar as it is spoken by an authentic genius—is even more otherworldly than the voice of a dead person, since it taps into a realm of eternity that is beyond any individuation. Monologue, through Schopenhauer, becomes *otherworldly* language.

The least sympathetic way to describe Schopenhauer's *World as Will and Representation* would be to call it a manifesto of the elite, which explains why Great Minds must be left to their own devices and freed from any social obligations.[20] As I have shown in the example of his strained delineation of genius and madness, the work of social distinction (the sorting of the privileged from the millions) stands at the center of Schopenhauer's discussions. The great irony of his elitism is that it is construed in a highly readable language, mostly free of specialist terminology and jargon, and was conducive to widespread popularization. To put it plainly: it is much easier (and arguably more enjoyable) to read Schopenhauer than it is to read Kant or Hegel, and this is a likely explanation for the belated popularity of his *World as Will and Representation*. In its striking accessibility, Schopenhauer's work sketched out for a general readership how to take a "retreat into darkness." Any curious reader is thereby provided with a complete cosmological picture that ought to (according to Schopenhauer's book!) be accessible only to a select few. We can read Schopenhauer, without having to achieve any of this knowledge for ourselves through art or askesis, and learn that the world is three things: (1) an illusion, or "veil," (2) the will, and (3) nothing. These revelations, which Schopenhauer's system places along a diachronic trajectory of discovery, have the power to become (in the imagination of the reader) a fixed model of a multilayered universe of worlds in the plural, with images on the top, the will below them, and nothing but darkness below it.[21] The book is an adventure story; the "genius" and the "saint" serve as generic avatars onto which readers can imaginatively project themselves so that they too can shuttle from one layer to the next, imagining the world, the will, and the void.

Georg Lukács had a theory as to why this multilayered ontology would have been so appealing to a wider, educated bourgeois readership. Far from presenting a genuinely otherworldly vision, Schopenhauer's philosophy was actually, Lukács argued, an artful expression of the real existing alienation that defined capitalist society in the nineteenth century. By locating his redeemed individual in a total void, Schopenhauer was simply imitating the compulsory egoism and isolation of the bourgeoisie. I refer here to Lukács's discussion of Schopenhauer from *The Destruction of Reason*, a work that has been widely discredited for constructing a simplistic notion of "irrationalism" but that nonetheless contains valid and incisive summaries of certain thinkers' works, including that of Schopenhauer.[22] In Lukács's critique of Schopenhauer, he suggests that *The World as Will and Representation* functions by doubling the everyday egotism of economic life:

> But with Schopenhauer, the dismissal of conventional, cosmically inflated bourgeois egotism is similarly enacted in the individual spiritually isolated from society, and it even marks a heightening of this isolation. From aesthetic enjoyment to saintly asceticism, the individual's pure self-sufficiency is celebrated more and more in Schopenhauer's professed surmounting of egotism as the only exemplary moral attitude. To be sure, this "elevated" egotism was meant to appear, in sharp contrast to ordinary egotism, as a turning away from illusion and the "veil of *maya*" (i.e., the life of society) in which conventional egotism is bogged down. It is presented as a sympathy with all things resulting from the insight that individuation is only an illusion, and one that conceals the unity of all existence.[23]

According to Lukács, Schopenhauer performs an act of copying whereby commonplace egoism is duplicated and displaced into another unified world underlying our own, merely material social world. Whereas the social for Schopenhauer is a space of permanent nonrelation, competition, and coercion, the unified world below is a space of shared darkness. Lukács's discussion of Schopenhauer recalls Jürgen Wertheimer's note about how literary writing around 1800 oversaw a general "withdrawal of the individual out of the space of social relations into the vacuum of absolute dialogue."[24] If Rousseau's solitary walker and Goethe's Werther had undertaken that withdrawal in order to recover the freedom of the self that cannot be realized *under given social conditions*, Schopenhauer recommends withdrawal to recover a unity that can be practically realized *under no circumstances*, that is, it can only be encountered and embraced *beyond any context*. According to Lukács, this dream of total darkness, of a vacuum beneath the world, is nothing but rampant egoism trying to become something else, which it cannot be under any existing circumstances: a selfishness that can only cease to be selfishness if it is transported into another dimension. Schopenhauer—with his ideal types of monologic misanthropes—succeeded in creating a hyperbolic and otherworldly copy of familiar individualism. The "void" penetrated by his elite group of metaphysical outsiders is (Lukács might have added) simply a copy of the real existing void of modern society, diagnosed by modern social theory, in which we are connected to one another only through relations of economic dependency. Following Lukács, we could further speculate that Schopenhauer's popularity was due both to the accessibility of his prose and for the way that his nihilist philosophy provided an unfamiliar picture of a very familiar kind of isolation. Monologue, as presented in *The World as Will and Representation*, is the discourse of an individualism that exceeds all known individualism. This nihilist monologue reiterates and revises a preexisting form of everyday alienation that is painful and numbing, and makes this alienation into something transcendent, inspired, rebellious, and even (despite its misanthropy) more humane. To negate the world with speech and achieve "the verbal epitome of loneliness and isolation" becomes a noble task, and the misanthrope becomes a kind of hero.[25] Monologue becomes the *art of alienation*.

Dostoevsky's Underground Monologue and the Art of Alienation

If there is a modern literary work that solidified monologue as an art of alienation, it is Fyodor Dostoevsky's 1864 novella *Notes from Underground*. Whereas Schopenhauer was a theorist of nihilist monologue, Dostoevsky was a practitioner. Whereas Schopenhauer sincerely subscribed to nihilism as a philosophy of life and gave monologic characters a privileged status in his system, Dostoevsky's novella showed what nihilism would *sound* like as speech, constructing a single uninterrupted contexture that gives voice to extreme alienation.[26] Lukács's description of Schopenhauer's thought as a "heightening of . . . isolation" can be applied to the Underground Man in a modified sense.[27] His ceaseless monologue is, on the one hand, a simple symptom of isolation: he lives alone and unhealthy in a garret and has nobody with whom to share his lament, so he channels his rage at contemporary society into an imagined speech that he writes down (and that is in turn provided to the reader). But the Underground Man *heightens* this isolation, developing his own particular idiosyncratic style of self-negation. He artfully invents an accompanying set of expressive metaphors that begin and end with the claustrophobic image of the "Underground." Taking up his own alienation as his primary theme, he heightens this alienation to the level of a verbal art––creating in the process a manner of narration that in turn spawned (some would claim) a good portion of modern European literature. Indeed, there is no shortage of emphatic claims regarding the monumental influence of Fyodor Dostoevsky's 1864 novella *Notes from Underground* within the literary history of the last centuries. According to Joseph Frank, "Every important cultural development of the past half-century . . . has claimed the underground man as its own."[28] Wolf Schmid has written that the *Notes* constitute "the first important work of a new genre of first-person narrative," which would become "fully developed and established" by the middle of the twentieth century.[29] Similarly, Brian McHale has called the Underground Man the "founder" of an entire "tradition of radically unreliable modernist narrators."[30] I would add that the Underground Man canonized the technique of verbal nihilism.

The Underground Man provides the template for characters who think and speak in a "vacuum" or "void," or at the edge of an "abyss."[31] Emptiness proliferates around him in all its variants: physical, social, emotional, spiritual, existential. Such a literary character is not simply alienated from this or that thing (that is, a particular society, living humanity, nature). As a verbal creature, this character exists as an ongoing process of incessant and ever-intensifying alienat*ing*. He is constituted thus through a special form of character-construction, which Mikhail Bakhtin claimed that Dostoevsky invented: the Underground Man is an "infinite function," as opposed to a static literary character, which is an "immobile and finite substance."[32] What the reader takes from the text is a dynamic verbal habit of nihilism. The Underground Man's nihilism is therefore not a fixed belief system (as with Schopenhauer) or a result of his innate character but a way of speaking and existing against the world, which is permitted to evolve from page to page.

With this literary practice, Dostoevsky's underground speakers offered visions of emptiness that supplemented and diverged from Schopenhauer's metaphysical imaginary of the void. When Rado Pribic writes that the general trajectory of the *Notes* is a "plunge into the void," he echoes and amplifies the hyperbolic rhetoric of the Underground Man himself, with its infectious and (for many readers and writers) irresistible negativity.[33] My argument is that this spatially and visually intricate hyperbole of the monologic speaker, who claims to exist in a "void" and "underground," lent a special significance to the monologue as an embedded literary form. The Underground Man created a new "brand" of verbal self-isolation. Monologue, for those who write in the wake of the underground type, has become a kind of verbal eraser of the world that performatively creates the emptiness that it describes.

Wherever it is encountered in his works, Dostoevsky's "underground type" is a highly self-conscious misanthrope whose voice represents the "verbal epitome of total isolation."[34] The underground type was (according to the author) expressed most succinctly in the figure of Goliadkin in the 1846 novel *The Double* and later canonized in the unnamed "Underground Man" from the 1864 novel *Notes from Underground.*[35] As a figure common to both of these novels, the underground type can be described as a character who lives in a vacuum of his own fashioning, talking to nobody. Both *The Double* and *Notes from Underground* present speakers who become engulfed by their own voices: interpersonal interaction is replaced with self-address, and social antagonisms are replaced with self-reproach. As with Schopenhauer's genius and madman, the underground type's monologue has an absence-effect. The speaker extricates himself from context—foreclosing any possibility of human community—by producing an unprompted and unlistenable discourse. But whereas Schopenhauer and Dostoevsky are focused on characters who are "becoming nothing," the German philosopher and the Russian novelist differ sharply in their accounts of the causes and consequences of antisocial monologue.

Dostoevsky's underground type is characterized by a particular kind of monologic, hyperconscious "voice regulation,"[36] which has the effect of projecting a "vacuum"[37] around the speaker. This technique is significant because, for Dostoevsky, the vacuum is not a preexisting metaphysical fact that must be discovered through a philosophical quest. It is something that is *made* through linguistic practice, out of materials borrowed from the social world. For Schopenhauer, the void uncovered by monologue is a given, an underlying fact of the universe. By contrast, a broad range of emotional, intellectual, and institutional relationships are implicated in the vacuum projected by Dostoevsky's underground type. His own private "Nothing" is made from the stuff of society. No matter how much social context is *absented*, it is never fully and finally *erased*. This difference between Schopenhauer and Dostoevsky is partly grounded in their chosen genres of writing. When Dostoevsky creates characters, he always provides them with a vivid social life. The concept of the "type" that Dostoevsky applied to his "underground" characters describes a specific practice of literary realism, which is pedagogical as well as poetic: the literary work undertakes the (sociological) task of representing the member of a certain social class or subgroup while also fictionalizing and poetizing the characteristics of that class so that the character takes on "mythic proportions."[38] Dostoevsky's construction of an "underground type" differs from Schopenhauer's typology of outsiders (madman, genius, saint) first of all because of its implied dialectical relationship to an ever-changing social reality. The underground type is presented—to quote Dostoevsky's authorial footnote—so as to "elucidate the reasons why he appeared and had to appear among us."[39] The literary work retains a sociological intention, however eccentric it may seem.

This relationship—separation *from* and proximity *to* society—is already suggested in the spatial connotations of the term "underground." The outsider's place is not "up" here with us, in public view, but it is directly "under" us. The shared, public space of the surface and the isolated space of the underground border on one another. Schopenhauer's outsiders are much further away from everyday life. He is interested above all in the chosen few who are on a permanent pilgrimage to the void. Dostoevsky's characters inhabit a void that is (so the author suggests) simply the dark underside of the everyday social world. The underground types of *The Double* and *Notes from Underground* are at least partly grounded in a particular time and place: they inhabit the largely anonymous society of mid-nineteenth-century St. Petersburg and belong, as René Girard writes, "to that pretentious and lamentable bureaucratic class whose mentality the writer deems extremely significant."[40] The antisocial underground type, in other words, is born out of a particular, middling position of administrative authority, which is neither totally destitute nor totally depraved, inhabiting neither the lower depths of the social hierarchy nor any elevated position of power. As Dostoevsky would make clear both in his subsequent diary entries on *The Double*, and as well as within the text of *Notes from Underground*, this middle social position is home to those intellectuals who will propagate radicalisms of all kinds (atheism, socialism, political nihilism, or anarchism). They are the everyday aliens that give birth to revolutionary politics. Within Dostoevsky's literary treatments of the underground type, this middling position between power and powerlessness becomes crystallized in a practice of monologue. In this monologue, the speaker makes innumerable claims regarding his sovereign knowledge of and autonomy from the world while also actively erasing and absenting himself through the very same speech. The underground type is, then, both a representative of a social class and the embodiment of a self-nullifying discursive style. He is both a seat of weak authority and a hidden cell in which all authority may be negated. In this way, Dostoevsky's prose translates the features of a given social class (the bureaucrat-intellectual) into a literary form that can then serve as an allegory for a common nihilist condition, in which all of "us" (to quote Dostoevsky's authorial footnote) are implicated (*NU*, 3). This condition, without transcendental values or authorities committed to the common good, is commonly understood as European secular modernity and was poignantly described by László Földenyi as the "*gray* hell" of "contemporary Western culture" defined by scientific rationality and extreme self-consciousness.[41] The monologue of one isolated "type" thus conjures an emptiness that we in turn can experience as an emblem of modern life.

The widespread appeal and influence of Dostoevsky's monologues might be connected to the versatility of the "underground" as a metaphor. In both *The Double* and *Notes from Underground*, the monologues of the underground type conjure emptiness through intricate metaphors of subterranean space. These metaphors, which connote isolation, damnation, and coldness, are integral to explaining the origins and meanings of monologue as a mode of discourse. Whereas Schopenhauer posited monologue as a mode of abyssal speech by locating it within a metaphysical model of the universe, Dostoevsky's novels characterize monologue through overdetermined spatial metaphors of "falling" and "going down," which carry a range of psychological, social, and metaphysical implications. Everywhere you go, there may be some kind of underground hidden away. "The" underground is not only in Saint Petersburg; it is anywhere, and anyone can go there.

Conjuring Abysses in *The Double* and *Notes from Underground*

This universal accessibility of the void––its proximity to the everyday––is already evident in *The Double*. In this novel, the protagonist's incessant monologues are represented as his way of talking himself into an abyss in the course of his daily routine. *The Double* tells the catastrophic story of a person who, to paraphrase Mikhail Bakhtin, attempts to replace social interaction with soliloquy, relying on his own inner "second voice" as a substitute for the voices of other people who would validate him.[42] Goliadkin is a low-level bureaucrat who is obviously envious of his superiors at work, and who embraces modern notions of individual self-reliance to a pathological extent. His ideas of independence feed his monologues, with which he is continually "justifying himself in his own eyes by various irrefutable reasons."[43] Goliadkin tries to survive in the social world through a continual practice of verbal auto-affection, talking himself up to be something bigger and better than others consider him to be. However, his self-justifications point back to his sense of eternal inadequacy, suggesting irremediable lacks in his social self (he is never smart, skilled, or suave enough). This incessant self-justification finally culminates in a complete loss of reality, triggering an experience of the uncanny and supernatural. The major turning point of the novel is Goliadkin's confrontation with his doppelgänger, the supremely confident and instantly popular Goliadkin Jr. While Goliadkin Jr. triumphs within St. Petersburg society, the original Goliadkin Sr. is scornfully packed off to an insane asylum. Within the narration, "abyss" emerges as central term for describing the direction and origin of Goliadkin's story. The "abyss" is his failure, humiliation, and captivity. Where and how does the abyss appear?

The opening of an abyss underneath Goliadkin is foreshadowed in the second chapter of the novel, as Goliadkin pays a visit to Dr. Krestyan

Ivanovich, who has previously prescribed him medicine for the treatment of an unspecified condition. During this appointment, the doctor tells Goliadkin that his treatment "should consist in a change of habits," specifically that Goliadkin should try to be more sociable: "you should visit friends and acquaintances, and along with that be no enemy of the bottle; likewise keep merry company" (*TD*, 11). Concerned that Goliadkin might be leading a "melancholy" way of life, the doctor politely seeks out information about Goliadkin's social relations or lack thereof. The doctor's attempt at information gathering prompts Goliadkin to deliver an extended monologue in which he takes over the doctor's role as observer and judge of healthy sociability. In his rambling speech, Goliadkin articulates his knowledge of, and adherence to, a range of social norms: "Mr. Goliadkin, still smiling, hastened to observe that it seemed to him that he was like everybody else, that he was his own man, that his diversions were like everybody else's . . . that he could, of course, go to the theater, for, like everybody else, he also had means, that he worked during the day, but in the evening he was at home, that he was quite all right" (11). This breathless declaration of conformity displays Goliadkin's internalization of a set of social values (self-reliance, industry, wealth, cultural prestige) but also confirms the doctor's suspicions that Goliadkin is basically antisocial, because he *does not let the other talk*. Goliadkin's claim that he is "his own man" is both true and untrue. His words are uttered for his own benefit, to shore up a sense of stable identity. But Goliadkin's incessant, unstoppable delivery suggests that his sense of autonomy is dependent on a continual and forceful labor of verbal auto-affection that permits no listeners or respondents. As such, his confidence is a fragile façade that could vanish as soon as Goliadkin loses control of his own voice. As Bakhtin argued, Goliadkin has resolved to live without the voice of the other: he wants to replace society with his own monologue. Such a way of life is, as suggested in Goliadkin's stammering and forced facial expressions, dangerously exhausting and supremely unstable. It is hard for the reader to listen to his monologue with a straight face.

Dostoevsky makes it easy to pathologize Goliadkin, and he sets a sort of trap for the reader: if we think Goliadkin is crazy and insufferable, then we as readers stand on the side of the doctor, who appears in the last scene as a demonic figure with red eyes, just as Goliadkin is being committed to an asylum. In order to avoid falling into this "trap," I want to instead consider an interpretation that tries to take Goliadkin's words at face value. In his first monologue before the doctor, Goliadkin demonstrates that he is trying to live out the idea of a rational, self-interested member of managerial class, who owns property and lives only for himself, as "his own man" (11). Given his solitary habits and his suppression of external voices of authority, we could say that Goliadkin takes these ideas more seriously than, for instance, the doctor with his recommendation of drinking and merriment. The discourses of rational egoism that define Goliadkin's subjectivity are, after all, not his own: his self-image is modeled on "everyone else" and therefore has universal validity.[44] Through his incessant repetition of the same points, in order to irrefutably justify himself, he helps to solidify and make permanent a set of emergent social norms that, he has learned, are proper to his class status. Incessant, dense monologue is his way of conserving the egotism that society has taught him. He knows that he needs a void around him, in order to be a proper citizen and "man." The problem is that he goes further than anyone else around him, making this personal void into a bottomless "abyss," into which he then plunges. Still, it is a *private* abyss *of his own making*—and therefore the proper product of a self-reliant middle-class subject.

The image of the "abyss" first appears in an extended passage narrated in free indirect speech, which immediately precedes the appearance of Goliadkin's double. Goliadkin has humiliated himself by attempting to force himself into a party hosted at the house of State Councillor Berendev, a higher-up who was "once Goliadkin's benefactor" (*TD*, 30). To everyone's horror, Goliadkin tries, uninvited, to dance the polka with Berendev's daughter, Klara Olsufyevna, whose birthday is being celebrated. Fleeing the humiliating scene, Goliadkin crosses out of the threshold of the house and finds himself on the verge of another threshold: "finally, he stumbled, it seemed to him that he was falling into an abyss; he was about the cry out—and suddenly found himself in the yard" (42). "Abyss" here is a metaphor for Goliadkin's emotional devastation. But the threshold of the abyss is established in the next chapter as an *actual* boundary between the world and the nonworld, which Goliadkin does in fact cross. Goliadkin goes into his own abyss, *for real*. In carrying out this erasure of social reality, he actually *conforms* to the rules of the social world around him.

As Goliadkin tries to assume and ventriloquize external social authorities, he becomes his own annihilator and constructs his own abyss. At the start of the fateful chapter where his double appears, Goliadkin begins by fleeing the "destructive gazes" of Andrei Filippovich, his distant superior in the bureaucratic hierarchy. The narrator makes the gap in authority between Goliadkin and Filippovich comically clear in detailing a labyrinthine chain of command: Filippovich is "head of an office in the place where Mr. Goliadkin also served in the quality of assistant to his section chief" (8). Filippovich's gaze at Goliadkin is, then, a downward gaze from high above. This is where Dostoevsky explicitly adopts the vocabulary of nihilism. Feeling this and other downward gazes, Goliadkin is "annihilated—annihilated totally—in the full sense of the word."[45] Goliadkin is reduced to a nothing. Instead of denying his own nullity, he himself now looks to adopt the work of making himself into a nothing, doing the work of oppression that others have been begun: "Mr. Goliadkin now wanted not only to escape from himself, but to annihilate himself completely, to be no more, to turn to dust. In the present moment he paid heed to nothing around him, understood nothing that was going on around him, and looked as if indeed neither the unpleasantness of the foul night, nor the long way, the rain, the snow, the wind, nor all this harsh weather existed for him" (*TD*, 44). Like any good nihilist, Goliadkin yearns for nothingness, attempting at once to nullify everything in his environment as well as himself. His self-renunciation liberates him from persecution—that is, according to the narrator's external viewpoint (who says that it "looked as if" the world around Goliadkin has ceased to exist for him). However, something separates Goliadkin's inclination toward nothingness from the transcendental nihilism of Schopenhauer. Even as he is yearning for the void, he ventriloquizes external social forces within his inner monologue, as relayed by the narrator in free indirect discourse. The very same words of self-justification that he uttered in the doctor's office reappear in the narrator's free indirect discourse, suggesting that Goliadkin is still firmly committed to modern jargon of self-reliance: "Mr. Goliadkin hastened at once, as was his wont, to assume a completely special air, an air which showed clearly that he, Goliadkin, was his own man, that he was all right" (46). Goliadkin's monologue of self-justification continues even as he strives for his own annihilation, and the world around him vanishes. This is not a contradiction; it is actually consistent with Goliadkin's character as established thus far. Goliadkin remains self-reliant in a perverse sense: he demonstrates that he is his own man by copying and amplifying the oppressive voices of society within his self-directed monologue. If he is to be annihilated, he is going to do it himself. For this reason, we can see the refrain "I am my own man" as a sort of magic protection spell that conjures an abyss beneath Goliadkin. When the abyss does appear, Goliadkin demonstrates his autonomy by completing the work of self-nullification *by himself*. Being self-reliant, nobody needs to push him down:

> His position at that moment was like the position of a man standing over a frightful precipice, when the earth breaks away under him, is rocking, shifting, sways for a last time, and falls, drawing him into the abyss, and meanwhile the unfortunate man has neither the strength nor the firmness of spirit to jump back, to take his eyes from the yawning chasm; the abyss draws him, and he finally leaps into it himself, himself hastening the moment of his own perdition. (*TD*, 49)

The abyss, then, has emerged as a metaphor for the self-nullifying operation of Goliadkin's ongoing inner monologue. His speech, antisocial yet strongly socially determined, has brought him to a point of no return. But this threshold is not, as for Schopenhauer's genius, a portal into a comforting "*Nichts*" beyond any social context. Goliadkin's abyss is a condensation of the antagonistic forces that characterize society. Therefore, his fall into the abyss is only the *beginning* of the unhappy story in which he will be humiliated countless more times. In this way, *The Double* explores the idea of an abyss that is immanent to the social world, one that opens up right in the Petersburg street on which Goliadkin is walking home. Society reproduces itself by making abysses, or more precisely: by making us make abysses into which we willingly plunge. *The Double* literalizes and visualizes this process by illustrating in downright fantastic terms the process whereby the individual's monologue of self-reliance opens up the abyss into which he falls.

The name that Dostoevsky will later give to this immanent abyss that underlies modern society is, of course, "the underground." In *Notes from Underground*, Dostoevsky posits subterranean space as a metaphor for the isolating, destructive consequences of modern rationality. The "Underground Man" is a former bureaucrat and intellectual who was once enamored of Enlightenment ideals of reason and historical progress, which he now sees through and repudiates to such an extent that he believes that "any consciousness at all is a sickness" (*NU*, 7). If Goliadkin's monologue was partially associated with individual pathology and the naive overzealousness of a petty bureaucrat, the monologue of *Notes from Underground* is presented as the ultimate voice of modern experience. This difference can be related to the distinct temporalities of two novels. Goliadkin loses his world suddenly, during the course of a normal workweek, and finds himself swept up in a fantastical, episodic farce involving his doppelgänger. The process of nullification in *Notes from Underground* is, by contrast, drawn out over an agonizing length of time and is already well advanced at the beginning of the novel. When the novel begins, the world is already gone for the protagonist; there are no characters to speak of except for the Underground Man and his imagined listeners. When the Underground Man finally initiates the narrative of his younger years in the novel's second section, he is separated from these dramatic episodes by an unbridgeable temporal divide. He lost his last chance to make meaningful contact with another human being, and it is now too late for him. Given this temporal position, the "underground man" speaks authoritatively *from* and *about* the abyss that is immanent to modern society. As both specimen *of* and guide *through* the underground, his antisocial discourse provides the reader with an exhaustive account of why community is impossible in the age of "hyperconsciousness."[46] His monologue is the native language of the underground, and he exhaustively develops a set of extended metaphors that express and explain the subterranean vacuum in which his voice resonates.

Of the many striking images that the Underground Man uses to describe his own incessant speech, perhaps the most striking his is description of his "babble" as "a deliberate pouring from empty into void" (*NU*, 18). Such a pouring, he suggests, is equivalent to intellectual discourse as a whole:

"the sole and express purpose of every intelligent man is babble" (18). Rhetorically, the Underground Man locates his speech within a paradoxical economy of emptiness. Babble seeks to fill the vacuum, but it does this by adding more emptiness to the vacuum. The drive to fill in the emptiness has the effect of increasing emptiness, subtracting more from the void. What connects this rhetoric of the "void" to *The Double*, then, is the idea that the void is both a cause *and* an effect of a speaking subject's monologue. In following the Enlightenment mandate of embracing one's own intellectual autonomy and speaking alone as "one's own man," the speaker finds himself alone in a universe where even emptiness is vanishing. And while this image does not make much sense with regard to the laws of physics, it serves to undermine the entire undertaking of *Notes from Underground* as a text, in which the reader is also implicated. If we are listening to this voice, we too would be located in this void that is becoming emptier with each successive word. Of course, the broader realist framework of *Notes* (which assures us that we are reading the notes of an isolated former bureaucrat) encourages us to take this statement about the "void" as a rhetorical flourish, which expresses anguish over the futility of intellectual labor. Nonetheless, Dostoevsky's novel—like *The Double*—lays the groundwork for future literary works that would take its antisocial imperative more seriously than Dostoevsky himself did. In Kafka's "Description of a Struggle," for instance, the "Praying Man" actually apparently *does* literally unmake the world around him by "pouring empty" into it. The impossible spatial configurations suggested by the Underground Man's discourse—his construction of a void in place of the world—would be revisited and radicalized in experimental fiction over the course of the twentieth century, conjoined with the voids of other thinkers of nihilism, including Schopenhauer and Nietzsche. Pouring empty into void would eventually become a literary phenomenon.

Dostoevsky's imagination of the void again diverges sharply from Schopenhauer's. Whereas the emptiness of the void was for Schopenhauer a final state of repose freed from suffering and individuation, the void of the underground is cramped and clogged with the detritus produced by its isolated inhabitant, along with remnants of the vanished social world. The "empty" has an overwhelming shape and volume. Early on in his monologue, the Underground Man provides an image of how the "loathsome, stinking underground" was built up and fortified through an ongoing, cumulative process whereby consciousness deposits more and more "filth" (*NU*, 11). It is, again, the modern intellect with its "hyperconsciousness" that initiates this process. Hyperconsciousness, here, is synonymous with Enlightenment rationality. The enlightened act of self-reflection is described not as a means to self-knowledge but rather as a form of self-devouring narcissism. The Underground Man captures the self-destructive workings of hyperconsciousness with the metaphor of a mouse-hole: "The wretched mouse, in addition to the one original nastiness, has already managed to fence itself in with so many other nastinesses in the form of question and doubts; it has padded out the one question with so many unresolved questions that, willy-nilly, some fatal slops have accumulated around it, some stinking filth consisting of dubieties, anxieties, and, finally, of the spit raining down on it from the ingenuous figures that stand around it like judges and dictators" (11). Much like Goliadkin's monologues of self-reassurance, the underground monologue is made out of the stuff of social life, infused with the voices of the authorities that denigrated and doubted the speaker in the past. This most solitary of all discourses, which seeks to create a protective shield around the subject and extricate it from any social context, is also a memory bank, a kind of catalogue of the antagonisms that accompany socialization. The monologic act of pouring emptiness into void is by no means a way of forgetting; rather, it is an attempt to turn the injurious languages of the social world into an indestructible shelter, where the subject can live to the end. The monologue is an excessive reiteration of speech already circulating in the social field, endowing old insults with renewed significance.[47] The Underground Man shows, at the same time, that this shelter is continually being destroyed and rebuilt, suggesting that it never provides the permanent protection that one had hoped for. He speaks of how, after the mouse has built its fence of discourse, it swipes this construction away and "immerses itself in cold, venomous, and, above all, everlasting spite" (11). These two movements, self-immuring and its revocation, cogently describe how the Underground Man's monologue is constructed: he voices elaborate polemics, turns them against himself, and then abandons this polemic for another. The verbal construction and fortification of the underground is an infinite and impossible task. The metaphor of the mouse-hole is, then, structurally analogous to image of "pouring from empty into void": the solitary speaker seeks to establish a vacuum around him, which is never empty enough (18). The incessancy that defines the Underground Man's speech—and comprises his major contribution to subsequent literary tradition—stems from a striving toward a nullity that can never be reached. The world will never be empty enough, and the self will never be absent enough. The nihilist position of the Underground Man must be performatively established, again and again. For the sake of nullity, the monologue must go on.

The *Notes* are not a manifesto, and the Underground Man never arrives at a stable philosophy of nihilism that could be extracted from and enacted outside his transcribed monologue. Yet even if the political consequences of the *Notes* remain debatable, the basic consensus regarding Dostoevsky's novel is that that the Underground Man stands as a polemic against the progressive, rationalist visions of society, which want to eliminate "the chaos and darkness and cursing" from human affairs (31). The verbal nihilism of *Notes from Underground* is directed against all utopian and progressive ideologies of the nineteenth century, as the Underground Man refutes the possibility of completing and perfecting *any* human-made and human-sanctioned institution. As a retort to the socialist ideals of Nikolai Chernyshevsky's 1863 novel *What Is to Be Done?*, the Underground Man declares that it is "better to do nothing!" (37). The subterranean structure of the "wretched mouse," as the Underground Man's alter ego, can be understood as a polemical counterpart to a utopian ideal of "new economic relations" envisioned by idealists such as Chernyshevsky (24). For the Underground Man, the absurdity of such relations consists above all in their claims to permanence. The socialist vision of a human society is mockingly referred to through the image of a "crystal palace," and as "a crystal edifice, forever indestructible" (25, 35). The Underground Man juxtaposes the rational-mathematical design of such a monumental structure to his own futile fortification of the "loathsome underground," a fence of filth that must be continually built out of bile, broken down, and rebuilt (11). Dostoevsky's text attacks European secular modernity through negative imitation. The torturous underground monologue, a monstrous product of "hyperconsciousness," means to hold up a mirror to liberatory Enlightenment projects that want to establish social freedom based on sovereign knowledge of human nature.[48] The Underground Man posits the solitude of his own voice as the natural consequence of the intellectual culture around him. He tells his spectral listeners at the end of the novel: "I have merely carried to an extreme in my life what you have not dared to carry out halfway" (129–30). This is why, as Viktor Erlich has argued, the Underground Man suffers "all the disadvantages of loneliness, yet has none of its fringe benefits—genuine privacy, freedom from those one detests."[49] His monologue claims to ventriloquize in solitude what society is already thinking and claims to make visible the future consequences of contemporary idealism. The Underground Man's past is society's future. The second section of the novel, "Apropos of the Wet Snow," recounts the Underground Man's last lost chance to connect meaningfully and philanthropically with another human being; the story ends with philanthropy turning into misanthropy, as the Underground Man insults and humiliates the young prostitute Liza, whom he claimed he intended to rescue from destitution. After the novel's conclusion, the Underground Man claims that this *analeptic* revisiting of the past is in fact a *prolepsis* of society's own dim future, in which philanthropy (socialism, utopianism, secular humanism) will inevitably devolve into misanthropy. The social will become the antisocial, and the permanent "crystal edifice" will reveal itself as a purgatory.

If the underground monologue was foundational for modern prose, as has often been suggested, it is perhaps due to its complex claim to radicalism. The underground monologue claims to be more radical than any political radicalism and to have understood the contradiction at the core of modernizing projects that would make human beings into "unprecedented omni-men" (*NU*, 130). Literature comes to represent, to borrow Schopenhauer's term from another context, "pure knowledge" of the course of world history. It exists closer to the threshold of the future than any future-oriented radical project. Literary monologue imbibes and surpasses the ideas of all revolutionary political ideologies, including socialism, anarchism and political nihilism, as well any variety of Enlightenment democratization. The underground becomes the privileged place for understanding the workings of *all* politics. It is no coincidence that Dostoevsky would later refer to political radicals *en masse* as "underground Nihilist scum."[50] With Dostoevsky's construction of the "underground type," he sought to fashion a template for understanding and exposing the essential misanthropy and self-destructiveness of any and all revolutionaries. The underground type—further developed in a range of canonical characters including the criminal Raskolnikov, the anarchist-atheist Ivan Karamazov, and the nihilist Nikolai Stavrogin—could appear to readers as the de facto protagonists of radical, revolutionary modernity.[51] An appealing aspect of the *Notes from Underground*—if it is read as a political allegory—is that it claims to distill the ambitions and failings of revolutionary thinking into single, breathless monologue delivered in the underground. It is the solitary yet universal voice of the political. And so, when the Underground Man mines the "verbal epitome of total isolation," he is also making an apocalyptic revelation.[52] Antisocial speech reveals the hidden truth of the social.

Schopenhauer and Dostoevsky traced a new trajectory for the development of literary monologue in the nineteenth century and onward, as they decoupled monologue from selfhood, rendering it instead as a conduit for the articulation of nullity (the nullity of politics and society, or the nullity of the universe). Rather than subscribing to Rousseau's slogan "nothing but oneself," they addressed a "nothing" that is the antithesis of this self. In distinct ways, their accounts of monologue abandon an emphatic notion of a "self-articulating subject"[53] that can fortify its autonomy through a withdrawal from the social realm into "the vacuum of absolute dialogue."[54] With the development of nihilism as a dedicated philosophy and as a sociopolitical position, monologue indeed remained a language of the "vacuum," but not a vacuum where a self-determining subject can experience freedom to the fullest. The vacuums of Schopenhauer and Dostoevsky are not free, inner spaces of subjectivity. Rather, they express an allegedly factual nullity that underlies the subject as well as all society. Schopenhauer's and Dostoevsky's very different approaches to nihilism converge in foregrounding monologue as a medium for probing this nullity that lies at the core of the given world. "Talking to nobody" is significant not because one "talks to nobody but oneself," but because it cuts through the pretenses of positivity that are held in place through conventional modes of social discourse. When someone talks to nobody, they locate themselves in the threshold of an occluded domain that goes unacknowledged in the course of everyday social life. For Schopenhauer, this occluded domain is the "nothingness" that is the underlying truth of the world-as-appearance, which is always the objectivation of the same will, at every point in time across all history, and at every point in space across the entire universe. For Dostoevsky, the occluded domain of nothingness revealed by monologue is the vacuity of human reason and self-consciousness, which have (blasphemously) claimed a higher status than religion. Both writers embraced a form of misanthropy by suggesting, in their own distinct ways, that the world's true nullity cannot be revealed in dialogue with any other human being. Rather, the world's nullity can only be revealed by absenting oneself from the social realm and erasing one's own markings of individual identity. With these negative conceptions of solitude, Schopenhauer and Dostoevsky reinterpreted and utilized the experience of the "emotional paralysis" of the misanthrope, as described by Novalis back in the romantic period.[55] That abysmal condition of "the human being [who] stands alone as a perishable force" and "slowly begins to consume himself" was for Novalis a deplorable condition with certain dubious advantages.[56] On his way to freezing completely, the misanthrope enjoys a special intellectual freedom and wit because all bonds to the outside have been severed. Novalis's description of the pros and cons of misanthropy only appeared in a stray observation alongside other miscellaneous reflections. However, for Schopenhauer as for Dostoevsky, the self-consuming misanthrope is no longer only of incidental importance. The person who speaks from under a shield of "frost" and communicates with nobody is granted access to a fundamental nullity that covertly underlies human thought and action and that constitutes the unity of the world as we know it. However much their works disagree, they are complementary in that Schopenhauer furnished a nihilist metaphysical framework that privileges monologue, whereas Dostoevsky innovated a literary form of monologue that concretizes nihilist thinking in a verbal practice of "voiding," or "annihilating." The resulting artistic product is a self-consuming and incessant contexture, which perpetually generates new metaphors expressing the speaker's separation from any outer world. Monologue, in the works of both writers, is a discursive genre that is not primarily disposed toward self-expression or self-discovery. Rather, monologue is a verbal technique that conjures a vast absence and consequently locates the speaker within the resulting void. For Schopenhauer, the truly isolated person exists outside of the universe; for Dostoevsky, the isolated (fictional) character regards his placement in the void as the most fundamental reality––even if it is obvious to the reader of *The Double* or *Notes from Underground* that this character still really is present in (and "morbidly preoccupied with") the social world.[57] With Schopenhauer and Dostoevsky, the anticommunicative character, who attests to the impossibility of community, becomes a heroic protagonist who daringly crosses the boundary into an unknown nothingness that is invisible in the normal course of social life. An enduring myth of misanthropy is, if not invented in these works, transfigured and preserved for posterity.

Nietzsche and the Universalization of the Underground Outsider

Friedrich Nietzsche subsequently constructed a historical framework that could accommodate Schopenhauer and Dostoevsky together, as two instances of passive, or "*Imperfect* Nihilism."[58] All of their outsider-figures (genius, madman, underground type) are characterized by radical withdrawal from the world rather than by any act of destruction. None of them perpetrate actual violence. For Nietzsche, only an authentically destructive attitude would earn the description of "complete," perfect nihilism. Being characterized by contemplation and verbal activity rather than by action, the monologic outsiders of Schopenhauer and Dostoevsky can be understood through Nietzsche's model as inchoate, *weak* instances of nihilism, in which "spiritual strength" is "fatigued."[59] In Nietzsche's narrative, the nihilisms espoused by Schopenhauer, and illustrated through fiction by Dostoevsky, can appear as separate symptoms of a longer process of decline. For Nietzsche, the strategies of self-absenting described by Schopenhauer and Dostoevsky become the markers of a historical threshold where the nullity of existing values comes to light, and where it becomes clear that these values have cumulatively led to a devaluation of worldly life. Schopenhauer's genius and madman and Dostoevsky's Underground Man, then, become legible as figures that faithfully and zealously play along with devaluation, espousing inaction above all else.

In *The Twilight of the Idols* from 1889, Nietzsche created a precise basis for comprehending the characters of Schopenhauer and Dostoevsky together, by developing a general theory of the outcast. In this text, the antisocial character is of interest above all as an untimely figure whose potential goes unrealized because of the stagnation and mediocrity of the present age. Whereas Schopenhauer located his antisocial types on the threshold of a realm *outside* of time, and Dostoevsky's Underground Man was presented as a symptom of the *present*, Nietzsche projects the meaning of his outcasts into the *future*. The antisocial, including but not limited to the "criminal," is a figure of a time-to-come. Nietzsche initiates his discussion of "*The criminal and his like*" with reference to the "Siberian convicts" depicted in Dostoevsky's 1862 fictionalized autobiography *House of the Dead*, "hopeless criminals for whom no road back to society stood open."[60] Nietzsche finds in Dostoevsky's descriptions of the criminal the markings of degenerated strength, and it is precisely these criminals who (for Dostoevsky, according to Nietzsche) are "carved from about the best, hardest, and most valuable material."[61] In the structure of exclusion that Nietzsche imagines here, it is always those persons with inborn strength who will be expelled from society; whoever would be strong enough to bring about a (truly *new*) future must be located outside of society. Proceeding from this idea of the criminal, Nietzsche goes on to posit a general category of "creatures who for some reason or other fail to meet with public approval," of which criminals are one subset.[62] In order to unify this general category of socially unsanctioned outsiders, Nietzsche imports the Sanskrit term *Chandala*, the name of the caste of untouchables from the ancient Hindu Laws of Manu.[63] It is significant that Nietzsche relies here on an ancient Sanskrit term in order to posit his general category of outsiders. By ascribing a "Chandala-feeling" to all those who lack public approval, Nietzsche roots his discussion of social identity–conferral in an imagined version of the ancient past, in what David Smith called "Nietzsche's India," which "was not the real India or any known land."[64] This land could provide a spectral origin for the general phenomenon of the antisocial as encountered in modern Europe. For Nietzsche, after all, the Laws of Manu reflected "pessimist values" that determine the Christian heritage into the present age of nihilism.[65] By invoking the Sanskrit term, Nietzsche subsumes the entire range of instances of social exclusion under an original legal code of exclusion. Nietzsche can thus assume a unified history of exclusion and pinpoint a particular category of outcasts within that history.

Within his imagined history of exclusion, Nietzsche is not interested in just *any* oppressed figures, but in particular those outcasts who "have, for a while, the grey and fatalistic mark of the Chandala on their brows: *not* because they are regarded as Chandala, but because they themselves feel the terrible chasm which separates them from all that is traditional and honorable."[66] This distinction between actual untouchables and those who *feel* like untouchables is apparently important, since Nietzsche is narrowing his range of concern to those antisocial types who feel excluded *because of their untimeliness*. Their exclusion is a secret that they keep for themselves, based in awareness of their own eccentricity. Nietzsche's discussion here is anything but a call for a general solidarity with the oppressed. As much of an elitist as Schopenhauer, Nietzsche is honing in on the "pioneers" who are conscious that their own nature is at odds with socially sanctioned values.[67] It is significant that Nietzsche's class of outsider-pioneers is distinguished not simply by their social status but also by their lack of public approval or assent, in German, "öffentliche Zustimmung." Nietzsche is interested only in individuals who have tried and failed to attain recognition and notoriety, and not in downtrodden and oppressed *groups*. The general grouping of "*The Criminal and his kind*" encompasses only those special individuals who display the *potential* to transform the world but cannot realize this potential in the given circumstances.

In illustrating this class of "creatures who . . . fail to meet with public approval," Schopenhauer and Dostoevsky remain crucial touchstones. Without explicitly referencing Dostoevsky's 1864 novel, Nietzsche employs the metaphor of the "underground" to demarcate the kind of person he is talking about: "The thoughts and actions of all such natures are tainted with a subterranean mouldiness [die Farbe des Unterirdischen]."[68] It should be noted here that Nietzsche first discovered *Notes from Underground* in a bookstore in Nice, and that his nominalization of the adjective "unterirdisch" echoes book's French title, *L'esprit souterrain*.[69] Through this intertextual gesture, Dostoevsky's Underground Man makes a cameo in *Twilight of the Idols*, abstracted into a "color" that identifies all pioneer-outsiders. Nietzsche extends the metaphor of the underground further, explaining that "everything in them is of a paler hue than in those on whose existence the sun shines."[70] Whereas Dostoevsky's Underground Man made clear that he had willingly embraced the underground, Nietzsche's underground type was forced into "excessively prolonged time underneath."[71] Following Nietzsche's discussion, the reader is compelled to see the underground types (such as Goliadkin and the Underground Man) as case studies of pioneer-outcasts, whose potential has been foreshortened by the life-denying values of European culture. In short, Dostoevsky is positioned here as a writer who describes the mental effects of the degeneration that Nietzsche sees as being characteristic of European culture. Thus, Nietzsche praises Dostoevsky as "the only psychologist from whom [he] had anything to learn" and is interested in his writing as "testimony" illustrating the internalized pessimism of the age.[72]

It is no coincidence that Nietzsche discusses underground types immediately after explicating his "concept of Genius," which is defined thus in terms of "explosives" that transform and benefit humankind.[73] In his discussion of the outcast, Nietzsche suggests that great men ("the man of science, the artist, the genius, the free spirit, the business man, and the great explorer") have historically been driven underground and marked by the "Chandala-feeling."[74] This is the fault of religion, through which "the *priest* represented the highest type of man."[75] Nietzsche implies that path from the underground to greatness would require a proactive destruction of the devaluing values of the age. The outcast would need to *act* on his exclusion, moving from passive to active nihilism. The verbal nihilism of the Underground Man would need to be externalized into a destructive urge that brings about a *tabula rasa* of morals. In underscoring the futurity of the underground type, Nietzsche was actually *embracing* a danger that Dostoevsky's late fiction would patently warn against: the horror scenario of violent anarchism. To embrace the anarchist position that "everything is permitted," uttered by Ivan Karamazov, would be for Nietzsche a historical leap forward, up and away from the self-denying condition of Goliadkin and the Underground

Man. With his discussion in *The Twilight of the Idols* Nietzsche lays out a possible reinterpretation of the underground monologue. The monologue, as an act of "speaking to nobody," would now become an indicator of an as-yet untapped power, whose explosive potential has been turned inward. If there is a language of the future, it would *need* to be a monologue, delivered to nobody. This, in fact, is a recurring theme in Nietzsche's writings. Nietzsche fashions himself and his fictional avatars as ones who "speak to nobody" in *Thus Spoke Zarathustra: A Book for Everyone and No One,* and in the preface of *Human, All Too Human.* In the latter, he confesses that his books thus far have been addressed to shadows, not to any group of "free spirits" that exists yet. Speaking to nobody, one speaks into the future.

Schopenhauer, the other thinker of the abyssal monologue, is negatively present in Nietzsche's discussion of "*The criminal and his like,*" as a sort of spectral opponent. By presenting the figures of the underground as the true counterparts of the "genius," Nietzsche is clearly taking his own advice from a few pages earlier: "one should in the first place *deny Schopenhauer.*"[76] More precisely, Nietzsche is polemically correcting and reframing Schopenhauer's account of genius in *The World as Will and Representation*, which according to Nietzsche is part of the pessimist philosopher's "forgery" of all cultural achievements of humanity. Schopenhauer is guilty of having made genius into a mode of sheer denial, positing it as the antithesis of the will-to-live. By locating the genius's contemplative activity in a realm of pure knowledge beyond time and space, where there is no pain or desire, Schopenhauer foreclosed the possibility that the genius could ever change the world. But for Nietzsche, the genius is by definition explosive: he radically exceeds the framework of his time "irrevocably, involuntarily, just as a river involuntarily bursts its dams."[77] It is only through such reckless acts that the genius becomes the "benefactor" of mankind: "humanity has been much indebted to such explosives."[78] Given his essentially interruptive and untimely role, it makes sense that Nietzsche's genius is characterized in "one of the stages of his development" by "a feeling of hate, revenge and revolt against everything that exists, that has ceased to evolve."[79] This revolt-feeling of the underground is unthinkable in Schopenhauer's metaphysical system.

By denying Schopenhauer, Nietzsche inserts the genius into an evolutionary narrative of becoming, in which alienation (qua the "underground") is a significant yet only temporary stage. Schopenhauer's pessimism makes self-denial into a permanent feature of genius. As such, he can be considered an accomplice to society's devaluation of genius. Dostoevsky provides a corrective lens, allowing us to study the psychological impact of pessimism. Whereas Nietzsche praises Dostoevsky as "the only psychologist from whom I had anything to learn,"[80] he mocks Schopenhauer as a "case of the first rank [for a psychologist]."[81] By making Schopenhauer into a patient and Dostoevsky into the doctor, Nietzsche assembles a narrative trajectory for understanding their different discourses on nihilism. Schopenhauer epitomizes the ruling pessimism of the age and perpetuates the ascetic, "Christian interpretation" of life. Dostoevsky, according to Nietzsche, studies the self-destruction induced by pessimism and thus points the way to redeem and redirect pessimism's latent energy. Schopenhauer *endorses* the weakness and degradation that Dostoevsky diagnoses.

Even if his notes on "European nihilism" were only fragments that remained unpublished during his lifetime, Nietzsche can be credited with having invented a unified narrative of nihilism, which retroactively folded a range of intellectual positions into a single cultural genealogy. Thus, the atheist metaphysical nihilism of Schopenhauer and the moral-political nihilism diagnosed by Dostoevsky could become discrete stages of a longer sequence of emergence and overcoming. By projecting a genealogical continuum of pessimism-nihilism-anarchism onto the intellectual history of the nineteenth century, Nietzsche enabled a rereading of his intellectual antecedents as distinct stages of a development that have culminated in his *own* position, which has already heroically overcome nihilism. From Nietzsche's own avowedly postnihilist standpoint, the different misanthropic comportments imagined by Schopenhauer and Dostoevsky can reappear as omens of a radically transformed future. The misanthrope, who shuns the world from a position of isolation, correctly (for Nietzsche) recognizes that there is no existing community worth belonging to. But in his descriptions of geniuses and "great men," Nietzsche suggests that conventional misanthropy (human hatred of humanity) is not enough: the strongest person would no longer be simply hateful of humanity, since such hatred entails negative attachment of "*ressentiment*." Daniel Cottom has argued that "[Nietzsche's] misanthrope is not a figure of humanity's disappointment with itself but rather an outsider to all its conventions, not excluding its conventional self-loathing and self-destructiveness."[82] Nietzsche's misanthrope, first embodied by Zarathustra, achieves a position *ahead* of humanity, awaiting the "as-yet unknown mates" who will bring about the "new world order."[83] Hope for a future community can only arise once one recognizes—in the manner of "great men"—that that worthwhile community is impossible *for now*. Worthwhile community will remain impossible, Nietzsche suggests, until the values that unite every other known community have been transcended. This, again, is why Nietzsche insisted that he had no listeners and had only invented listeners for himself as part of a "hermit's shadow play."[84] All speech that is worth speaking must remain monologue *for now*, until an adequate set of addressees enters the world. Once Nietzsche formulates his evolutionary models of pessimism and nihilism, the monologue thus becomes a verbal form that is "haunted by the future."[85] The communicative void in which monologue is located, in Nietzsche's conception, is an *interval* between one world and another radically different one. Alenka Zupancic has illuminated

Nietzsche's understanding of the misanthrope-genius as "dynamite." The role of dynamite is to "blast open, within a given practice, a kind of vacuum," in which something new can come about through an event.[86] "This vacuum is the privileged place," Zupancic writes, "from which it becomes possible to create, as well as to see or perceive what has been created."[87] The verbal nihilism of Schopenhauer's and Dostoevsky's eccentrics, who *fashion* vacuums for themselves through monologue, can become (through Nietzsche's reinterpretation) the basis for a heroic remaking of the world. Given Nietzsche's insurmountable influence over so much literary modernism, we might say that his revisionist vision was interpreted (by many twentieth-century writers) as an invitation to revisit the different "vacuums" of his nineteenth-century predecessors. To those readers who would identify themselves with his project of overcoming and transvaluation, Nietzsche issues an *antisocial imperative*. It is *necessary* to be alone, to dwell in a void, and to experience the world as nothing, in order to recover one's "will." This void is unavoidable for anyone willing to retrace Nietzsche's footsteps; one must temporarily inhabit the roles of the rejected, underground genius and the destructive anarchistic spirit. Through Nietzsche's thought, Schopenhauer's and Dostoevsky's models of monologue become stepping-stones on the way to a new world beyond the void.

Around the same time that Nietzsche was revising and refining the nihilisms of Schopenhauer and Dostoevsky, a very different model of an "unavoidable void" was emerging in the relatively new academic field of sociology. Ferdinand Tönnies's 1887 book *Community and Civil Society* and Émile Durkheim's 1897 work *On Suicide* constructed scientific models of modern society as a field of emptiness. They focus on circumstances in which traditional communal ties and shared values have vanished and have been replaced by the impersonal mechanisms of economy.[88] Sociology, like nihilist letters, posited an "unavoidable void," which became an ineluctable historical fact with the rise of capitalism and the modern bureaucratic state. Participation in such an economy makes everyone, at least potentially, into de facto nihilists. The literary culture of nihilism considered in this chapter does not necessarily contradict such sociological observations regarding the increasing emptiness of modern life. Rather, literary nihilism repeats and reiterates this emptiness to the point of excess. As Lukács would say, literary nihilism "heighten[s]" the prevailing "isolation" diagnosed by social theory.[89] Writers such as Schopenhauer, Dostoevsky, and Nietzsche took control of alienation by turning alienat*ing* into a verbal art. Once alienation was been refined into an art, creative writers began (perversely, as it were) to sympathetically appraise the misanthropic postures posited by their antecedents, discovering in this misanthropy a form of liberation. The status of the "untouchable" outcast became desirable.

Chapter 2

✦

Unworldly Anarchism
Gustav Landauer's Nihilist Community

Through nineteenth-century discourses on nihilism, the form of the monologue gained a special status, acquiring two contradictory capacities at once. Monologue became both a verbal eraser of the world and an instrument for ushering in a *new* world of the future, which would be otherwise inconceivable to anyone anywhere at present. An outsider's monologue that epitomizes absolute alienation could, paradoxically, become a means for overcoming alienation. Toward the beginning of the twentieth century, creative writers began to experiment with this strange suggestion and its accompanying paradoxes. The German-Jewish anarchist writer Gustav Landauer, who began his literary career steeped in the vernaculars of nihilism, developed a vision of solidarity that would originate in extreme alienation, moving "durch Absonderung zur Gemeinschaft" (through separation to community).[1] In Landauer's early prose, it is necessary to reach the "verbal epitome of loneliness and isolation" in order to arrive at a radical conception of community beyond competitive individualism, exploitation, militarism, and the state.[2] Misanthropy is the starting point for benevolent anarchy. Landauer appropriates the most extreme forms of negativity furnished by nihilist discourse and borrows from its spatial imaginaries of voids, vacuums, abysses, and undergrounds. It is in these subrealities, which underlie the world in its concrete sociological and geographic dimensions, that Landauer carves out a place for a romantic vision of political anarchism.

The first written work in which Landauer undertook such an experiment is his novel *The Death Preacher* from 1893, written at the height of the European decadence movement. In its final scenes, the novel celebrates a utopian anarchist vision of "free living and free associations," as conjured by the misanthropic intellectual Karl Starkblom, who has lived in isolation for years following the death of his wife in childbirth and the voluntary termination of his career in law.[3] Starkblom's idea of free association is not culled from the humanist tradition of the Enlightenment: it is mined from the abysses of nihilism. These abysses are already presented in hyperbolic form both in the novel's title and first sentences—helping to "brand" the novel as a work of proper nihilism, affiliated with Schopenhauer, Dostoevsky, Nietzsche, and others. Verbal nihilism is both the core theme of this text, as well as its most salient formal strategy. The title points directly to a scene in Nietzsche's *Thus Spoke Zarathustra*, where the titular character Zarathustra announces the necessity of a verbal nihilism with the words: "The earth is full of those to whom departure from life must be preached."[4] In short, the world needs death-preaching. The nihilist affinities continue: the novel's short preface, which contextualizes its fictional biographical narrative within the wider history of the universe, immediately invokes Schopenhauer's dismissive description of life on earth as "mouldy film [that] has produced living and knowing beings"; Landauer's narrator speaks of "a greenish mold" that "encrusted . . . the entire curvature of the earth" (compare to Schopenhauer: "on this crust a mouldy film has produced living and knowing beings").[5] This general mood of misanthropy is augmented with a description of "consciousness" as a "sickly seed," which echoes the nihilist appraisal of consciousness voiced by Dostoevsky's Underground Man, who claimed that "any consciousness at all is a sickness" (*NU*, 6–7). These dismissals of life and consciousness are matched with a dismissal of all human society. The earth's "puny beings" are "nothing for themselves and therefore had to rely on one another and feud with one another."[6] Here, another nihilist joins the company: the condemnation of human society as a gathering of *nothings* is clearly inspired by the individualist proto-anarchist Max Stirner, for whom there were good and bad "nothings"; he disparaged the *weak* nothing of human society and celebrated the *triumphant* "nothing" that he claimed as his own identity: "I am not nothing [*Nichts*] in the sense of emptiness, but I am the creative nothing, the nothing out of which I myself as creator create everything."[7] Humanity's default position, however, would be the "nothing in the sense of emptiness." Landauer's narrator has internalized this lesson, siding with Stirner against everyone else. Accompanied by the ghosts of Stirner, Schopenhauer, and Dostoevsky, the novel's preface gives the sense that humanity is a collective of *nobodies*, living on a *nowhere* planet, with *nothing* in our minds.

There is a noticeable ideological mismatch between Landauer's political agenda and his literary antecedents for *The Death Preacher.* Apart from Stirner, none of the writers of nihilism mentioned above can be properly called "socialist," or even "anarchist." Even Stirner, the nihilist most closely associated with the Left, represents the extreme egoist and libertarian wing of anarchism, which dismisses all forms of collectivity in favor of an absolute, sovereign "I" that purports to take ownership of the entire world: anarcho-solipsism. The nihilist "brand," imprinted onto the cover and introduction of *The Death Preacher*, would not seem conducive to the sort of romantic leftist utopianism for which Landauer is known. There are no shared political intentions behind the works of Schopenhauer, Dostoevsky, and Nietzsche, but each has been with some justification called "reactionary" in that they dismiss most modern, materialist interpretations of the world, which hold that alienation is a consequence of social inequality and could be remediated through redistribution. They provide no blueprints for social justice. A side-by-side comparison of the "underground" characters in Dostoevsky's novels with the general human outsider-types in Schopenhauer's and Nietzsche's writings does not produce a unified picture of how exclusion and self-exclusion work, nor do these discussions recommend any "change" to social systems that would minimize such instances of exclusion. Schopenhauer, Dostoevsky, and Nietzsche insist on the *necessity* and *truthfulness* of extreme alienation. Espousing misanthropy, they polemicize against the emancipatory ideals of both republicanism and socialism, which had emerged out of the Enlightenment and came to shape the notions of historical progress in the nineteenth century (Hegel and the Hegelians being the most obvious example). In Schopenhauer, Dostoevsky, and Nietzsche, the emphasis on the importance of monologue can be understood as a polemic against all progressive, egalitarian political projects, whether republican, reformist, or revolutionary in nature. Schopenhauer's models of withdrawal from life leave no possibility for a transformative, collective action that would diminish social suffering; he is an unapologetic, self-avowed monarchist. Dostoevsky's Underground Man polemicizes against the "crystal edifice" of a rationally planned social utopia, insisting that it would cave in to antisocial impulses out of the citizens' inevitable boredom with perfection (*NU*, 35). Nietzsche's outsiders, marked by the "color of the underground," are not to be understood as an oppressed mass that should revolt but as potential figures of singular greatness; their strength is clearly opposed to the degenerate, Christian "weakness" that Nietzsche abhors in the socialists, who blame others for their own suffering.[8] In each case, the language of misanthropy makes a mockery of political plans for an egalitarian society.

So, how does Landauer's hero Karl Starkblom end up an anarchist and a lover of all, if Landauer's novel begins under the auspices of these nihilist influences? How did Landauer himself become an avowed anarchist, if this was his literary and philosophical heritage? Unless you are an orthodox Stirnerian, *misanthropy* would seem to have no place in classical anarchist thought. Anarchism, by most accounts, requires a basic optimism regarding human capacities for coexistence. George Woodcock writes that anarchists "may not believe that man is naturally good, but they do fervently assert that man is naturally social."[9] The novelist and essayist Iljia Trojanow recently provided a sympathetic and open definition of anarchism as "a lifelong project, where one does not succumb to the cynical insight that suffering is necessary."[10] It is the opposite of pessimism and misanthropy. Anarchism's broad negation of all existing hierarchies relies on a positive sense of possibility, a hopeful conviction that another world is desirable and possible. While Nietzsche considered anarchism to be one potential outgrowth of pessimist thought, classical political anarchism is characterized by a resolutely activist stance that insists that some form of positive change is always immediately possible.

Gustav Landauer stands out as an intriguing exception to this strategic optimism of classical political anarchism. Already in his earliest writings, Landauer sought to synthesize the claims of philosophical pessimism and political anarchism, fashioning ideas of "unworldly anarchism" and "misanthropic socialism" that run against the orthodoxies of both political movements (*DT*, 98). Landauer does not just love misanthropy; he loves paradoxes. The intriguing conceit of Landauer's early writing is that the misanthropic intellectual, who passionately hates the world and labors to forget humanity, would be the best possible candidate for a humanist anarchist. Landauer suggests that a truly free form of collectivity, unmarred by inequalities and hierarchies, must begin in a self-constructed isolation chamber. Only through the most intense isolation—in a "rant" where speech devolves into noncommunicative nonsense—can the subject arrive at a proper vision of anarchy. This is because, when Landauer's outsider reaches a moment of dissociation where the self is negated, a chaotic web of connections is revealed, out of which the self was forged and out of which new worlds can be created. Landauer's fictional and philosophical stories about human life tend to culminate in this revelation of generative anarchy.

Why would Landauer need this strange model of dissociation in order to make way for a positive image of anarchic community? It may have been because of the author's long-standing pacifism, which turned out to be one of his enduring contributions to German intellectual culture of the early twentieth century (for instance, Martin Buber's opposition to World War I was influenced first of all by Landauer's stringent antimilitarism).[11] How could pacifism be compatible with pessimism? If we turn to the internal debates of the anarchists, an answer emerges: Landauer followed his anarchist predecessor Mikhail Bakunin in embracing creative destruction, but he could not abide by Bakunin's approval of spontaneous violence as a way to clear the path toward a new society. Consequently, Landauer needed to develop an analogous version of creative destruction that did not involve advocating actual violence against other people. This pacificism is explicitly stated in Landauer's 1895 essay "Anarchism in Germany," which insists that the anarchists' "propaganda of the deed" must aim for the "rebirth of the human spirit" through emphatic language and must not involve killing people; indeed, Landauer denies that real anarchists would ever "suppress other opinions with violence" (fremde Meinungen mit Gewalt [unterdrücken]).[12] It is for this reason, I would speculate, that Landauer was drawn to the practices of *verbal* voiding (as opposed to embodied, *violent* voiding) offered by literary nihilism. Through nihilist speech, it is possible to void our internalized, engrained images of the world and develop a sense for new possibilities without ever leaving the land of literature. Fiction is the place to make the anarchist *tabula rasa* happen.

Landauer's philosophical anarchism, with its emphasis on interior transformation, placed him at a distance from the varieties of practical political anarchism that emerged in Catalonia and Andalusia in the early twentieth century.[13] Yet, within the context of German literary culture, Landauer can be seen as a kind of unlikely unifier of the late nineteenth century's cultural dissidents as he strove to harmonize the political language of the leftist workers' movement with that of the intellectuals who embraced the pessimist metaphysics of Arthur Schopenhauer. His idea was that the pessimist refusal of the world, perfected in Schopenhauer's philosophy, could be modified and made into the basis for a free and equal society. Disgust, for Landauer, was the most authentically revolutionary affect. In the essay "Anarchism in Germany" mentioned above, Landauer names the negative, misanthropic sentiments that were his primary reasons for embracing an anarchist politics of revolt. He suggests that his own anarchism has grown out of a wholesale misanthropy that holds all people equally responsible for the misery of mankind: "For me it is above all the disgust for the humanity that surrounds me, the rage at the comfort of the privileged who tolerate seeing their happiness built on the rubble of failed existences and degraded beings, and the no less intense rage at the lowest of the oppressed people," who, Landauer explains, are born as equals to the privileged but die with no more than the "bones that they left behind as the rubble of their tireless struggle for life."[14] Landauer's politics begin with the dissolution of all sympathies, a hatred of both rich and poor. Only by letting go of all attachments and alignments can a new world come into being.

Landauer's pessimistic depiction of social life has a programmatic significance: he is working to build an alliance between Germany's circles of self-described anarchists and its milieu of pessimist, literary intelligentsia associated across Europe with the up-and-coming fin de siècle. He claims that his misanthropic social vision is shared by many "intellectuals of Germany . . . who are very far from feeling solidarity with us anarchists" (Gebildeten Deutschlands . . . , die doch sehr weit davon entfernt sind, sich mit uns Anarchisten solidarisch zu fühlen").[15] Landauer explains that these intellectuals are characterized by a love of Schopenhauer, who is "often the comfort of their sleepless nights" (der Trost ihrer schlaflosen Nächte).[16] These are unhappy insomniacs, for whom the darkest moments can only be brightened by reading the darkest philosopher of them all—by moving from bad to worse. Yet this uncompromising negativity, Landauer suggests, could be creatively redirected in the service of a future free society. He explains that the pessimist intellectuals diverge from anarchists above all in their resolute insistence on the *impossibility* of ever creating a free society in place of the prevailing misery. Landauer describes this attitude as a "general despair and skepticism, the belief that such a future [of free living and free associations] could never, ever grow out of the present" ([die] allgemein[e] Verzweiflung und Skeptizismus, [der Glaube], daß nie und nimmer aus der Gegenwart eine solche Zukunft erwachsen könne).[17] The pessimist intellectual is a misanthrope with a radical sense of impossibility who finds *nothing* worth continuing or cultivating in the current world. For Landauer, this sense of impossibility can only be a starting point; negativity must be transformed through emphatic, vocal propaganda that is linguistic and nonviolent. It makes sense, then, that Landauer closes his essay by quoting Schopenhauer as an anarchist rallying cry (!): "Life is short and the truth works far and lives long: let us speak the truth" (Das Leben ist kurz und die Wahrheit wirkt ferne und lebt lange: sagen wir die Wahrheit) (*WWR1*, xvii).[18] Ending with the preface of *The World as Will and Representation*, Landauer suggests that an alternative history of nihilism has yet to be written, which shares in Schopenhauer's quest for truth, but turns his disgust with the world into the basis for social liberation, mutual aid, and peace. Such a narrative of passage from impossibility to possibility is a consistent feature of Landauer's early writings. From the early 1890s, Landauer sought out ways of imagining how the antisocial could be the precondition for a new social existence, how solitude could create solidarity, and how a nihilist sense of nothingness could be the precondition for an abundant and inclusive human community.

Marxism Meets Nihilism in *The Death Preacher*

The Death Preacher is not only an individual life story of the tortured intellectual Karl Starkblom but also the site of an ideological struggle between competing philosophies of its era. To summarize the story told by Landauer's *Death Preacher*, it makes sense to begin without the protagonist and point to the two competing models of collectivity that figure most prominently in the text: the institutional collectivity of the Socialist Party, and the dispersed collectivity of European nihilist intellectuals, also known as "decadents." Both of these collectivities are firmly located in the historical moment of the 1890s. The year 1890 saw the expiration of the antisocialist "Socialist Laws" previously passed by the German parliament, paving way for the consolidation (and electoral successes) of the Social Democratic Party.[19] The early 1890s also brought broader recognition to the literary and intellectual movement of decadence, as exemplified by Max Nordau's 1892 book *Degeneration*.[20] When the narrator of *The Death Preacher* calls this historical moment a "chaotic, anarchic time" (*DT*, 22), it is both descriptive and prefigurative: the point of the story is both to document and *harness* this "chaos" and stage a productive collision between decadent aesthetics and socialist ideology. In short, the novel is meant to make a mess of existing social boundaries so that something new can come out of them. This ideological cacophony is supposed to create new community that includes both the proletariat and the déclassé bourgeoisie.

Midway through an expository biography of the novel's protagonist, the narrator zooms out to map the scope and scale of Europe's two competing collectivities of decadence and socialism. Interestingly, both of these movements of relative "outsiders" are positioned as the most salient historical forces of the time. There is no mention of empires that cross Europe and colonize the rest of the world, or of emergent nationalisms that challenge these empires. The German emperor and the institutions that support him are nowhere to be seen. There are, rather, two bands of rebels. The first "band" described is composed of solitary, suicidal nihilists and includes the protagonist Karl Starkblom. They suffer from what might be called "decadence syndrome"[21] and comprise a community without any direct contact or communication, bound together by their morbidity and isolation:

> Back then there was a small band of such people in Europe, who like Karl Starkblom . . . were dragged . . . from one despair to another, who sooner or later stole away from human society into solitude with inevitable determination, who knew nothing of one another and wanted nothing from one another, who constituted no union and no party, whose disgust was too great and whose faith was too weak to love anything in the present and to hope much from the future.
>
> Solche Menschen, die ähnlich wie Karl Starkblom . . . von einer Verzweiflung der andern geraubt, früher oder später mit unabwendbarer Bestimmtheit sich aus der menschlichen Gesellschaft in die Einsamkeit hineinstahlen, gab es damals in Europa eine kleine Schar, die nichts voneinander wußte und nichts voneinander wollte, die keinen Verein bildete und keine Partei, deren Ekel zu groß und deren Glaube zu schwächlich war, um in der Gegenwart etwas zu lieben und von der Zukunft viel zu erhoffen. (*DT*, 22)

This collective of misanthropes is defined through negativities. Being ignorant of one another and indifferent toward one another, they lack any institutional or organizational structure. Bound together by a shared sense of nullity, they are a "they" that represents the zero degree of human collectivity. The small "band" of nobodies is defined by a principle of noncommonality. They collectively adhere to the nihilist principles that (according to the narrator's introduction) underlie the universe as a whole. Being invisible to one another, and without ever speaking to one another, they constitute a telepathic network of isolated minds that is more authentically cohesive than whatever is known as "society." The supernatural, spiritist bond between them is confirmed by the narrator's description of how sensory energy circulates within this "band" in the instance of each member's death: "Now and then one of them killed themselves, and it ran through the limbs of the others and they honored the unknown dead by asking themselves why they were still waiting for death" (*DT*, 22). Their perfection as a collective is maintained by the world's inattention to them: "But these were just totally isolated appearances [*Erscheinungen*], half or entirely crazy eccentrics posing no danger, to whom the world paid no further attention" (22). The inactive, nihilist collectivity is then juxtaposed to the mass movement of Social Democracy, a "completely new teaching" that comes from "a completely opposite side" (22). The "organized mass of the hungry" has become a "world power with which the mightiest statesman and the smallest village preacher had to reckon" (22–23). A single speech act—the concluding line of Marx and Engels's *Manifesto of the Communist Party*—has triggered this global mobilization:

> Workers of the world, unite! This call stretched across the whole world and shook the oppressed awake and bound them to a common cause; to the liberation of humanity from anarchic commodity production and circulation, to a communist production and distribution of need, to the destruction of blind egoism; to the demolition of national differences; to the creation of a true humanity and humaneness.
>
> Arbeiter aller Länder vereinigt euch! Dieser Ruf zog durch die ganze Welt und rüttelte die Unterdrückten auf und verband sie zu gleichem Zwecke; zur Befreiung der Menschheit von der anarchischen Warenproduktion und Zirkulation, zur kommunistischen Herstellung und Distribution der Bedürfnisse, zur Vernichtung des blinden Egoismus; zur Zertrümmerung der nationalen Gegensätze; zur Herstellung einer wirklichen Menschheit und Menschlichkeit. (23)

With this nonsyntactic listing of the familiar goals of the Socialist International, *The Death Preacher* clearly takes on a didactic function, providing the reader with basic lessons in the motivations of the political Left. As with the collectivity of nihilists described before, the narrator binds these general political tendencies back to the intellectual biography of the novel's protagonist Karl Starkblom, who had heard this "call" of socialism during his youth, having read Marx "pretty thoroughly" (22). The dispassionate tone of the narrator's account, however, hints at a general mood of disillusionment with the promises of the Socialist Party, and a desire to triangulate a new form of collectivity that is neither purely nihilist nor socialist in the usual sense. The conceit of *The Death Preacher* is that these two social options can be "wed," and alchemically forged anew, within the isolation chamber created by an extended monologue.

The bifurcated structure of the novel makes this possible: the majority of the novel relays a biographical narrative in which the protagonist experiences the social and ideological divisions of his time. Yet the centerpieces of the text are two interpolated monologues, composed by the protagonist and delivered (imaginatively) to a nonexistent audience. These monologues construct a void at the center of the novel out of which a putatively radical vision of anarchy is born. As crystallizations of extreme nihilism, these discourses serve as a substitute for political violence: the voice sweeps away the old world through incessant speech and installs an anarchist utopia of indiscriminate kinship and mutual aid. To be sure: this is an absurd and hubristic project, but one that anticipates postmodernist ideas of a "community without community," a "virtual," "negative," or "inoperative" community that begins with an absence of community.[22] In issuing his apologia for extreme solitude, Landauer prefigures a line of literary affinity that leads across experimental writing—and poststructuralist theory—of the twentieth and twenty-first centuries.

Why, then, have so few readers heard of *The Death Preacher*? Given its creative experiments with canonical nihilism and its fascinating combination of radical political positions, why was the novel ignored by readers, most critics, and major publishers? There are general answers to these questions: Gustav Landauer has remained a figure who attracts readers interested in anarchism, utopianism, and modern Jewish Messianism. As such, he is best known for his political writings and cultural criticism rather than for his prose fiction. Landauer was active as an essayist from his adolescence until his death, but he composed his corpus of narrative prose relatively early in his career, in a period of just over a decade, beginning with the novella *A Boy's Life* (*Ein Knabenleben*) in 1891, continuing with *The Death Preacher* in 1893, and ending with a volume of novellas, *Macht und Mächte* (*Power and Powers*), published in 1903. Landauer's earliest prose was praised in private correspondence by none other than the great German realist novelist Theodor Fontane, but as Landauer continued to publish his work he found little public recognition.[23] What happened to this promise? The best answer, frankly, has to do with the artistic quality of what Landauer wrote next. As a work of literary fiction, *The Death Preacher* is unquestionably marred by a certain amateurish overreach of ambition, as noted by both contemporary and posthumous critics. The literary scholar Philippe Despoix has called it "a twenty-year-old's credo," a view that Landauer himself was inclined to adopt in the afterword of the 1903 edition.[24] The influential socialist theorist and politician Eduard Bernstein (1850–1932), who published the only known contemporary review of *The Death Preacher* in the Social

Democratic Party journal *Die Neue Zeit*, considered the novel a moderate failure, with a few redeeming narrative twists. Bernstein unfavorably called Landauer's book a "Tendenzroman," that is, a work that transparently reflects a political ideology.[25] The term "Tendenzroman" was cogently defined by Friedrich Engels as a work intended "to glorify the social and political views" of its author, and so is distinct from a properly realist work that allows the reader to make a "political analysis" without directly voicing an ideological stance.[26] Because it clearly announces its allies, *The Death Preacher* is not good realism. Bernstein summarizes the expression of political tendencies in *The Death Preacher* in this description of the novel's protagonist: "The retiree and legal counsel Karl Starkblom, Landauer's hero, is a socialist in the best sense of the word, namely, not a socialist in the sense of German Social Democracy. He is, like the writer of this novel, an 'independent.'"[27] We could bracket Bernstein's skeptical, ironic appraisal of the protagonist's "independent" socialism as the prejudice of an established Social Democratic Party politician, whom Rosa Luxemburg would later criticize for his gradualist, reformist tendencies.[28] But Landauer himself, in his 1903 afterword to *Der Todesprediger*, insisted on the paradoxical nature of the novel's political tendency, which he named with two complementary phrases: "So it's something like misanthropic socialism, unworldly anarchism [menschenfeindlicher Sozialismus, weltabgewandter Anarchismus] that one finds in this book" (*DT*, 98). In other words, *The Death Preacher* is a "tendency novel" expressing political tendencies embraced by *nobody*, which are *nowhere* in practice, and which immediately evoke a sense of impossibility. It is "tendency literature" for an alien world. Landauer succeeded in creating a novel that would please nobody, forging an intellectual-political alliance that was fated to irrelevance.

A Biography of Disgust

In terms of story line, *The Death Preacher* has at least the skeletal structure of a realist novel, sketching the tortured lifelong education, and final redemption, of a bourgeois character. The hero, Karl Starkblom, is born sometime in the mid-nineteenth century to a middle-class family. The lives of his seven siblings chart out the different privileges and instabilities of their class: Karl himself is educated in the university; his brother Adam is educated as a merchant and becomes a successful plantation owner in Haiti. The other siblings achieve varying degrees of wealth and destitution: one brother becomes a business owner, another a military officer, and another a craftsman, while his sister becomes a "woman of the streets"; and his brother Hans vanishes entirely after traveling to Haiti (5). Karl stands alone among them with his spiritual-intellectual passions. In his adolescence, Karl

Starkblom is interested in studying philosophy and solving "the puzzle of the world" (6). In the shorthand biography that fills the first proper chapter, Starkblom wavers erratically between misanthropy and sociality. During his adolescent school years, he simply feels no "need for contact" with his peers, but at university he temporarily unlearns his antisocial inclinations, joining his fellow students at the "beer table" and becoming "sociable, carefree, harmless, and full of joie de vivre" (6). He meets a "pretty girl," and they become engaged (7). The wavering between solitude and society repeats, neutralizing any sense that Starkblom is progressing or growing up; the constant setbacks add up to a cyclical, if not static, biography. Once engaged, Starkblom begins to unlearn his conversation skills and again feels uncomfortable in society. Almost as soon as he marries, his wife (who is largely undescribed, and whose prior life is unnarrated) dies in childbirth along with their infant. Starkblom withdraws again from humanity, entering an extended period of mourning in which he turns to his books and leaves his career behind. In an unfortunate turn of his fortune, Starkblom's brother Adam, the plantation owner, dies and leaves him a small inheritance with which Karl is able to buy a small house in the countryside in southern Germany.[29] To quote Eduard Bernstein's review: "He moves into a small villa at the foot of the Black Forest and—philosophizes, philosophizes, philosophizes on the meaning of life until he has philosophized himself into a complete disgust with the world and humanity."[30] For a humanist socialist like Bernstein, disgust would be a political dead end, but for Landauer—and for his fictional hero Starkblom—disgust is cast as an unlikely, unpleasant, yet ostensibly productive beginning for political engagement. The compulsive iteration of what Bernstein calls "disgust, disgust, disgust" (Ekel, Ekel, Ekel) accurately describes the affective intensity of the protagonist's inner life, which leads him to his vision of unworldly anarchism.[31] It is sheer nihilism, rather than progressively acquired wisdom, that ultimately leads Starkblom toward transcendence and redemption.

Starkblom becomes politicized almost by accident. After a long tenure of disgusted solitude in his forest home, Starkblom ventures back down from the hills to the city, where he coincidentally (that is, after reading a flyer posted outside) becomes ensnared in the reading groups of the Social Democratic Party, then with a cohort of antiparliamentary socialists. Inspired by their anger, Starkblom renounces his bourgeois origins and becomes a celebrated socialist agitator, delivering speeches to enraged and euphoric crowds of workers. This new political career is cut short, however, when Starkblom is plagued by inner doubting voices during an important public speech and suffers an epileptic fit that shocks and scatters his large audience. He then withdraws (again) into his countryside home, writing a series of pamphlets in which he transcribes his own sprawling monologues, which are addressed to the entirety of humanity.

With these monologues, the biographical narrative of Landauer's text retreats behind an incessant stream of verbal nihilism, which is relayed *in toto* to the reader without any mediating narrator. The text becomes "preachy" in the literal sense that the protagonist's death-sermons completely disrupt the narrator's discourse. In the first of his monologue-pamphlets, Starkblom renounces socialism forever in the name of death, which he declares to be the world's true liberator. In the next monologue, he intensifies this declaration by presenting the vision of a suicidal death-cult that takes over the world and finally voids the entirety of humanity, leaving an uninhabited planet to return to the cycles of nature. The actual impact of these monologues on the continuing biographical narrative is almost fantastic: Starkblom's second pamphlet finds virtually no readers, but a Frenchwoman named Marguerite living in a commune in Paris discovers it in a back-alley bookshop and resolves to leave her lover in France and to visit Starkblom in Germany. Two days later, Marguerite is at Starkblom's door, where she hopes to lift him out of his suicidal depression. The two engage in philosophical debate over nihilism and the meaninglessness of life and immediately fall in love. Soon Marguerite's former lover, Hans—who turns out to be Karl Starkblom's long-lost brother—joins them in the house in southern Germany. At fantastic speed, the novel undergoes a total mood shift. Hans has brought with him the reprinted gallows speech of the bomber Ravachol, a real-life self-described anarchist who was sentenced to death for killing members of the Paris judiciary. As they read Ravachol together, the narrative is again interrupted with an interpolated sermon. Moved by the condemned anarchist's words, Starkblom becomes convinced that the anarchists are a group with a noble goal, and thus inspired, they all avow their support of anarchist socialism. The novel ends with the reprint of Starkblom's final monologue-pamphlet, where he announces his commitment to a new, as-yet-nonexistent revolutionary community, which will take shape under the auspices of his new familial bonds to his wife and unborn child. The narrative arc of the novel concludes with reproduction: Starkblom withdraws into solitude after the death of his first wife and her child, and he returns to humanity through his second wife's pregnancy. In anticipating fatherhood, he discovers his own revolutionary voice and promises to "give birth" to a future revolutionary mass with this voice. Twice married, he is ready to oversee the marriage of all humanity.

Because it ends as a success story, it makes sense to read *The Death Preacher* as a classic tale of *Bildung*, whereby the hero must pass through a phase of disillusionment (in this case, nihilism) in order to achieve a mature and constructive perspective on life. However, it may actually be more useful to recapitulate the novel using Eduard Bernstein's mocking description of the hero's discourse as an expression of "disgust, disgust, disgust." That is to say, the novel records an excessive repetition and intensification of a single negative affect, culminating in a downright *otherworldly* form of disgust so extreme that it engenders a unique form of utopianism. In essence, Starkblom is shouting *No, no no!* with increasing volume and abrasion, until he breaks through the boundaries of the world. These *no*'s are the red thread of the novel. The narrative of Starkblom's philosophical and political education is peppered through, from the very beginning, with nihilist insights that intensify with each iteration. We read that, as a student, Starkblom "noticed all at once that misery and pain permeated all of humanity and the whole world," from "philosophical despair" to "social misery" (9). This nihilist insight is not portrayed as a reflection of his adolescent mind but rather appears as an eternal truth, which negates the entire idea of an individual life story as mandated by a realist novel: "It seemed to him that he had thought and felt everything exactly in this way . . . a long, infinitely long time ago, probably more than a thousand years ago" (9). The nihilist wisdom of the novel is already in place before the beginning of time.

Starkblom's sense of omniscience makes his misanthropy into a kind of universal empathy because it provides a position from which all suffering, across the entirety of time and space, can be recognized at once. There is a precedent for this combination of solitude and empathy in classical nihilist thought: Schopenhauer described sainthood as a condition of universal empathy, whereby a person comes to understand that individual suffering is at one with the suffering of all other beings (this being the portion of Schopenhauer's thought that is indebted to Buddhism). Having retraced the solitary steps of Schopenhauer's saint, Landauer's protagonist aims to do something completely beyond the scope of *The World as Will and Representation*: he wants to *change* the world and its suffering. He rediscovers an adolescent desire, written down in a diary from when he was sixteen: "I want to dedicate my services to humanity; I want to speak a new word [neues Wort] that no one has spoken yet" (*DT*, 9). Withdrawing into intellectual solitude in his newly purchased villa outside the city, Starkblom attempts to discover this "new word" within himself. The discovery does not come easily; Starkblom's quest to serve humanity carries him even further away from it.

Instead of curing his misanthropy, Starkblom's newfound solitude allows him to cultivate and refine his sense of universal disgust. The major event that punctuates this period is an encounter in the city with an acquaintance from his youth, who has become a successful factory owner. Their short meeting at a restaurant further confirms Starkblom's misanthropy and yields a new iteration of his nihilist "digust," which is now directed at language itself: "Strange, really strange how two people who have essentially nothing in common, can nevertheless speak, even though their characters are so completely different that one must misunderstand the other" (*DT*, 20). Dialogue perpetuates the social order because it upholds the illusion of a common ground that does not really exist. Consequently, Starkblom finds that he must speak to nobody because doing so is his only path toward a new form of "contact" (Umgang) (21). From here on, Starkblom is on a quest to discover a "new word" that transcends reason and bypasses rational assumptions about language as a medium of intentional, multidirectional communication (9). As it happens, Starkblom finally discovers this new language through a public meltdown (in the manner, familiar to today's political culture, of an orator who has a "meltdown" in front of a large audience).

In the next narrative sequence, Starkblom becomes an active socialist, only to watch his political convictions melt away almost immediately. As noted above, Starkblom's socialist episode begins with a coincidence: after seeing a poster while on a rare stroll in town, he attends a political debate for the upcoming parliamentary election, followed by a Social Democrat reading club called "Humanity" (Menschheit). At these meetings, Starkblom finds he can identify with the negative affects circulating in the angry crowds. At the debate, he is inspired in particular by an anarchist speaker's rage toward both capitalism and social democracy. The anarchists' refusal to acknowledge the legitimacy of any election, and their refusal to vote, resonates with Starkblom's philosophical misanthropy. But it is also the racism of the politicized workers that appeals to him: at the reading group "Humanity"—and this is certainly the most disturbing scene of the novel—Starkblom identifies emphatically with the anti-Semitism of the proletarian crowd, nodding approvingly when a young worker forcefully ejects two men who are "apparently merchants with pronounced Jewish features" (offenbar Kaufleute mit ausgeprägt jüdischem Typus) (30). Otherwise an outsider among the workers in attendance (because of his bourgeois status), Starkblom can relate to the openly violent misanthropy of anti-Semitism. In her critique of this unsettling scene, the literary scholar Corinna Kaiser writes that it "is not the anarchist humanist Landauer writing here. . . . What is expressed here is much more a death-fixated misanthropy, which is influenced by Schopenhauer's pessimism and above all by Nietzsche's doctrine of the Übermensch," which in turn played no small role in shaping Nazi ideology.[32] In Kaiser's view, if Landauer is to be a model of progressive politics, we need to distinguish between his humanist and misanthropic moments.

It is true that the later Landauer is much more humane and politically inspiring as a leftist figure than was the young Landauer. The anti-Semitism of his early writings faded as Landauer's attitude toward his own Jewish identity evolved from aversion to avowal by the early 1900s. By the time Landauer penned the speech "From Separation to Community" and published it in the 1903 book *Skepticism and Mysticism*, his writing had taken on the appealing, benevolent tone that would mark most of his subsequent prose. This same benevolence even resonated in the empathetic words that Landauer reportedly spoke to the right-wing Freikorps soldiers who brutally murdered him in Stadelheim Prison in Munich following the overthrow of the Soviet Republic of Bavaria in May 1919: "You don't know yourselves how terribly you've been betrayed."[33] Whatever Landauer was actually thinking in this moment, his words still echoed the socialist ethics for which he was known. Not least for this reason, it makes sense to distinguish between a young nihilist Landauer and a mature humanist-pacifist Landauer. Nevertheless, it is also true that around 1900, Landauer consistently sought to undo the distinction between misanthropy and humanism, justifying nihilism and pessimism as necessary stages toward the recovery of a more fundamental mystical bond between all beings; the young Landauer who wrote *The Death Preacher* already cultivated the communal ideals of the older Landauer. The narrative arc of *The Death Preacher*, with its reiteration of "disgust, disgust, disgust," eventually leads toward a utopian humanism, implicitly justifying each preceding iteration of disgust as a necessary, preliminary step to be overcome. Unfortunately, one such iteration of disgust is late nineteenth-century anti-Semitism, which scapegoated Jews for the inequalities of capitalism. Because of these moments of bigoted misanthropy, the nuanced nihilism of Landauer's writings appears much less appealing than the pragmatic, humanist socialism of Eduard Bernstein, who was himself unconvinced by Landauer's novel. The alternative that Landauer offers is not better just because it is "alternative." It is impossible to defend *The Death Preacher* in this regard. If one wants to engage in apologetics (and this is not my goal), the most forgiving thing that that could be said about the novel is that its racist nihilism is eventually superseded by cosmic nihilism, in which humanity is verbally voided as a whole, culminating in a vision of a depopulated planet. The particular disgust with Jews, which erupts during the socialist episode of the protagonist's life story, eventually morphs into universal disgust. Yet it is impossible to forget or forgive the scene in light of the subsequent history of National Socialism and the Holocaust, and it provides a sobering reminder that Landauer's novel should be handled with a critical, historical distance.

As suggested above, the short socialist episode of Starkblom's story mainly serves to elaborate and intensify his disgust with dialogue, which drives forward his quest for a "new word" (*DT*, 9). This quest for a "new word" is ultimately a quest for a form of monologue that will transcend the individual's own voice and abolish the distinctions set up by the pronouns "I" and "we." This monologue should, in turn, reconfigure the idea of human collectivity that underwrites socialist politics. As part of this quest, Starkblom must become a socialist so that he can subsequently revolt against socialism's language of collectivity. Already at the moment of his political conversion at the workers' meetings, it is clear that Starkblom cannot articulate his own vision of solidarity in a language that is understandable to most members of the working class. The epiphany of his visit to the socialist reading club "Humanity" comes when he articulates a nihilist notion of collectivity that is based in the indistinctness and instability of the self; he tells one worker, without being understood, that he does not believe he is a "sole" entity (Ich glaube nicht, dass ich einzig bin) (40). He explains that his own solitude already contains the negativity of the entire world. As a "lonely, dispersed" part of the larger world, he is capable (in a Messianic manner) of taking up all the pain of the world into himself and saving others from it: "The soul of a human being is set up so that, once one has used all pain and despair of an entire life to reach something and hold onto it, he can spare others from this misery, by making the complete result of his life comprehensible" (40). So, more than any other person, he has experienced the unity of his own extreme suffering with the suffering of the rest of the world (this is essentially identical to Schopenhauer's sainthood). He actively *wills* himself to suffer more than all others so that he can stand ahead of the rest of humanity and make visible for all the totality of all suffering. He is destined to show the world that it is united in pain. Misanthropy becomes an intentional project of *going ahead of humanity* in order to experience the full potential of the world's isolation and oppression *before others do*. In this passage, Landauer is grappling with another nihilist predecessor besides Schopenhauer: when Starkblom says he is not single or unique (einzig), he is channeling and inverting Max Stirner's egoism, the subject of which is *der Einzige* (as in the title *Der Einzige und ein Eigentum*, in English, *The Ego and Its Own*). Unlike Stirner's egoism, which denies the existence of anything outside the individual self, Starkblom offers an egoism that is programmed to *encompass* the entire world and transcend mere individuality. The point of his remarks, in the context of the socialists' meeting, is to put forth a philosophical-spiritual program that outdoes socialism's claims of political unity through a revelation of cosmic unity. No existing political language can verbalize this unity. Only the relentless monologue of verbal nihilism can perform the work of unification.

There is an element of surprise, then, in the novel's plot: the text of *The Death Preacher* turns to sheer verbal nihilism just as Starkblom seems to have discovered a political cause that he can wholeheartedly embrace. His disillusionment is almost fantastically abrupt. Not long after attending the socialist meetings, he rises to prominence as a socialist agitator, known across Germany. Then, one night, he suddenly finds it impossible to speak from a single political position, and his socialist speech is swept up in a self-abolishing verbal stream. He can no longer repeat the conventional language of revolt, calling the workers to unite and destroy both the state and capital. Suddenly, he is interrupted by what the narrator calls "an inner laughter and rebelling" (ein innerliches Lachen und Aufbäumen) (42). This turning point arrives during a lecture to a large audience in a hot and badly ventilated hall somewhere in western Germany, where Starkblom means to describe the functioning of a future socialist society. As soon as he tries to educate the crowd, though, Starkblom's own voice revolts against him. He hears within himself a mocking slew of injunctions and insults: "Give it up, man! It's all wrong! There's no point!" (Mann gib's auf! Es ist alles falsch! Hat alles keinen Sinn!) (43). The culminating blow dealt by this inner, doubting voice is the question, "what do other people matter to you?" (was gehen dich denn andere Menschen an?) (43). Misanthropy prevails as a demonic voice from nowhere shatters Starkblom's one vision of philanthropic selfhood and supplants it with another. If Starkblom has until now managed to fashion himself as a conscious political agent who shares goals and practices with other socialists and workers, the demonic voice offers a vision of self that is defined by its nonrelation to others. Here again, the influence of Max Stirner's *The Ego and His Own* comes to the fore, in its wholesale refutation of the very idea of community: "No, community, as the 'goal' of history hitherto, is impossible."[34] A Stirnerian language of misanthropy erupts within Starkblom's public speech, disrupting his attempted verbalization of a unified socialist future of humanity. The scene is explosive: it is not simply that Starkblom has uncovered his own "true" inner thoughts. Rather, the demonic voice emerges out of him as a creative-destructive force that does away with the collective *and* the individual. The moment is stringently nihilist because Starkblom has cut ties both with others, and with the one he used to be. There is no community, but there is also no self.

Verbal Nihilism and the Work of Revocation

What remains, beyond community and self, is the creative-destructive energy of monologue. From this point onward, Starkblom's voice is characterized by inner "rebelling" or "rising up," which prevents him from locating himself in any one coherent position or taking on any one political perspective. This experience of self-loss is punctuated by a dramatic, seizure-like collapse: "Then he made a suppressed scream, led his hand to his head and fell down" (43). This convulsive transformation, like so many of Landauer's themes, has an intertextual resonance. In later scenes, Starkblom will refer to himself as an "epileptic," alluding to Dostoevsky's depictions of the epileptic seizure.[35] Both for Myshkin in *The Idiot* and Kirillow in *The Demons*, the epileptic seizure was a form of mystical dislocation, briefly placing a person in a realm of "timelessness" and "eternity."[36] Something similar happens to Starkblom, who has a not so much epileptic as a "Dostoevskian" seizure. The fact that Starkblom is marked as "epileptic" seems to have more to do with this literary inheritance than with Landauer's direct engagement with the symptomology of the disorder; Starkblom, too, has an experience of timelessness in the sense that he can no longer locate himself in, or speak from, any single individual position. Landauer appropriates the seizure as a trope of self-overcoming, indicating a radical break from the confines of individuality.

A formal principle of *The Death Preacher* is clarified and amplified at this moment of "inner laughing." Starkblom's "inner laughing" and accompanying seizure are part of a general form of *revocation* that comes to define the narrative rhetoric of *The Death Preacher* as a whole. When Starkblom calls out for socialism but then immediately finds himself revoking and revolting against his own words, he is compulsively performing a form of verbal nihilism that works through perpetual revocation and voiding of whatever has been previously uttered. One word for this perpetual revocation would be *metanoia*, the act of revoking what one has just said (employed quite gratuitously by Dostoevsky's Underground Man, who negates essentially every one of his own statements). Metanoia is not only a rhetorical but also a psychological and theological term: it can refer to an abrupt experience of transformation (changing one's mind) and to a rhetorical device (whereby a speaker refutes something that he has just said). Metanoia, both as a rhetorical device and as a form of mental experience, is a defining form of *The Death Preacher.* In it most extreme instances, metanoia has an unnatural, transgressive effect: it is a form of revocation that violates and revises reality as previously defined by the narrator. By revoking his own individual utterances, Landauer's hero also revokes himself as a literary character and reveals (in place of where "he" was) an invisible world beyond human individuation. Thus, metanoia leads into a radical instance of metalepsis, the overthrow of the hero's own voice by an anonymous and otherworldly voice. At the moment when Starkblom the socialist speaker collapses before the crowd, a new voice emerges out of nowhere, which leaves no firm individual identities intact, revealing an unspeakable unity behind these identities. These tendencies of metanoia and metalepsis are most intensely concentrated in the nihilist monologues that become the centerpiece of Landauer's novel.

To underscore the philosophical significance of these monologues, it is helpful to examine the theories of individuality and collectivity that Landauer developed just two years after *The Death Preacher* in his 1895 series of essays entitled "On the Developmental History of the Individual."[37] In these works, Landauer adopts the unified universe furnished by Schopenhauer's will but purifies it of its sinister valences as a force that naturally causes suffering. Landauer does not speak of a "will" but rather of a "whole" of which every apparent individual is a part, a "great community" (groß[e] Gemeinschaft) of the universe.[38] This whole appears to us through our sense organs as a series of discretely appearing bodies. Yet beyond these bodies' appearance in time and space, they are composed of great, otherwise invisible yet definitely indivisible communities. In short, Landauer espouses a holistic cosmology while working against an atomic definition of the individual as a discrete unit that cannot be decomposed into smaller units. He hopes to replace this atomism with a vision of individuals as the singular manifestations of a *collective*, whose unity is always metaphysically guaranteed. For instance, the collectivity of the human species, as a "bodily community," is "inescapable"; our dependence on our ancestors cannot be escaped, and thus such a community exercises a "force" (Zwang) and places the human individual under its "spell" (Bann).[39] What we call "individual," or "I," is in fact an indivisible community of indivisible communities. Landauer feels that language itself is a reactionary force that staves off this underlying reality, and so he must himself adopt a language that contradicts itself: it is only through perpetual self-correcting (rhetorical metanoia) that we can break through its illusory façade into the more fundamental underlying reality (a kind of narrative metalepsis that permits the self access to an otherwise inaccessible level of existence).

The monologues at the middle of *The Death Preacher* carry these tendencies of metanoia and metalepsis to a new extreme. After Starkblom's epileptic fit, he publishes two pamphlets containing extended nihilist monologues, which are provided for the reader in full. These two embedded texts take up the task of positing an "I" that is also a multitude, which in its solitary monologue affirms its belonging to a cosmic community, whose cohesion is guaranteed outside time and space (a great whole). One could go so far as to say that, in Landauer's novel, community is known and authenticated only through collapse of the categories of time and space. Community is the implosion of reality as we thought we knew it, and so a central purpose of Starkblom's monologues, in their protracted interruption of the novel's main narrative, is to perform such a collapse of time and space. The monologue—echoing Schopenhauer—signals the removal of the individual speaker from any particular location *here* or *now*, producing a disembodied voice that crosses between unconnected points in time and space. The ultimate effect is (to borrow a term from quantum physics) a "nonlocality" of voice: speech emits from more than one place at a time and thus appears ubiquitous. In achieving an apogee of mental suffering, the speaker shows that he "belongs" to the universe.

The monologues in these missives follow from Starkblom's desire to utter a "new word" to humanity. They are difficult to categorize as they combine a number of genres in a kind of monstrous conglomerate: the political agitation speech, the philosophical essay, the religious prophecy, the clinical self-diagnosis, and finally (by Starkblom's own admission) the classified personal ad. The monologues mix genres in order to verbalize a negativity so extreme that it can both (*a*) void the entire history of human achievement in both the abstract and material realms, and (*b*) revoke the identity of the individual speaking subject who performs this voiding, so as to (*c*) arrive at a formless darkness out of which the world could be created anew. Then, something like "love" becomes possible. It is only in the final moments of verbalizing the void that basic ideas of sympathy, mutual aid, and the primary need for companionship can finally be expressed.

In the first transcribed monologue, Starkblom self-corrects his socialist speeches (metanoia) by revoking the last traces of his humanist ideals and establishes that life is a fundamental mistake. In the second monologue, Starkblom conjures an apocalyptic fantasy in which he himself plays the role of "Death Preacher" who brings about the end of human civilization through a crazed, pseudo-Dionysian suicide cult. This second monologue performs a twofold violation, or metalepsis: first, the monologue superimposes a hallucinatory reality directly onto the communicative reality of the missive, treating this imagined apocalypse as if it were really occurring in the present moment of communication. Second, the speaking-writing individual "Starkblom," who presents this apocalyptic vision, finds that he himself is incapacitated and erased by his own vision, so that he cannot finally uphold a coherent distinction between himself as a hallucinat*or*, and the hallucinat*ed* horror he is describing. Having conjured a posthuman void in which he himself is implicated, Starkblom uncovers a primary need for sociality and ends by asking for the companionship of one other person who would accompany him into death. His nihilist rant turns into a plea for partnership. In this way, misanthropic isolation (*Absonderung*) of monologue finally creates the precondition for community. The final metalepsis of the monologue violates the textual boundary between speaker and listener, as Starkblom reaches out to the reader for a companionship that might rescue him from the void.

The first "Missive of Karl Starkblom to the Human Race" is subtitled "Rejection Letter to Socialism" (Absagebrief an den Sozialismus) (*DT*, 44). The text basically reads as an update of the polemics in the first half of Dostoevsky's *Notes from Underground*, where the narrator refutes the humanist pretenses that want to create a "crystal edifice," or an egalitarian heaven on earth. In this "rejection letter," the attitudes that previously led Starkblom to embrace socialism (the mood of revolt, anger at the human condition, the desire for global collectivity, a millenarian desire for *tabula rasa*) are recast in order to refute all institutional and extra-institutional varieties of socialism. Starkblom is not, like Dostoevsky's Underground Man, "disillusioned" in the sense of having witnessed in practice the limitations of intellectual idealism. He is not disappointed with some particular instance of political failure. Rather, Starkblom refuses socialism out of a preternatural awareness of the nothingness of humanity and the universe, to which he gives the name "death." Death, in *The Death Preacher*, is never merely the end of a single human life. Rather, it is an agglomeration of two models of nullity borrowed from nihilist philosophy: Schopenhauer's *Nichts*, in which the universal will finds repose, and Stirner's conception of the self as a "creative nothing" out of which the ego can entirely determine its universe.[40] One might say that the locution "death" for Starkblom serves the function of a reset button that cancels out all concrete determinations and values and makes it possible to start over again. "Death" is an imagined *tabula rasa* that will allow Starkblom to rethink the nature of community anew, starting from the blank page of nothingness.

In order to underscore his refutation of humanism, Starkblom's monologue proceeds by fabulating a new, antihuman collectivity that is opposed to the "community of human beings" (Gemeinschaft der Menschen) presupposed by socialism (44). The members of this fictional mass, he insists, are his true listeners. These listeners, as a sort of revolutionary base that will bring about the apocalypse, are united through their hatred of life. It is clear, from Starkblom's descriptions of them, that this antigroup is none other than that "band" of suicidal nihilists, or decadents, that was introduced at the start of the novel's second section as the antipode to the global collectivity of socialists. In Starkblom's monologue, he names these "brothers" as privileged "listeners" and establishes their superiority over the devotees of any particular political ideology. These imagined listeners, like Starkblom, are aware of the limitations of every political ism (socialism, communism, anarchism, idealism, individualism). Having moved past the values asserted by each of those ideologies, these sovereign outsiders became pessimists who "had lost their beliefs as well as their longing for life" (47). Starkblom installs himself as the leader of these "disgusted," "chosen" ones who form the vanguard of his imagined revolution (47). As he mentions this subculture, Starkblom abruptly shifts the addressee of his speech away from humanity in general and claims instead to be staging a private communication to his putative "brothers." As such, he makes it difficult to discern the "here" and "now" of his discourse. His description is shot through with hallucinatory interpolations that make the nonexistent existent, conjuring a present that is absent for the reader:

> They are standing in the first row, and their hearts are open to me there, and they are waiting for the word that I shall speak. And when I speak the word "death," it sounds ripe and familiar to them, they have become mellow and understand me and follow me. I
> bless you, my brothers, our paths come from different births, but now they have found each other and will remain together.

> Sie stehen in der vordersten Reihe, und ihre Herzen liegen mir offen da, und sie harren des Wortes, das ich sprechen soll. Und wenn ich das Wort ausspreche, das Wort "Tod," dann klingt ihnen das schon reif und vertraut, sie sind mürbe geworden und verstehen mich und folgen mir nach. Ich segne euch, meine Brüder, unsere Wege kom-

> men aus verschiedenen Geburten, aber nun haben sie sich gefunden und bleiben beisammen. (48)

What Victor Erlich wrote of Dostoevsky's Underground Man can be applied to Starkblom's rant: "It is not so much the prevalence of 'I' as it is the repeated and avowedly futile use of 'you' . . . that underscores the total vacuum into which the monologue . . . projects itself."[41] The abrupt cancellation of one addressee (humanity) and its replacement with another (the subculture of death) underscores the communicative void that Starkblom will later articulate with the futile address: "My friends who are not here" (55). When Dostoevsky's Underground Man conjures such a "vacuum" through futile second-person address, it carries a socially critical connotation, highlighting the "*preposterous* social situation in which the speaker finds himself" (that is, a social situation that is not a social situation at all).[42] In Landauer's novel, the communicative vacuum, in which the addressee is simultaneously present and absent, is endowed with a mystical meaning. The conceit of Starkblom's discourse is that, in removing himself to this communicative vacuum, he can approximate a state of nonexistence, a living death where time, space, and causality are transcended (96).

As noted above, a crucial juncture in Starkblom's biography was his discovery of the failure of dialogue to produce understanding. In this monologue, the problem of communication is ostensibly "solved" through the idea of a magic word—"death"—that names the substratum of all existence. Language can create consensus und mutual understanding only insofar as it expresses a universal refusal. Only the vocabulary of death can cross class boundaries, solidify solidarity, and authorize a single leader. Gathering together the different pessimist discourses of the nineteenth century, Starkblom claims to have concocted the recipe for undefeatable political unity that is not a "world power" but an "antiworld power." Starkblom's "Rejection Letter to Socialism" is presented as the turn in the tides of history, when the world is finally converted from socialism to nihilism (he even concludes the monologue by attempting to recruit readers into his cult of death and commit suicide with him). The task of his next monologue is to imagine how this history might proceed further and culminate in the end of human civilization. The absurdity of Starkblom's undertaking is made clear at the start of this monologue. As it turns out, Starkblom's first missive did not have the effect its author intended, and nobody wrote him to join his community of death. As such, his second published monologue, entitled "The Vision of the Death Preacher. Second Missive to the Human Race," does not pretend to reflect the world as it is. Rather, this second outpouring of verbal nihilism is explicitly marked as an otherworldly "vision" and proceeds as a work of speculative fiction. A character named "Starkblom" does appear in this other world, but the surname is now applied to the speaker's alter ego, "Starkblom the Death Preacher." Adopting this hallucinatory avatar, the "second"

Starkblom can conjure an *apocalyptic* void far surpassing the scale of the *social* void experienced by the "first" Starkblom in the preceding portions of the novel. In the place of everyday emptiness where the first Starkblom lives with "nobody," the second Starkblom envisions the absolute "nobody" of a posthuman world. Through the creative work of nihilist monologue, Starkblom turns himself from a misanthropic "underground type," into an imagined harbinger of global destruction. Perversely, it is through this horrific process of transposition and hallucination that Starkblom finds a path to new community.

The first step of Starkblom's second monologue is to acknowledge that everyday emptiness, which characterizes the life of Landauer's protagonist. At the outset, Starkblom establishes that the "listeners" he had invoked in his first missive (the "band of death") have not actually materialized. Nobody, in fact, has come forth to join him: "My words have not found any answer at all, no strong reverberation" (*DT*, 55). Expecting that he would be cheered for writing his first pamphlet, he finds that "nothing of the sort" has happened (55). This would seem to be a turning point where Starkblom would decide to "pack it in"; he would understand the essentially ineffectual nature of his misanthropy and would be able to laugh at the hubristic claims of his first pamphlet. And indeed, Starkblom calls his own earlier expectations "ridiculousness upon ridiculousness!" (55). But instead, he embraces absurdity. Starkblom finds that his failure perfectly corresponds the goals he had set for himself. He now addresses his speech to "My friends who are not here" (55). The community that Starkblom now invokes is more purely nihilist than even his imagined "band of death": *nobody at all* belongs to it. Starkblom then performs a narrative conjuring act whereby this rhetorical "nobody" is translated into a real corporeal mass of followers who listen with raptures to the sermons of "Starkblom the Death Preacher." The community of death-loving "friends" that he invoked in his first monologue are concretized into a voracious, aggressive crowd poised to dominate the world and commit mass suicide. The crowds converge around Starkblom's promises to do away with the basic conditions of human subjectivity: the crowds need to converge in a collective, and then individuality and rationality and, by extension, suffering, will finally come to an end. Now, his revolution can begin.

Starkblom's monologues of agitation and mobilization are flavored with citations of the nihilist literary tradition. When the alter ego "Starkblom the Death Preacher" addresses the masses, he promises a form of unity that recalls Schopenhauer's transcendence of individuation:

> This I still want to say to you all: one and nothing—they are the same. Individuation and difference created the world in the first place. If the world is one again, then there is nothing left, Nothing is there, absolutely Nothing.

> Denn wisset, das will ich euch noch sagen: eins und nichts—das ist dasselbe. Die Besonderung und die Verschiedenheit erst hat die Welt und Leben und Bewusstsein erzeugt. Ist die Welt erst eins, dann ist nichts mehr, dann ist das Nichts da, das absolute Nichts. (62)

There is, of course, a clear analogy between these promises and the promises that Starkblom delivered earlier when preaching socialism. Instead of agitating crowds of workers with visions of an egalitarian workers' society, Starkblom now agitates the masses with a pastiche of Schopenhauer. A philosophical inheritance associated with extreme solitude and contemplation becomes a mobilizing mechanism on par with the slogan "Workers of the world, unite!" In this way, *The Death Preacher* slyly sends a signal to the intellectuals of the decadence movement, asking them to consider what it would look like if their discourse were made into a mechanism of political mobilization. What if Schopenhauer were the new Marx?

Landauer's work with nihilist intertexts is also evident in Starkblom's discourse on epilepsy. He imagines how this illness, as a key motif of decadent literature (inherited in this case through Dostoevsky), could become a political rallying cry: "We are all epileptic, in all of us there lives something that strives against life" (56). This idea of "epilepsy" echoes certain characters of Dostoevsky and also has much in common with Schopenhauer's models of self-denial as achieved through art and asceticism. Starkblom suggests that epilepsy is a liberating condition that can free us from the strictures of time, space, and causality. This is precisely the liberation that Starkblom's alter ego promises to his imagined masses: "You will return home to unconsciousness. You will no longer ask why. The idiocy of this 'purpose' madness has died with you. Nature is one again, everything is beautiful, and nothing is felt but its own one beauty. Time has died with you, and cause and effect live no longer" (57). This sermon makes sense when understood as a translation of Schopenhauer's thought: the misery of living as an individuated self (caught within the chains of time, space, and causality) must be transcended if one wishes to escape suffering. However, the Death Preacher's prescription—that humanity follows its inner "epileptic" drive toward death—is glaringly anti-Schopenhauerian since the philosopher clarified his opposition to suicide in the first volume of *The World as Will and Representation*.[43] Landauer's hero remains a rebellious reader of the classical nihilists, drawing conclusions that were never contained in the original texts.

Alongside these intertextual allusions to classical nihilism, Starkblom's vision conjures images that connect clearly to the contemporary artistic movement of decadence. In describing the exploits of his fabulated death-cult, he invokes the decadent theme of the necropolis, which he expresses in painterly visual detail:

> Everywhere, in all cities, they have thrown the statues of princes and generals in the marketplaces from their pedestals, and with the stone and iron rubble have smashed in the windows of castles and palaces of the living. And on the pedestals, they have placed colossal skeletons, deified figures of death, and they have thrown off their clothes and dance around the portrait of death.
>
> Sie haben überall, in allen Städten, die Statuen ihrer Fürsten und Heerführer auf den Marktplätzen von den Sockeln geworfen und mit den Stein- und Erztrümmern die Fenster der Schlösser und Paläste der Lebenden eingeschlagen. Und auf die Sockel haben sie kolossale Gerippe gestellt, vergötterte Todesgestalten, und sie haben ihre Kleider von sich geworfen und tanzen um das Bildnis des Todes. (57)

Here, Landauer's hoped-for alliance between anarchism and decadence qua pessimism becomes concretely manifest as gothic fiction. This morbid "palace revolt" lives out the anarcho-socialist dream of spontaneous expropriation and smashing of the state, recalling at once the Paris Commune, a Dionysian orgy, and the medieval *danse macabre.* With its odd fusion of vivacious revolution and macabre religious ritual, this passage confirms the affinities of Landauer's writing to the aesthetics of fin de siècle symbolism.[44] Like many of his literary contemporaries of the 1890s, Landauer employs imagery of a dead city for the "concretization" of a pessimist philosophy inspired above all by Schopenhauer.[45] In his vision of a world saturated with death, Landauer was reiterating a common fin de siècle theme: "the dead city as an image of the world's madness," with the difference that here that madness and the dead city are an *alternative* to the endless suffering that defines the world.[46]

Dissociation and New Community

Landauer's text engages in a kind of coquetry that wants to please a range of audiences: Starkblom creates a morbid mélange that might appeal to the tastes of a fin de siècle bohemian intellectual with its nods to Schopenhauer, Stirner, Dostoevsky, Nietzsche, and the decadence movement, but it could also speak to the revolutionary spirit of the contemporary workers' movement. However, this mixture of sources is destined to please nobody: the text resolutely presses these intertexts together into an explicitly indigestible language so convoluted and violent that it "revolts" even in the mouth of the speaker who produces it and finally renders him incoherent. The protagonist winces at his own words: as Starkblom (as the narrator of the "missive") quotes the speeches of his fabulated character Starkblom (the Death Preacher), he himself becomes affected by its negativity and is suddenly dislocated from the spatial, temporal, and causal chain of his own narrative. Just as he is reporting on the crowd's joyous responses to the Death Preacher, he loses control of what he is narrating:

> The mass of death-happy ones becomes bigger and bigger.—Hah, where is he? Everything disappeared before my eyes? I see nothing more. I hear nothing more. I am lying on the ground and am groaning and feel my body. Where is this Starkblom? Starkblom, where are you?
>
> Größer und größer wird die Masse der Todesfrohen.—Ha, wo ist er? Alles schwand meinen Augen? Ich erblicke nichts mehr. Ich höre nichts mehr. Ich liege auf dem Boden und stöhne und betaste meinen Leib. Wo ist dieser Starkblom? Starkblom, wo bist du? (57)

As soon as the narrator becomes a witness to the vision of his alter ego's morbid excesses, he is thrown into a state of disorientation, darkness, and uncontrollable convulsion that bring about a narrative paralysis, and for a moment nothing more can be told. His story about the self-annihilation of humanity triggers—as if by reflex—a form of narrative self-erasure, where the "I" is unmasked as an illusion. Dissociation (the loss of personality and personhood) is the destination. The failure to communicate is the whole point.

This quest for dissociation plays out sentence for sentence within Starkblom's monologue; each time he announces his desire for the annihilation of humanity: "Oh, I would not speak to you if I knew how to murder you all!" (*DT*, 58). Even the most emphatic statement is refuted and retracted. Verbal nihilism, here, consists not only in the threat of violence but in the ongoing self-erasure of the discourse. The initial threat to "all" of humanity morphs into an apologia where the speaker's earlier desire to kill is explained as a desire to rescue humanity from suffering: "I don't want anyone to come after my death, who would experience the same thing" (58). He only wants to save everyone. Then, this apologetic "I" turns into a subject of pure renunciation, which does not want to kill but simply wants *nothing*: "I don't want" (58). From here, the speaker expresses disgust at his own outburst of disgust: "I am revolted by my last thought. I am revolted by solitude" (58). Through this process of revocation and regret, the impression of any locable, embodied "I" dissipates into a stream of ephemeral moods. In this way, quite perversely, Starkblom's act of death-preaching has a productive outcome: it makes the individual recoil from himself, disown his own discourse, and declare his dependency on others. This process of deindividuation recalls Schopenhauer, who theorizes morality as the outcome of empathy, in which the distinction between self and other is overcome.[47] For Starkblom, this sense of empathy is gained through verbal violence, where the individual recoils from himself. If Schopenhauer saw ascetic practice as the path toward empathy, Landauer's protagonist attains something akin to empathy by displacing himself with shocking utterances: hearing his own murderous threats, he becomes another and thus ostensibly recovers an inclination to community. The grotesque indulgences of the "Death Preacher" monologue are thus justified, in the context of Landauer's novel, through the pretense of a self-shocking meditative practice whereby the subject convinces himself of the illusory nature of the solitary and self-sufficient "I." This is where the negative becomes positive, and community springs from solitude: just as nihilism undoes the self, nihilism undoes itself, and the text reveals a primary need for outward relation, a "you" that can give substance to the "I" that is on the verge of dissolution.

This may sound fairly benevolent, but one should not underemphasize the gratuitous fabulations of violence that transport Starkblom from misanthropy to a love of community. The fabulated apocalypse of the Death Preacher involves a violent anarchy that exceeds most leftist visions of liberation, where looting and public sex lead to infanticide and mass murder, as "countless individuals and couples are already dying, the newborn children are almost all killed" (*DT*, 59). These disturbing fantasies fulfill the auto-affective function of Starkblom's monologue: he is horrified by his own words. The lonely speaker, in the echo chamber of his own monologue, drives himself *out of his mind* with gratuitous images of horror. One brief narrative thread illustrates this drive toward excess: a young man addresses the murdering masses and suggests that humanity is not doing enough to destroy itself. He says collective suicide will be useless if there are still sentient beings living on Mars, because "We cannot reach them there" (60). He emphasizes that what is being achieved is "almost" nothing but still not pure nothingness: "Not only humans, not only animals, not only this earth, no, the entirety of nature, we must be able to destroy the whole world! And can we do that?" (60). The void created through Starkblom's vision, in other words, may never be complete.

Anxiety about the incompleteness of the void results, first of all, in more extreme forms of horror, culminating in one of the ugliest passages of Landauer's novel: after the young man's zeal in pursuing the "good cause" is questioned, he demonstrates his commitment to nihilism by perpetrating an act of sexual violence, raping a "beautiful fifteen-year-old girl," then killing her and himself by jumping out of a window. This is a turning point in the monologue, as the vision of sexual violence triggers an epileptic fit in Starkblom. He now completely loses control of himself both as the narrator of the apocalypse and as its primary protagonist. Not only is humanity dissolving, so is the vision of dissolution: "Everything swam before Starkblom's eyes. That was the familiar sign. The attack threatened again" (60). This "attack" spells the final dissociation and dissolution of Starkblom as a cognizing subject. What Starkblom calls the "outpourings" of his "crazy brain" culminate in a revocation of himself as a hallucinator. Whenever Starkblom verbalizes a worst-case scenario, he nullifies himself (60). As with Dostoevsky's characters, this "epileptic fit" places the subject outside of time and space: the convulsive Starkblom can briefly inhabit the excluded middle between existence and nonexistence, overcoming the parameters of individual subjectivity. Of course, this causal link follows a deeply disturbing logic, since it purchases transcendence of the self through visions of gratuitous violence against women. The misanthropic vision incorporates toxic misogyny and instrumentalizes the resulting shock-effect.

The culminating shock-effect of Starkblom's vision arrives when he forces himself to confront the final consequences of the Death Preacher's monologues. Within the span of a single paragraph, the second Starkblom's verbal nihilism triggers the suicide of all humans, who collectively drown themselves.

> "This I want to tell you all again: one and nothing—it's the same thing. It was separation and difference that first created the world and life and consciousness. If the world is one, then nothing is anymore, then there is nothingness, absolute nothingness." And then they dove into the floods—all of them. And after a short time the laughter and singing and fearful screams were silent—for a few also screamed—and the earth was empty of people far and wide. But the Rhine flowed on calmly, and soon the animals of the forest came and perked up their ears and drank from the cool waters, and the world of plants grew up around the whole earth and covered the rubble of human inhabitations, and a singing and jubilation of the birds rose up like never before, and the flowers shone and scented in sweet splendor as never before, and the trees rustled and told it to the wind, and the storms howled it onward, and the earth boomed vocally along its course: he was dead, he was dead! the great tormenter!
>
> "Das will ich euch noch sagen: eins und nichts—das ist dasselbe. Die Besonderung und die Verschiedenheit erst hat die Welt und Leben und Bewusstsein erzeugt. Ist die Welt erst eins, dann ist nichts mehr, dann ist das Nichts da, das absolute Nichts." Und dann stürzten sie sich hinein in die Fluten—allesamt. Und nach kurzer Frist war das Gelächter und der Gesang und das Angstgeschrei verstummt—denn einige schrieen auch—und menschlos war die Erde weit und breit. Der Rhein aber floss ruhig weiter, und bald kamen die Tiere des Waldes und spitzten die Ohren und tranken aus kühlen Gewässern, und

> grün umwucherte die Pflanzenwelt die ganze Erde und umspann die Trümmer der Menschenbehausungen, und ein Singen und Jubilieren der Vögel erhob sich wie nie zuvor, und die Blumen leuchteten und dufteten in süßer, nie erhörter Pracht, und die Bäume rauschen und erzählten es den Winden, und die Stürme heulten es weiter, und die Erde brauste klingend ihre Bahn dahin: er war tot, er war tot! der große Peiniger! (62)

With the ensuring vision of "absolute nothingness," Starkblom fully loses control over his own monologic discourse, finding that all of his purported identities as a speaker have been voided. The depopulated landscape conjured in Starkblom's monologue actually prompts him to back *away* from the void; the absolute misanthropy of his monologue triggers in him a need for a minimal human relation. No longer able to maintain his nihilist posture on his own, Starkblom finally totally loses his capacity for monologue and reaches out (through a language of bodily gestures) to others who might provide him with minimal companionship. The hallucination of his total domination and destruction of humanity turns into a plea for help.

> And now I grab my head and the inclined reader may do the same. He may calm himself, he is still alive, and I will not murder him. I however am Starkblom, not Starkblom the Death Preacher and not Starkblom the epileptic––only Starkblom the first, Starkblom the Suffering One and the Starkblom the Dying One.
>
> Und jetzt greife ich mir an den Kopf und der geneigte Leser tue desgleichen. Beruhige er sich, er lebt noch, und ich werde ihn auch nicht ermorden. Ich aber bin Starkblom, nicht Starkblom der Todesprediger und nicht Starkblom der Epileptische—bloß Starkblom der Erste, Starkblom der Leidende und Starkblom der Sterbende. (*DT*, 62)

It is now no longer the *world* or *humanity* that has been reduced to "nothingness"; rather, Starkblom makes the crucial discovery that *he* is nothing without *some* other. Instead of voicing the strength indicated by his name (the German *stark*, meaning "strong"), Starkblom becomes a node of embodied fragility and pain. He ceases to be a soliloquizing and visionary subject and stands now as a gap to be filled. He is nothing but a lack of community, one who needs another to hear him and respond. Starkblom realigns his identity in negative terms: he is simply one who is fragile and mortal, and these are his primary characteristics. With this new iteration of himself, Starkblom defines himself in terms of a previously unvoiced need: the minimal need for difference and relations in the face of total negativity. As such, he confesses in a pathetic tone that he is just looking for one (einer) who could die with him. His entire nihilist monologue has concluded by exposing the prima-

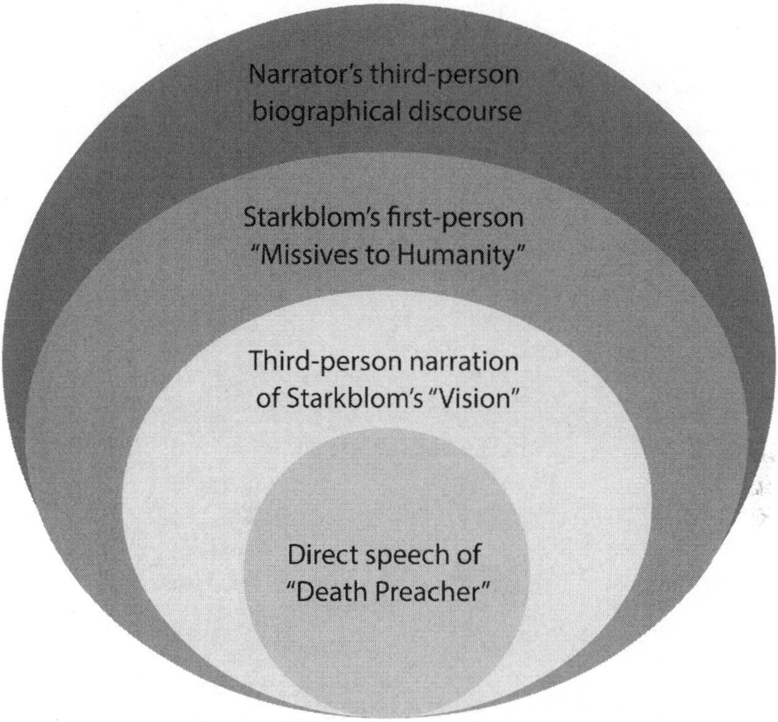

Initial arrangement of layers.

ry relationality of the self, which cannot even die if it is alone. As the self threatens to vanish, a minimum of sociality asserts itself over and against any idea of autonomous selfhood. This sociality asserts itself, moreover, by a move away from language as a medium of interaction, toward an acknowledgment of shared embodiment. By grabbing his head and suggesting that the reader is doing the same thing at the same time, Starkblom transitions from verbal to bodily communication. From the epitome of nihilism, the minimal need for community is allowed to appear.

In formal terms, the text's step from nihilism to community corresponds to a violation of the hierarchy of discursive layers that initially lent stability to the dilated middle section of the novel. Up until this point, Landauer's novel was clearly structured through a model of progressive embedding, with the nihilist speech of the Death Preacher contained within three discursive frames (see above diagram). As the narrative focus of the novel steps back from the innermost frame (the one containing Starkblom's "death preaching," it seems that the outermost frames have been either eliminated or distorted beyond recognition, so that the reader is not initially returned to the authoritative discourse of a narrator, but rather

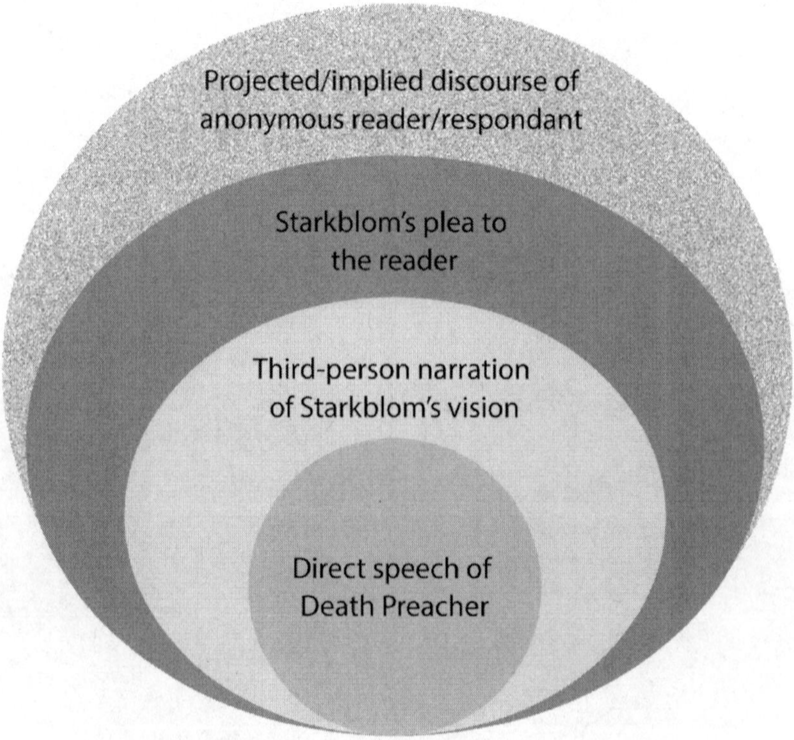

Eventual arrangement of layers.

the outermost frame is now determined by an anonymous *reader* standing outside the bounds of the text. The following illustration shows how, at the end of Starkblom's monologic missive, the outermost narrator's discourse is implicitly displaced, making room for the undefined discourse of an anonymous respondent (see above diagram).

As the illustrations suggest, Starkblom's outward cry to the reader is an instance of metalepsis, a transgressing and renegotiating of textual boundaries. By narrating his own bodily gestures alongside those of an unseen reader and locating these gestures in a shared "now," Starkblom has transgressed the boundary between intratextual actions and extratextual actions. This outward reach across boundaries, in turn, establishes a bond between the otherworldly, apocalyptic vision of the Death Preacher and the everyday solitude involved in the practices of European literary culture. In the end, the simple solitude of reading and writing is not so different from the absolute solitude of a depopulated planet because both of these experiences of emptiness refer back to a fundamental need to *reset* relationships. One moves to the brink of emptiness in order to learn how to back away from it. In the wake of extreme nihilism, the familiar frames have vanished and been replaced with an implied, extratextual vantage point occupied by an other on whom one is existentially dependent.

In *The Death Preacher*, this experience of transgression and transformation provides the basis for a new set of sociopolitical visions, creating a blueprint for both familial love and socialism. For Landauer's hero, there can be no socialism, no family, and no anarchism without an intense and solitary experience of self-loss, where the "I" loses all guarantees of integrity and substantiality. As Starkblom steps out from the innermost discourses of his self, he finds that the very conditions that make the utterance of "I" possible have changed. The "I" is now entirely predicated on the answer of an absent other, denoted as "the inclined reader" who would be willing to step down into the nadir of nihilism that the "I" occupies. In this situation, the pronoun "I" does not refer to some stable and preexisting identity but rather is a *call for rescue by another* from the edge of the void. When language no longer makes sense, and the speaker loses his sense of what "I" means, his speech indexes nothing but a primary dependency. For Landauer, the speech that uncovers this truth must be a monologue that negates everything and denounces all need for human contact and human survival. This is how one moves "through isolation to community." By subjecting himself to a vision of an apocalyptic void and approaching the threshold of complete verbal deterioration, Starkblom can begin to think of how the self *and* the masses are isometrically related: both are an anarchic plurality of possibilities. Through his monomaniacal monologues, Starkblom hits upon the primary volatility of all fixed identities.

Elsewhere, I have emphasized the absurdity of Starkblom's (and Landauer's) undertaking in *The Death Preacher*. Some of this absurdity might be by design, particularly in light of how the novel ends. In backing away from the precipice of the void, the *Death Preacher* concludes as a comedy. Almost without transition, Landauer's protagonist leaps out of his hallucinated apocalypse into a fast-paced marriage plot: immediately after the publication of the Death Preacher's "Vision," a young Frenchwoman named Marguerite arrives at Starkblom's doorstep, who has discovered his texts through a bookseller in Paris (78). She is already in love with him and ready to remedy his nihilism and depression. After a long textual segment filled with the work of voiding performed by a masculine voice, a feminine voice arrives as a savior to fill in the void, rescuing the male speaker from nihilism. Starkblom himself is quite conscious of this gendered "rescue operation" and its corresponding model of heterosexual coupling. During a later conversation with Marguerite, he likens his own nihilist discourse to a personal ad in a newspaper taken out by a lonely middle-aged man seeking a companion (*DT*, 76).

Virtual Revolution

The happy ending of Landauer's novel is in many respects preposterous, given how quickly a male fantasy of a perfect woman (young, adventurous, and fertile) materializes before Starkblom's doorstep to save him, after she has read his transcribed nihilistic monologues. The conceit of this happy ending is, in any case, that there is no absolutely fixed boundary between literature (his missives) and life (their marriage). The virtual relation of literary communication constitutes the legitimate basis for future human community. Both the marriage of Starkblom and Marguerite, and the revolutionary political community for which he hopes, are first constituted in the virtual sphere of literature. That is to say, the creation of community needs nothing more than writing desks, printing presses, and booksellers. Indeed, this celebration of literature's virtual relations lends credence to Yossef Schwartz's argument that Landauer produces an "almost postmodern celebration" of ephemeral, plural "identities and realities."[48] The conjuring-voiding act of imaginative literature is, for Landauer's hero, the source and destination for communal identity.

If Landauer, as Schwartz suggests, presents an early version of political postmodernism, he also prefigures postmodernist fiction's ontological pluralism. Each of the "visions" of Landauer's novel is a "flickering reality, both there and not there."[49] The final political vision of *The Death Preacher*, just like its vision of romantic love, also "flickers" between hallucination and concrete mobilization. In his closing monologue-missive in the novel's final pages, Starkblom soliloquizes his desire to "wed" fallen bourgeois intellectuals (the decadents of his time) with the revolting ranks of workers, marshaling these bohemians "in the field of the future, in the camp of the proletariat" (im Lager des Proletariats) (*DT*, 97). At one point, he makes mention of a worker standing next to him, who has materialized out of nowhere to reproach him for uttering what "we" (the workers") have known practically "since before birth," amid an otherwise "incomprehensible" speech (97). The reproach smuggles a "we" of the workers into Starkblom's soliloquy, before turning to another collective subject, the "they" of bourgeois fin de siècle outcasts (97). What is the ontological status of these collectivities, which are allegedly present as Starkblom writes out his monologue? Is this alliance of avatars any more substantial than the fabulated suicidal masses pictured in the novel's middle section? The answer expressed in the novel's last dramatic scene is ambiguous. After saying goodnight to his wife, Landauer's hero goes to the window and reaches his hands out into the air, as if he were calling to his "people." Outside there is only darkness, punctuated by a few lights in the distance. This scene encapsulates the relation of isolation and community explored throughout the novel. The isolated subject with "nothing" in his field of vision but the black of night sees something indiscernible flickering in the distance: the initial beginnings of a formation of people, and of a human presence, stand out against a formless void. Starkblom's "people" is the virtual formation that can be projected from the threshold where he stands. His community is the minimal bundle of relations that jumps out of the darkness of the void. If we read backward from this final page, we can see the entire novel as an attempt to arrive at this positive community of the void, which overrides and replaces the morbid and murderous communities of the void envisioned in earlier sections.

Several times I have used the term "virtual" to describe the communities imagined in Landauer's *Death Preacher*. Virtual communities are, of course, a product of the Internet age, where we engage remotely with hundreds or thousands of named and nameless others. However, the concept of virtual community is not an entirely anachronistic term for the communities of *The Death Preacher*, which are always present in their absence, "there but not there."[50] Landauer himself described his idea of anarcho-socialist community by invoking the telecommunications technologies of his time, which eventually evolved into our current online world. Landauer suggests that there is a cosmic basis for telecommunications and its attendant virtual relations and that these technologies actually represent the most primordial form of community. In his 1903 book *Skepticism and Mysticism*, Landauer insists that both the telegraph and wireless communication would have existed long ago if humanity had first come into existence without eyes. It was the evolutionary emergence of eyesight, Landauer argues, that furnished us with the illusion of space and of separate individuated beings: "If we had no eyes, . . . we never would have hit upon the crazy idea of saying 'I' to this body here, but not to this book or this table or this woman."[51] Landauer goes on to suggest that it would have been possible, in this case, that "telegraph and wireless telephony" (Telegraphie und Telephonie ohne Draht) would have been familiar things long before the invention of eyesight.[52] In this alternate history, humans would *invent* eyesight, *after* telecommunications, and with their newfound vision they would not see a world of separate, distanced individuals but a single "I" that they already knew was connected. Landauer insists that the visible reality we commonly accept is an illusion: underneath our isolated, individual identities, we actually exist in a vast web of insoluble connections. Telecommunication is the hidden truth of the universe. In order to make this realization, a certain extreme nihilism is necessary: we must withdraw from society into a condition of radical soliloquy, isolate ourselves even further than society usually dictates. All the avatars that one adopts as an individual would seem to be merely ephemeral masks over an occulted unity. This mystical model of unity is, I would speculate, what allows Landauer to combine radical and revolutionary postures with socially conservative ones: Starkblom the "family man" and "property owner" marries Marguerite the "mother" and "bon vivant," but this traditional family structure is just one possible expression of the chaotic energy of the universe, which also erupts into revolutionary upheavals of the workers' movement, and the anarchists' propaganda of the deed. There is anarchy underlying every discrete person, place, and thing. This is the basic revelation of nihilism, triggered by the hero's verbal voiding of the world through monologue. Without actually destroying anything or physically hurting anyone with his speeches, Landauer's hero has brought about a private, virtual state of anarchy in which no identities or social formations have a fixed, permanent existence.

Anarchists have often debated how it is possible to confront coercive authority without engaging in coercive violence. Literature, at the end of Landauer's novel, is poised to resolve this dilemma. He seeks a solution among the most distasteful elements of nineteenth-century nihilism, in the company of Dostoevsky's antisocial underground types and Schopenhauer's ascetic misanthropes. Their art of verbal voiding emerges, in *The Death Preacher*, as a substitute for acts of political violence that would marshal and mobilize opponents to the state. Starkblom, in his utopian missive at end of the novel, speaks of allying workers and bohemians "on the field of the future" (97). Keeping the rest of the novel in mind, it would seem that this battle cry is not supposed to precipitate any actual bloodshed (Starkblom would rather stand at his window dreaming than lead his "troops" into some future war) (97). Civilization must be destroyed, the earth must be emptied, preexisting identities must be nullified, but only *virtually*, that is to say, *verbally*. To rephrase the slogan of a contemporary anarchist collective, it is a matter of *words not bombs*.[53]

However unconvincing it may be, *The Death Preacher* undertakes a staggering work of transmogrification, turning the darkest pessimism into a saccharine and ostentatious optimism. Landauer appropriates the antisocial postures of nineteenth-century nihilism in the service of an eccentric and jubilant "anarchism" that operates in and through literature but issues no immediate political demands. Landauer makes the social and metaphysical outsiders of Schopenhauer and Dostoevsky into protagonists of revolt. These characters subsume the political desires of the anarchists (freedom outside of any institutions, destruction of all authority) into their antisocial monologues, which relentlessly stipulate the impossibility and vacuity of all existing communities. This vocal insistence on the impossibility of all community becomes the precondition for alternative forms of togetherness that are yet to be written or realized, such as Landauer's holistic "world-self" (Welt-Ich).[54] For Landauer, the language of impossible community is actually the *preview* of a community that could emerge in another possible world.

Chapter 3

✦

Society of Nobodies

Franz Kafka and the Communal Vacuum

"Unworldly anarchism" was Landauer's term for his improbable fusion of nihilism and communitarianism (*DT*, 98). It was a tagline he attached to *The Death Preacher* ten years after its publication, while reflecting on what, if anything, might still make that novel worth reading. In what follows, I propose that Landauer's creative term "unworldly anarchism" can be used to describe a number of comparable literary experiments of the twentieth century, which proceed from pessimist and nihilist premises but conclude with the discovery of an anarchic community liberated from the fixed social identities of the given world. Unworldly anarchism is not so much a coherent political stance as a kind of experimental fiction that uses the instruments of nihilism to speculate on the creation of otherworldly communities. The nihilist's monologue turns into a medium for making community. In narrative works that play with this conceit, solitary characters are endowed with exceptional, if not fantastic powers: a lonely protagonist may erase the world around him, fall into an abyss that he has created for himself, and finally find there the conditions for affirmative community.[1] Unworldly anarchism, then, emerges through narrative experimentation, which swerves away from mimetic, realist norms and embraces the fictionality of fiction. As such, "unworldly anarchism" could be a useful way of describing a particular practice of fiction that is not restricted to authors who, like Landauer, self-identified as political anarchists. I will use the term to describe fictions in which nihilist monologue is taken seriously as an instrument of anarchic community. Such community is anarchic in the sense that it subverts prevailing models of social cohesion, conjoins total strangers, and violates assumptions about what is possible and impossible within a given narrative world.

In the fiction of unworldly anarchism, community is not an "immanent" presence, felt and experienced immediately by persons in close corporeal contact.[2] It arises through the transformations triggered by an intense experience of solitude. A younger contemporary of Landauer, Franz Kafka, coined a phrase that quickly captures the former's estranging complex of solitude and community: "a society of nobodies" (eine Gesellschaft von lauter niemand).[3] The phrase appears in the second draft of Kafka's first significant prose work, "Description of a Struggle" ("Beschreibung eines Kampfes"). As suggested by its title, this highly disjointed story focuses on a contentious relationship that plays out, at first, as a kind of interpersonal combat. The surprise hidden by the title is that, by the text's final section, this "struggle" or "fight" turns into a strange form of intimacy. This intimacy springs—much as in Landauer's *Death Preacher*—from the shared confrontation of a void, into which all solid identities threaten to vanish. Completed around 1910, "Description" is a highly experimental work that plays with logical impossibility, not least in the second draft's odd image of a plural nobody ("these nobodies," or "diese Niemand"). This plural nobody is both *nothing* (zero times any number is zero), and yet it is also a corporeal union with "lifted arms linked together" and "numberless feet treading so close" (diese vielen quergestreckten oder eingehängten Arme, diese vielen Füße durch winzige Schritte getrennt) (*BK*, 113).[4] In picturing a free, living community built on an absence of companions, Kafka's narrator voices an unworldly anarchism that echoes key ideas of Landauer's experimental writing—even if Kafka himself was only sporadically aware of Landauer's literary criticism,[5] his translation work,[6] and his involvement in charity work in Berlin's Jewish community.[7] Even if the two writers lived in the same world, their intellectual overlap was a matter of shared intellectual questions, hopes, and desires.

The possibility of a connection between Kafka and Landauer revives long-standing and highly controversial questions in the scholarship: was Franz Kafka an anarchist? Are his works at all sympathetic to the claims of political anarchism? By considering the affinities of a story like "Description of a Struggle" to the unworldly anarchism of Gustav Landauer, it is possible to productively build on this controversy without repeating its polemics or relying on discredited evidence. Several of Kafka's Czech contemporaries testified to the author's anarchist leanings and stated that he had attended the meetings of a libertarian socialist underground group in Prague around 1910. These testimonies were recorded by Klaus Wagenbach in his 1958 biography *Kafka* and subsequently affirmed by the widely discredited *Conversations with Kafka* published by the Czech novelist Gustav Janouch in 1968.[8] The idea that Kafka was an anarchist generated some excitement on the Left; also in 1968, an article by the scholar Mijal Levi was published in Buenos Aires, translated in 1972 as "Kafka and Anarchism," which affirmed "anti-authoritarian inclinations" in Kafka's youth, as well as in his mature works of fiction.[9] Such excitement was matched by the skepticism and dismissal of other critics. Another Kafka biographer, Ernst Pawel, dismissed the accounts of Kafka's anarchism as a "legend," writing that Kafka's reading of the Russian anarchist Pyotr Kropotkin alongside the memoirs of the Russian socialist Alexander Herzen "was probably as close to radical activism as Kafka ever got."[10] In response to such dismissals, recent scholars have tended to revise the biographical account of Kafka's anarchism by concentrating on the ways in which Kafka's fiction adopts familiar themes of anarchist thought, yet without insisting that Kafka's anarchism led to any significant involvement with radical political movements of his time. Mark Anderson suggested in 1990 that Kafka's social vision comes close to the individualist anarchism of Max Stirner,[11] and in the same year Joseph Vogl argued that Kafka had used "anarchist theorems" to pose the "question of community."[12] A deeper source analysis supports Vogl's thesis. For instance, Kafka's 1914 story *In the Penal Colony* depicts European overseas colonialism using clear fingerprint borrowings from the novel *The Torture Garden* by the French anarchist writer Octav Mirbeau.[13] Along similar lines, the French-Brazilian sociologist Michael Löwy has argued that Kafka's fictional works such as *The Trial* and *The Castle* capture "the impenetrable and incomprehensible character of the rules of the state hierarchy as they are seen *from below and the outside*."[14] In other words, Kafka's visions of hierarchal institutions overlap with the critical descriptions and diagnoses made by classical anarchist thinkers. Yet, even if Kafka agrees with the anarchists' diagnosis, is there any reason to believe that his response to opaque hierarchies was actually anarchist? Is there, anywhere in Kafka's writings, a vision of anarchic, nonhierarchal community that would not be as nightmarish and oppressive as existing institutions?

If Kafka's notoriously negative texts do contain such an "answer," they certainly do not express it in the same language as practical-political anarchists, who proclaim solidarity and mobilize *as* anarchists. However, Kafka's earliest visions of community in "Description of a Struggle" do resonate with the highly eccentric position staked out by Gustav Landauer with his idea of "unworldly anarchism" that drew equally from pessimism, nihilism, and socialism (*DT*, 98). Moreover, Kafka's texts explore the idea of community in the medium of antimimetic experimental narrative, where a strict distinction of "dream" and "reality" is useless—just as it was for Landauer. Kafka hardly espoused an activist agenda of "propaganda of the deed," but his paradoxical vision of community in "Description of a Struggle" can be productively compared to Landauer's idea of moving "through separation to community" (durch Absonderung zur Gemeinschaft), whereby antisocial postures uncover an unexplored substrate of togetherness.[15] The characters of "Description of a Struggle" find togetherness in a shared sense of nullity: they bond with one another as they are on the verge of a void where personal identity and corporeal integrity vanish.

Many of Kafka's works recall the paradoxical bond of isolation and community that Gustav Landauer theorized through his "unworldly anarchism." Rainer Nägele has written that Kafka's works contain a "strange new communality and commune" characterized by a "paradox of a singular solitude and insularity, which at the same time is bound up, at its deepest level, with its time and its world."[16] More recently, Vivian Liska has shown how Kafka located himself in "the borderland between loneliness and community," seeing solitude as a mode of relation.[17] The text that perhaps most cogently captures an image of solitary community is the short prose piece "At Night" ("Nachts") in which a solitary insomniac imagines himself to be the night watchman who guards all the anonymous sleeping inhabitants of the city around him.[18] The specter of solitary community also crops up in the final scene of *The Trial*, as Josef K. wonders whether the sole witness to his execution, raising their arms out of the window of a nearby tenement, is in fact "everybody" (waren es alle?),[19] possibly in the sense of "all humanity." However, given that the phrase "society of nobodies" belongs to the extended project of "Description of a Struggle," it makes sense to seek out the contours of Kafka's unworldly anarchism through a close reading of Kafka's first completed story, written in the first years of the twentieth century. In the "Description," community arises out of monologues of verbal nihilism. Characters speak to nobody; they intensify their own alienated condition; they erase the world around them with words. In this way, they become the members of an anarchic community that takes shape beyond the strictures of the given world.

Unworldly anarchism, in Kafka as in Landauer, begins with verbal nihilism that places the "world under erasure" through relentless monologue.[20] The character in "Description of a Struggle" who epitomizes the strategy of verbal nihilism is the nameless "Praying Man" (Der Beter). The Praying Man appears in the ontologically problematic middle section of the story, where the world tends to "flicker" in and out of existence, and where the difference between hallucination and fact is nullified.[21] The centrality of the Praying Man was noted by the German philosopher Günther Anders, who argued that "Description of a Struggle" exemplified Kafka's interest in recording the trials of an outsider seeking acceptance within a human community. That story, Anders suggests, records "the desperate efforts which this unsubstantial and homeless creature makes in order to gain acceptance in the world."[22] In the Praying Man's monologues, he incessantly and interminably chains together preposterous claims that nullify himself along with the concrete context in which he is speaking. In Anders's interpretation, this scene illustrates the problem of social acceptance and recognition: "The conversation is simply soliloquy, in which the function of the second speaker is to merely ignore the first, misunderstand him, in fact to treat him as if he were thin air."[23] Anders very concisely captures the strange vision of anonymous intimacy that Kafka develops throughout the story. The Praying Man seeks acceptance by running up to a stranger and delivering a breathless soliloquy in which he insists that he be recognized as nothing. Attachment and acceptance do not begin with dialogue between characters but instead with one character demonstrating his solitude and nullity—his status as an "unsubstantial and homeless creature," in Anders's words—before another character.[24] By rendering himself an alien through nihilist monologue, the Praying Man finds a way of transcending alienation in a "society of nobodies."

When Kafka's Praying Man insists to another that he be recognized and treated as "thin air," he introduces a metafictional discourse into the world of the text: he wants to be *as weightless as a fictional character.* His self-nullifying monologue vocalizes an insight that is already obvious to the reader of Kafka's text: that the Praying Man is an ephemeral figment of the imagination of a storyteller, who is in turn an ephemeral figment of the imagination of the author. Like any fictional character, the Praying Man is "unsubstantial."[25] Without the words on the page, without the endurance and expansion of his soliloquy through the spilling of more ink, he is fated to fade away. When he accosts the nameless Drunken Man on the streets of a nameless city and points out that he himself is a nothing, he is simply exposing the common condition of fictionality shared by both these characters. The Praying Man's monologue, like Kafka's story as a whole, posits an unfamiliar form of kinship between strangers, based in a shared experience of insubstantiality and ephemerality. In other words, the Praying Man demonstrates that strangers can connect over the common experience of being a nobody, poised at the threshold of nothingness.

By reaching beyond the narrative frame in which he is embedded and pointing to the fictionality of his existence, the Praying Man exposes a common groundlessness. He exhibits the extreme vulnerability of his own existence as a mere figment, inviting his listener to recognize an analogous groundlessness in his own existence. The naming of this null community is a constant concern of the Praying Man's monologues in other parts of the text: he speaks of how "one's body could vanish" (dass die Körperlichkeit entschwindet) (DS, 44; *BK*, 89) and suggests (in a famous passage published elsewhere as "The Trees") that "we" are all like rootless trees that are only apparently and inauthentically attached to the ground (DS, 45; *BK*, 89). The collective subjects (the "we") invoked in these utterances all share the ephemerality and unreality of fiction. As a whole, "Description of a Struggle" invokes an expansive and broadly inclusive community of groundlessness, which implicates the positions of both author and reader, both of whom are implicitly robbed of any firm grounding or authority. As the Praying Man imparts his insubstantiality to strangers, the reader is called in as a corroborating witness who has the power to authenticate or notarize the new relationship between strangers, effectively saying: *Yes, these are ephemeral and unsubstantial creatures, and they belong together.* In other words, the metafictional gesture toward the reader is the point for the initiation of a solidarity based in a common insubstantiality and ephemerality.

The Praying Man declares that what he holds in common with others is the exposure to a void.[26]

In conjuring this community, however, the Praying Man engenders a form of narrative anarchy that pushes "Description of a Struggle" toward incomprehensibility, because it fabulates a self-contradicting fictional reality. Yet there is no reason to dismiss the text by saying (as I have heard one colleague say) that it "makes no sense." Kafka's narrative anarchy can be approached and appreciated using the analytic tools developed in the academic subfield of narratology by scholars focusing on postmodernist and "unnatural" narrative. For narratologists of the unnatural, the logical and ontological contradictions of a text should be *foregrounded* and appreciated on their own terms rather than marked in advance as a failure. Since the Praying Man can void and revise the fictional universe around him, he stands for a form of antimimetic fiction that permits logical contradiction as well as the revocation of virtual facts. The impossibility of the community represented is central because it challenges us to entertain a kind of relation that we (most likely) believe could never be realized in our world. The entertainment of impossibility, in turn, allows us to move beyond prejudices regarding what a community should be. Kafka's text does not describe an "immanent" community of a shared presence but rather one that violates the ontological framework in which its members are located: whatever exists between the characters could be voided at any moment.[27] The Praying Man makes this clear. Through the artful verbal nihilism of his monologues, he revokes the things and people that are ostensibly present in the world and declares them to be virtual or totally nonexistent. In this sense, he is a "main character." His voice most obviously and audibly de-realizes and virtualizes each of the narrative frameworks in which he is embedded. With his structural location at the very center of Kafka's story, he becomes the most important spokesman of the void, whose voice resonates outward through the entire story. By spreading the teaching "*I am nothing and so you, too, are nothing*," he spreads word of a way of living together that is less restrictive than conventional coexistence in the structures furnished by family, the workplace, social class, or any official political unity. Community might be sought out in a verbalization of ontological groundlessness.

Tellings and Retellings of Alienation

Not much happens in "Description of a Struggle," and what does initially seems quite petty. The story begins with a few spontaneous words exchanged between two young men over cake and liquor at private bourgeois party. The protagonist, who narrates in the first person, first sets up the story as a comedy of manners, as he explains to his interlocutor "how improper it is to talk about an amorous girl to a man sitting alone drinking schnapps" (DS, 10). This microscopic interpersonal scenario of awkward acquaintance, involving the solitary narrator and his romantically adventurous interlocutor, later turns into a pretext for a process of ontological unsettlement. The impossible breaks into the banal.

From this everyday scenario of acquaintance, the narrator will transgress the boundaries of known reality. He becomes "acquainted" with the abyss underlying his existence and learns of the existential dependency of his "world" on the fragile bonds provided by the circulation of language. In short, "Description of a Struggle" departs from quotidian reality, uncovers the unreality of that reality, and arrives in the end at an idea of how language might enable human beings to cope with their collectively "impossible" lives. As such, the text transports the reader from a familiar scene of social relations (the mannered motions of making acquaintance at a formal bourgeois party) into a strange vision of relationality, which pictures human lives as a brittle chain of solitary voices that hang uneasily over a void. The truly common ground in Kafka's story is not a shared "world" but a shared vacuum that underlies the mechanized, economic and social routines of the modern city.

The exposure of this vacuum follows a series of attempted escapes, as the narrator continually flees the social context in which he is caught. He first attempts to evade the attention of other partygoers by pulling his acquaintance out of the party and accompanying him on a walk to Prague's large city park on the Laurenziberg. Their stroll through the nocturnal streets is marked by an atmosphere of urban alienation and paranoia, as they are surveilled with suspicion by an anonymous watcher at an apartment window, and by the guests at the door of a wine tavern. The two men likewise remain perpetually suspicious of each other's intentions, and their ironic, frustrated interactions mirror the mood of distrust and danger in the empty streets. As the narrator and the acquaintance become alternately frustrated and infatuated with one another, the former finally takes flight from his companion: crossing a bridge over the Vltava, he abruptly abandons the fictional reality that he has established thus far and begins the story's second section, which tells of a series of phantasmagoric "amusements." These amusements play out in a different universe from that of the initial story, which critics and readers have commonly presumed to be the universe of the narrator's unhinged imagination. The fun, as it were, begins as the narrator rides his acquaintance like a horse into an "unfinished" mountain region (DS, 21; *BK*, 61). The third section of the novella resumes the initial, comparatively realist story of the two young men in Prague as they sit sparring on a bench in the park on the Laurenziberg. "Description of a Struggle," as the above summary suggests, is a work that is *full of vacuity*. Kafka's story offers, at first glance, a map of human relations as a state of perpetual and ubiquitous alienation. The reader takes in a panorama of impossible community.

Of course, this is already a familiar clichéd conception of Kafka's writing, and it is the position taken by the author's harshest critics, who see Kafka as nothing more than a symptom of bourgeois narcissism and political defeatism (read: spinelessness). Take for instance the 1966 essay "Dostoevsky and Modernism," by the Soviet literary scholar B. Burssow. He argues that European modernists such as Kafka had selectively appropriated Dostoevsky's topos of the "underground" in order to fashion an image of the human being "as a lonely creature . . . damned forever to solitude."[28] Developing a Marxist-humanist argument that closely resembles Georg Lukács's critique of Kafka, Burssow accuses him of having succumbed to total isolation. Kafka, Burssow argues, discarded the underlying humanist intentions of Dostoevsky's prose and fashioned protagonists who fully abandon themselves to the "underground hole" of their solitary consciousness.[29] From their underground perspective, Kafka's alien figures produce "a completely formless picture" both of the world and themselves.[30] Actually, I would argue that Burssow is right: Kafka's prose actually *is* seeking out a formless, and hence anarchic, picture of world and self. This vision of formlessness can, as Burssow correctly suggests, be traced back to a selective adaptation of themes and figures from the work of Fyodor Dostoevsky. The verbal nihilism of the Praying Man has structural similarities to that of the Underground Man, as both conjure an abyss through a chain of negations and self-negations. Indeed, Kafka's fiction sympathetically reevaluates the nihilist postures parodied and critiqued by Dostoevsky's fictions of the underground type. It is *good* to go underground, and to go even farther *below* the underground.

Burssow's claim that Kafka's characters *want* to be powerless underground types is particularly true in the case of "Description of a Struggle," which directly echoes both the setting and dialogue of Dostoevsky's *Double*.[31] Kafka's narrator-protagonist lives a life that closely recalls that of Dostoevsky's most pathetic character, the neurotic and antisocial civil servant Goliadkin. It is probably not coincidental that the impersonal urban world of *The Double* resembles the city of Prague imagined in Kafka's "Description."[32] Kafka's first story seems to be a deliberate rewrite of Dostoevsky's second novel. The first rendezvous of the narrator and his acquaintance, along the Vltava River in Prague, evokes the first encounter between Goliadkin Sr. and his double, Goliadkin Jr., at night along the Fotanka River in St. Petersburg.[33] More importantly, "Description" embeds nearly verbatim the words of Goliadkin within the voice of his first-person narrator; it is as if Kafka's story wants to depart from the same premises as *The Double* in order to arrive at different insights into the anonymous existence of an urban office worker.

The allusion in question comes from an early scene of *The Double*, as Goliadkin is seen speaking ceaselessly in the office of the doctor Krestyan Ivanovich. The doctor has told him he needs to "reorganize [his] whole life radically and in some sense break [his] character" (*TD*, 12). Goliadkin, ever given over to soliloquies of self-justification, insists that everything is fine for him: "[He] hastened to observe that it seemed to him that he was like everybody else, that he was his own man, that his diversions were like everybody else's . . . that he could, of course, go to the theater, for, like everybody else, he also had means, he had means, *he was in the office during the day, but in the evening was at home, that he was quite all right*" (11; emphasis added). The doctor will be proven right; Goliadkin's attempts to shield himself with a self-validating monologue will throw him into an "abyss" where he will experience a total loss of self and world (49). Kafka has his protagonist follow this same pathway to the abyss. In the first of the three sections of "Description of a Struggle," Kafka's first-person narrator recites almost word-for-word part of Goliadkin's speech of self-justification, when he is recounting the general structure of his night out on the town:

> I had merely been at a party, had saved an ungrateful young man from disgrace, and was now wandering around in the moonlight. That was all right, too. *All day in the office, evenings at a party, at night in the streets, and nothing to excess.* A way of life boundless in its naturalness! (DS, 12, translation modified and emphasis added)

> Ich war eben in Gesellschaft gewesen, hatte einen undankbaren jungen Menschen vor Beschämung gerettet und spazierte nun im Mondlicht herum. Auch das gieng. *Den Tag über im Amt, abends in Gesellschaft, in der Nacht auf den Gassen und nichts übers Maß.* Eine in ihrer Natürlichkeit grenzenlose Lebensweise! (BK, 125, emphasis added)

In good humor, Kafka's narrator is reassuring himself before the reader of the appropriateness of his lifestyle and the thoroughly quotidian nature of his night out. His phrase to describe the everyday life of the office worker ("Den Tag über im Amt") is strikingly similar to Goliadkin's. As with Goliadkin, this monologue of self-reassurance (that one lives an everyday life) sounds like a lie. And, as with Goliadkin, the enunciation of this self-delusion foreshadows an interruption of the quotidian cycle. For Goliadkin, this interruption comes in the form of the doppelgänger who will tear apart his life. For Kafka's narrator, this interruption comes in the form of a nameless "Bekannter," whom he meets "around twelve o'clock" (gegen zwölf Uhr), just as the everyday cycle through the office is about to resume. More specifically, what interrupts this cycle is the strong chance of intimacy between the two men. The narrator inwardly entertains the possibility that his acquaintance might be fascinated or infatuated with him, but he immediately guards himself against the moment the acquaintance tries to embrace and kiss him, as they are crossing the Charles Bridge over the Vltava River. Ignoring these advances, the narrator begins talking to himself in such a way as to extricate himself from the excitement of his acquaintance's embrace:

> Then I said to myself: "Why walk with this man? you don't love him, nor do you hate him. . . . So this person to you is indifferent—repeat it—indifferent." (DS, 20, translation modified)

> Da sagte ich zu mir: "Warum gehst Du mit diesem Menschen? Du liebst ihn nicht und Du hassest ihn auch nicht. . . . Also ist Dir dieser Mensch gleichgültig—wiederhole es—gleichgültig." (*BK*, 60)

Not unlike Goliadkin, the narrator is now mentally training himself to divorce himself from the situation. He issues demands to himself that he recite his own commands back to himself. And, like Goliadkin's own attempt at verbal self-insulation, this soliloquy marks the opening of a radical new narrative segment, where the protagonist's old sense of reality dissolves. Here, the story is punctuated with a second section, entitled "Amusements, or Proof That It Is Impossible to Live." The final sentence of section 1 sets up an entirely monologic, insular mode for section 2, unbothered by external reality or social relations:

> So walk on with him up on the Laurenziberg, . . . but let him talk and amuse yourself in your way, for in that way (say it quietly) you will best protect yourself. (DS, 20, translation modified)

> Also geh weiter schon auf den Laurenziberg, . . . aber laß ihn reden und vergnüge Dich auf Deine Weise, dadurch—sage es leise—schützt Du Dich auch am besten. (*BK*, 60)

With this inner discourse, the narrator trains himself to disavow his acquaintance and the world, to drop out of the present moment into a hermetic state of auto-affection. Generically speaking, this auto-affective discourse is reminiscent of the "hyperconscious" monologues of Dostoevsky's underground types, in that it serves to create a protective shield against the outside world, protecting against the risks and surprises of social interaction.[34]

The narrator's citation of Goliadkin accompanies a shift toward an "underground" mode of radically insular narrative. As soon as section 2 begins, the narrator makes clear that every narrative fact he posits (such as the existence of steep mountains) is only meant to serve his own desires;

every feature of this world is set with an eye to how it will affect the narrator: "Because I love pinewoods I went through woods of this kind" (Da ich Fichtenwälder liebe, gieng ich durch Fichtenwälder) (DS, 22; *BK*, 62). The "acquaintance" only enters into this world as a slave to the narrator's will; he is ridden like a horse and left to the vultures as soon as he is injured. Aggressive misanthropy is the first readily apparent theme of the story's middle section. The multiple subsections of section 2 demonstrate an active labor on the part of the narrator to declare before himself his own indifference toward those in the social field around him. If this were Dostoevsky's *Double*, then we would expect to watch the narrator be lampooned and punished for this indifference. In short, we would expect a moral tale that cautions against the abandonment of shared reality. We could, then, plausibly expect "Description of a Struggle" to be another morality tale of why it is dangerous to go underground and leave humanity behind.

However, ultimately, the interpolation of Goliadkin's words in "Description of a Struggle" accomplishes something else: it sets up the conditions for Kafka's author's peculiar version of unworldly anarchism, which in section 2 will perform an inversion of pessimism and solitude that partly recalls Landauer's *Death Preacher.* Over the course of this entire middle section, the narrator will discover how precisely such an indifference, which removes the self to a vacuum, can unexpectedly become a precondition for community. Although the narrative premises of Kafka's text are similar to Dostoevsky's, its conclusion is strikingly different. In section 2, the most intimate connections that emerge are between total strangers who talk past one another in self-absorbed monologues. The misanthropic posture, which wants to have nothing to do with others, is replicated again and again on the level of form: the ultimate structure of this middle section, before it collapses and concludes, is *a monologue within a monologue within a monologue within a monologue.* In this interweaving of monologues, Kafka's story establishes a tenuous "we." Community emerges in form through a recurring figure of inclusion. Again and again, one solitary voice is recursively embedded within another. As an instrument of embedding, monologue becomes a means of community.

Togetherness through Monologue

As the story's middle section progresses, one monologue is progressively interpolated within another. This process of interpolation culminates, finally, in the emergence of the Praying Man. The effect on the reader can be highly disorienting, since it takes special effort to keep track of who is quoting whom quoting whom, and so on. Therefore, I will briefly enumerate the different, telescopic layers of monologue: the (1) outermost monologue is the solipsistic soliloquy of the narrator, who has declared his total indifference to the social world around him and retreats into a fabulated, "unfinished" mountainous landscape, riding his acquaintance like a horse. Along his journey into this private world, the narrator comes across a Buddha-like "Fat Man" floating down a river, who delivers a (2) narrative monologue about how he met his friend, the Praying Man. Their encounter culminates in the delivery of another (3) narrative monologue by the Praying Man about his adventures out at night in the city, during which he delivers *another* (4) monologue, which itself is a citation of the (5) ravings of other anonymous speakers, recounting rumors that have been circulating about the city of Paris in its glorious superficiality. The Praying Man utters the most striking, and most-quoted, aphorisms of the story: he is the one who says that we are like trees in the snow, which are only apparently bound to the ground (*BK*, 89); he is the character who says that people "float" (*BK*, 77) and speaks of how often the houses of the city inexplicably collapse (76). It is the Praying Man who, generally, paints a picture of existence as being "there but not there," as a superlatively fragile weave of virtual existents stretching over a void.[35] In what follows, I will argue that his different utterances, which speak to the instability of any apparent ontological givens, have an *ontological* impact beyond their philosophical resonance as aphorisms. I will show that that the speeches of the Praying Man *anarchically revise* the narrative world of "Description of a Struggle" and enable an alternative conception of community that is impossible yet necessary. The Praying Man performatively calls a new community of the void into existence, which implicates all the subject-positions inscribed in the text (authors, narrators, characters, listeners, and readers). "Description of a Struggle" coheres around this progressive implication of all actors in the Praying Man's discourse.

This claim might be mildly controversial, considering that "Description of a Struggle" is commonly seen as a chaotic and confounding text, above all because of the story's middle section. The three pieces don't seem to ever fit. Section 2 is an extended narrative and ontological non sequitur that presents many sequences of time and states of affairs that are completely incompatible with the two outer sections of the story. On the macro level, "Description of a Struggle" displays ontological opalescence, saying that one world exists, then revoking it and replacing it with another, then revoking that second world and restoring the first.[36] There have been numerous critical attempts to "assemble" the broken puzzle of "Description of a Struggle" into a sensible whole, in order to rescue it from incoherence. Several critics have tried to explain the middle section's eccentricity by arguing that it represents an internal reality, as opposed to the external (urban, social) reality of the first and third sections.[37]

The dichotomy of "internal" versus "external" experience can be overcome, if we approach "Description of a Struggle" with tools of unnatural and postmodernist narratology. These tools offer a better grasp ontological poetics of the text, foregrounding its practices of world-making and world-erasing. I contend that this spatial model of inner and outer narratives misses the strangest aspect of Kafka's story: the "flickering" of the fictional reality posited by the narrator, which is subject to revision and erasure.[38] The technicality in Kafka's story that motivates my reading is the fact that the text never explicitly labels one section as reality and another as a dream. There is no marker saying that some parts happen "in the mind" and others in "the real world." When the narrator tells us that he is vanishing into a formless void on one page and on the next page says that he was sitting on a park bench at approximately the same time, we as readers are not provided with any explanatory discourse that tells us that the vanishing was a mere fantasy or that the park bench is the more solid reality. Kafka's story plays with the idea that "projected *existents*—locales, objects, characters, and so on—can have their existence revoked."[39] When the narrator, midway through the story, posits a surreal scenario that is fully incompatible with the initial narrative scenario, this is indeed a completely "unnatural" narrative move that does not allow for an easy distinction between fantasy and reality.[40] The insubstantial is substantial, and the substantial is vacuous. In the literary universe that Kafka creates for his readers, these are facts faced everywhere, by everyone. This is how "nothing" (vacuity, emptiness, insubstantiality) creates community.

As Kafka was beginning work on "Description of a Struggle," he wrote a letter to his friend Oskar Pollak expressing a vision of mutual aid. Kafka discusses how the act of writing a letter is like extending a rope to another person, "and if one stops, the rope is torn."[41] In the moment of interrupting the verbal stream that connects one being to another, both beings threaten to fall into an abyss: "Only if human beings tighten up all their powers and help each other lovingly do they maintain one another at a bearable height over an infernal depth, towards which they want to go."[42] Language is the medium of cohesion in this vision of brittle unity suspended over a void. This cohesion consists not so much in communication as in the assembly and maintenance of an uninterrupted string of words: "Among themselves they are connected with a rope."[43] The language that could sustain human beings over an abyss is an uninterrupted monologue, thrown across the void to another fragile being. An analogous model of human coexistence informs the structure of "Description of a Struggle" in its phantasmagoric section 2. The multiple, progressively embedded monologues of the narrator, the Fat Man, and the Praying Man are finally revealed to constitute a kind of verbal thread that tenuously keeps all these characters from vanishing into a vacuum, in which they will cease to be human, then cease to be anything at all.

The spectacular conceit of "Description of a Struggle" is that the monologic attestation of a common void could become a new, communal oral tradition that is passed on from one alien character to the next. The virtually infinite regress of the story's embedded narrative layers (a monologue within a monologue within a monologue, and so on) attests to the transmission and reproduction of this oral tradition of verbal nihilism. This abyssal community (built over an abyss, with a language that attests to the abyss) comprises the sole positive image of human togetherness in Kafka's text, which otherwise voices anxieties about the anonymity and coercion of all social life. Modern city life in particular, as depicted in this story, is marked by the fatal pairing of anonymity and false familiarity. It is impossible to know anyone. The anonymity is represented in the ephemeral motion of "passing street-cars" (vorüberfahrend[e] Straßenbahn) and "passersby" (vorübergehende Leute) (*BK*, 72; 91). False familiarity is found in the automatized sociability identified with closed circles of private bourgeois parties. The social world is a frightening aggregate of isolation and coercion. However, the fragile assemblage of voices in Kafka's text conjures an alternative form of intimacy, which sews together so many different instances of solitude. The unique form of Kafka's story—which collates monologues without ever assembling a stable image of the characters' shared world—leads to an antifoundational and anarchic imagination of community. This is not exactly the sort of imagined community that Benedict Anderson saw as being necessary to the formation of modern nationhood and that has become a common object of study in academic cultural studies.[44] If the "form of the novel" (to quote Jonathan Culler's paraphrase of Benedict Anderson) can serve as "the condition of possibility for imagining the nation," then we might say that the collated monologues of "Description of a Struggle" present a condition of possibility of imagining an emphatically baseless, *non-national* and also *nonfamilial* community, lacking the supporting structures of institutions or kinship ties.[45] To understand how this community works, I will explain how the Praying Man's verbal nihilism intrudes into and interacts with the rest of Kafka's text. This will provide an alternative way of understanding the unity of the two relatively realist bookends (sections 1 and 3) with the radical fabulations and interpolated narratives of section 2.

The Praying Man is first introduced in the innermost embedded level of the story's "Russian Doll" structure, section 2.3b (the second subsection of the third subsection of the second section). Here, he immediately appears as a character "inclined to monologues" that epitomize the idea of conjuring a vacuum.[46] In the frantic speeches that he delivers to strangers across the landscape of an unnamed city, the Praying Man somewhat resembles the fairy-tale character Chicken Little, who declared that "All the world is falling." The Praying Man repeatedly incessantly reiterates a set of interwoven messages, which I enumerate here:

1. He attests to his own nonexistence or near-nonexistence (saying he is unreal).

2. He attests the hyperbolic fragility of his seemingly stable environment, which he sees flickering in and out of existence, teetering over a void.

3. He cancels out the coherence of his own discourse, assembling streams of prose in which the initial speaking subject is obscured or erased by contradicting predicates. Statements predicated on the subject "I" develop in such a way that this "I" tends to vanish, or becomes radically indeterminate.

With these three simultaneous strategies of verbal voiding, the Praying Man reiterates and intensifies that effect of dramatic soliloquy noted by Johann Georg Sulzer, whereby "speaking alone" can distract the mind so thoroughly that a person "completely forgets whether he is alone or in society."[47] The Praying Man induces and practices a form of self-distraction, after which he cannot say whether or not he is in the world, much less in society. As Günther Anders has written, he aims to make himself into "thin air," along with everything around him.[48] He appears unprompted and uninvited in public spaces, attaching question marks to whatever fixed, stable entities he encounters. As such, the Praying Man should be considered an anarchic element within the wider continuum of Kafka's text. Inhabiting the centermost section of the text, the effects of his monologues (or nihilist "prayers") radiate into the surrounding layers of "Description of a Struggle."

An example of his verbal nihilism appears in section 2.3c in the "Story of the Praying Man," in which he recounts a visit to evening party (or society, "Gesellschaft"). At this party, he speaks to a young woman who points out that his speeches lack substance. She tells him that his words are "boring and incomprehensible" and that he is incapable of telling the truth (DS, 37). Rather than rejecting or disputing this accusation, the Praying Man goes on to vociferously affirm these allegations of insubstantiality in a way that exceeds the woman's criticism. He begins by simply describing the basic attributes of the setting around them, which he prefaces with the self-negating sentence, "I don't understand that" (DS, 37). From here, the Praying Man begins the work of verbal voiding. He utters a set of sentences about the partygoers that effectively cancel out the coherence of the social context in which he and the young woman find themselves.

> They lay their arms on the backs of chairs or they lean against the piano or they raise a glass tentatively to their mouths or they walk timidly into the next room, and having knocked their right shoulders against a cupboard in the dark, they stand breathing by the open window and think: There's Venus, the evening star. Yet here I am, among them. If there is a connection, I don't understand it. But I don't even know if there is a connection. (DS, 38)

> Sie legen ihre Arme um die Rückenlehnen der Stühle oder sie lehnen sich ans Klavier oder sie heben ein Glas zögernd zum Munde oder

> sie gehn furchtsam ins Nebenzimmer und nachdem sie ihre rechte Schulter im Dunkel an einem Kasten verletzt haben, denken sie athmend bei dem geöffneten Fenster: Dort ist Venus, der Abendstern. Ich aber bin in dieser Gesellschaft. Wenn das einen Zusammenhang hat, so verstehe ich ihn nicht. Aber ich wieß nicht einmal, ob das einen Zusammenhang hat. (*BK*, 80)

At first, the Praying Man simply undertakes the straightforward task of describing the people around him, apparently to give context for whatever argument or statement he will make next. Instead, the Praying Man ends by voiding the surrounding context with opaque utterances. Inadvertently recalling Schopenhauer's models of genius and madness, the Praying Man nullifies context (*Zusammenhang*) and conjures a darkness in its place (a darkness that is here implied by the low light of the windowed room, and the night sky beyond the window). The Praying Man's nullification of context has a particular semantic effect: it calls into question the coherence of society (*Gesellschaft*) as a concept. His description of the party transitions unannounced into a counterfactual story about certain unnamed guests at the party around him. Initially, what he says seems to be a simple description of shared reality, as he notes the locations and actions of different guests (they are leaning on the piano, raising a glass). Yet as he continues, the Praying Man inserts details that flicker between the mimetic and the antimimetic, making present-tense observations of things he cannot possibly be witnessing at the exact moment. It can only be the result of creative speculation when the Praying Man provides this description of invisible guests who are currently in another room, who bang their shoulders on a cupboard and glimpse Venus. Departing from the common communicative context in which he himself and the young woman are located, the Praying Man conjures a narrative about a paradoxically plural individual (a solitary "*they*") who retreats from the party to stargaze at the window. He attaches new predicates to this story that drastically obfuscate his own position as the narrator and describer of the scene: "Yet here I am in this company (*Gesellschaft*). If there is a connection, I don't understand it. But I don't even know if there is a connection" (DS, 38). Are these the words of the imagined guest, or his own? His utterances have become stringently unlocable, as it is unclear whether they address "this" world in which he speaks, or another, unseen world that is being improvised through narrative utterances. Everything solid here flickers.

The voiding action of his monologue becomes evident in the interplay between three words that reflect the broader problem of orienting oneself within a shared world: "society" (*Gesellschaft*), "connection" (*Zusammenhang*), and "evening-star" (*Abendstern*). The Praying Man's monologue describes a disjunction between the social and the cosmic: the guests cannot understand the connection between their location within society on the one hand, and, on the other, their position among the stars above. This moment of bafflement implies two feelings of absence: looking at Venus, they are absent from the party; and locating themselves in the party, they are absent from the universe. A coherent context (*Zusammenhang*) does not emerge out of this juxtaposition of the social and the astronomical. Locating itself at the threshold between society and the wider universe, the plural speaking subject loses the ability to orient himself within any context and questions the existence of *any* context whatsoever. The extreme ontological uncertainty of the Praying Man's monologue can be underscored in the following retranslation of it: "If there is a *context*, I don't understand it. But I don't even know if there is a *context*" (DS, 38, emphasis denotes my own modified translation). In the soliloquy of the window-gazing guests, the act of self-orientation ends by calling into question whether anything exists at all in a unity that could be called the world. The implication is that the self exists *nowhere*, in a void that can only be captured through the linguistic confusion of this self-revoking discourse but not directly described. In the wake of this ontological questioning, the association nominally implied by the concept of *Gesellschaft* is eclipsed by an incessant verbal dissociation. The incessant speaker absents himself both from the smaller grouping (*Gesellschaft* as the term for a bourgeois party or company), as well as from the broader field of *Gesellschaft* as the modern form of mass human coexistence. Looking out the window at Venus, the speaker's "I" becomes a void, which opens up in the space between the artificial social world and the ineffable and incomprehensible universe. One sentence at a time, the Praying Man exposes this void with his dissociative monologue.

It is not just that the Praying Man *is* alienated; through its incessant self-cancelling syntax, his monologue actively *performs* and *engenders* the alienation of an "I" from everything including itself. Alienation is a verbal achievement to be perfected. Beginning with a simple expression of feelings of solitude and social anxiety, the Praying Man's monologue creatively amplifies and expands these feelings so as to establish the impression of a complete vacuum. In the wake of his speech, the Praying Man leaves his listener (and reader) with the image of a total void. The different contradicting predicates attached to Praying Man's "I" make it uncertain whether the contexture of his utterances add up to anything at all, leaving the reader (like so many passages in "Description of a Struggle") "clueless."[49] The Praying Man has perfected the art of alienation within his monologues, and as such, he offers to the world (that is, to the young woman listening to him, and to the Fat Man listening to his account of himself) a linguistic form through which alienation can be propagated and shared in everyday communicative situations. Here, Kafka establishes a surprising understanding of how literature fosters or reflects collective experience. If Lukács argued that the novel as a genre captures the inescapable modern solitude that is passively shared by all,[50] Kafka develops at the core of his "Description of a

Struggle" a vision of how solitude could be *actively shared and propagated* by the anonymous aliens who inhabit the modern metropolis. By crystallizing the art of alienation in a verbal form that can be shared and imitated, the Praying Man provides others—his different fictional listeners, as well as the text's readers—with the linguistic template for a community based in nothing but an emphatic sense of nullity. As "Description of a Struggle" develops toward its conclusion, the text itself (in its multiple mutually embedded layers) becomes an agglomeration of isolated, alien voices that nonetheless breathe together in breathless monologues. In short, the text itself is a kind of *conspiracy* (breathing-together), exhibiting a multitude of alienated selves whose voices become conjoined in an otherwise empty world. Just as the text itself seems ready to "fall apart," its characters stick together.

The Praying Man offers the "glue" that enables this sticking-together, but the adhesive and cohesive functions of his speech do not become clear until the final pages of section 2. After his monologues have concluded, the worlds of "Description of a Struggle" are no longer the same. The hierarchy of narrative layers, occupied by different pairs of characters, collapse into one another in jarring and patently unnatural ways. Each subsection impacts the section in which it was embedded. As each monologue concludes and yields to the next outward layer of framing speech, a common theme jumps from one speaker to the next, permeating not just their speech but their environment. This common theme is *insubstantiality.* Insubstantiality, here, is the impression that the self, as well as the world, are threatening to vanish into nonexistence. This theme jumps from one frame to the next, altering each frame along the way.

The innermost frame is also an epitome of urban alienation, as the Praying Man quotes his own raving speech, delivered on the street at night to an unresponsive drunken man, wherein he recounts rumors of the insubstantiality of people and locales of Paris: that buildings there are made entirely of façades, and that people are made only of "sumptuous dresses" (zierlichen Kleider) (DS, 42; *BK*, 86). The Praying Man's message about the grandiose superficiality of Paris, which presents human life as a series of opalescent images without substance or duration, acquires a heightened reality in the next frame outward, in the scene that frames the Praying Man's monologue before the drunken man. On the other side of the quotation marks containing the Paris speech, the Praying Man reveals that his Paris rant was delivered at a moment when he was becoming acutely aware of the insubstantiality of the city around him. This was a moment when "everything" around him was ready to vanish and be replaced for a moment with a void:

> Perhaps it was that short quiet lull between night and day, . . . when everything stands still without our knowing it, since we are not looking at it, and then disappears. (DS, 43, translation modified)

> Es war vielleicht diese kleine, ganz ruhige Pause zwischen Tag und Nacht, . . . wo alles, ohne daß wir es merken, still steht, da wir es nicht betrachten und dann verschwindet. (*BK*, 87)

The Praying Man testifies to the existence of a vacuum in the seams of everyday life that opens up on the cusp between night and day. In the gap between units of measured time, a gap in existence opens up where the known world is momentarily and peacefully nullified. His testimony is echoed again on the next layer outward, in a remark he made that is cited directly by the Fat Man, where the Praying Man expresses a fear that his own corporeality might disappear. In the Fat Man's own monologue, which is on the verge of conclusion, the theme of insubstantiality (both of the body and the world) is reproduced in a description of how the Praying Man "blew away a few bruised little clouds" to reveal "the uninterrupted surface of stars" (DS, 46). Here again, the material fixity of the world disperses at a slight exhalation; the boundary between the earth and the cosmic void is ominously thin. Insubstantiality is not just something subjectively sensed or feared; it is "in the air." Here, a strange "interframe relationship" emerges, whereby the theme of the Praying Man's monologues shapes the discursive frame that contains it.[51] In narratological terms, the Praying Man has initiated an extended and highly unnatural form of ontological metalepsis.[52] His apparently paranoid claims—about how the world is a thin veneer that could easily vanish—radiate through each frame outward. With each metaleptic jump, they acquire a new validity. The impossible community of "Description of a Struggle" emerges through this interframe relationship.

This interframe relationship gains in scope and intensity as the Fat Man—whose own monologue embeds all of the Praying Man's utterances—ends his own speech, so that the primary narrator can resume his discourse. In these final paragraphs of the novella's second section, the claims of insubstantiality that passed from the Praying Man via the Fat Man now radiate into the discourse of the primary, first-person narrator introduced at the start of "Description of a Struggle." As the narrator ceases his citation of the Fat Man's monologue, everything around *him* rapidly drains away, and he is flushed into a "space that no longer owned any landscape" (Raum der keine Landschaft mehr besaß) (DS, 46; *BK*, 91). The narrator is left without any dimensions, threatened with suffocation, as he cries out: "What are our lungs supposed to do?" (Was sollen unsere Lungen tun?) (DS, 46; *BK*, 91). Not even the breath that carries his speech can be taken granted any longer; the very fact that he has even said these words seems impossible.

This last scene has a didactic function: something has been learned in the long sequence of amusements that the narrator initiated in order to shore up his indifference to the social world. In this final subsection, after the termination of the Fat Man's speech, the narrator finds that he himself—like each of the monologic speakers since the Praying Man—has been standing on the threshold of an ontological vacuum. The fragility and insubstantiality hinted at in the monologues of the Praying Man have been transported through Fat Man's monologue and now apply directly to him; he has learned about it, and now it defines his environment. There has been a kind of cross-contamination by way of quotation. The theme of insubstantiality qua disappearance has sprung from its containing frame into the next frame outward. This affects our narrator, as he is being sucked into a vacuum and can no longer produce narrative statements of any kind. As his body undergoes impossible contortions and he is about to vanish, he shifts from simple past tense to present tense and cries out to a collective addressee who had not previously existed in the text, who stands beyond the page:

> [My head] was as small as an ant's egg, only it was a little damaged, and so no longer totally round. I made begging rotations with it, for the expression of my eyes couldn't be seen, it was that small.
>
> But my legs, my impossible legs lay over the forested mountains and shadowed the village valleys. They grew, they grew! They already towered into a space that had no landscape, their length long since had reached out of my depth of vision.
>
> But no, that isn't it—I'm actually small, small for the time being—I'm rolling—I'm rolling—I'm an avalanche in the mountains! Please, passers-by, be so kind as to tell me how tall I am–just measure these arms, legs. ↢ (DS, 47, translation modified to correspond to original draft's diction and punctuation)

> [Mein Kopf] war doch so klein, wie ein Ameisenei, nur war er ein wenig beschädigt, daher nicht mehr vollkommen rund. Ich führte mit ihm bittende Drehungen aus, denn der Ausdruck meiner Augen hätte nicht bemerkt werden können, so klein waren sie.
>
> Aber meine Beine, doch meine unmöglichen Beine lagen über den bewaldeten Bergen und beschatteten die dörflichen Thäler. Sie wuchsen, sie wuchsen! Schon ragten sie in den Raum der keine Landschaft mehr besaß, längst schon reichte ihre Länge aus der Sehschärfe meiner Augen.
>
> Aber nein, das ist es nicht—ich bin doch klein, vorläufig klein—ich rolle—ich rolle—ich bin eine Lawine im Gebirge! Bitte, vorübergehende Leute, seid so gut, sagt mir wie groß ich bin, messet mir diese Arme, diese Beine. ↢[53]

After the narrator's bodily contortions, he undergoes a set of linguistic contortions that utterly transfigure the nature of the text we have been reading. Like Landauer's Death Preacher, Kafka's narrator finds himself revoking his own statements in an instance of radical metanoia ("but no!"). Even more jarring is the metaleptic conversion of the narrator's personal discourse into an out-

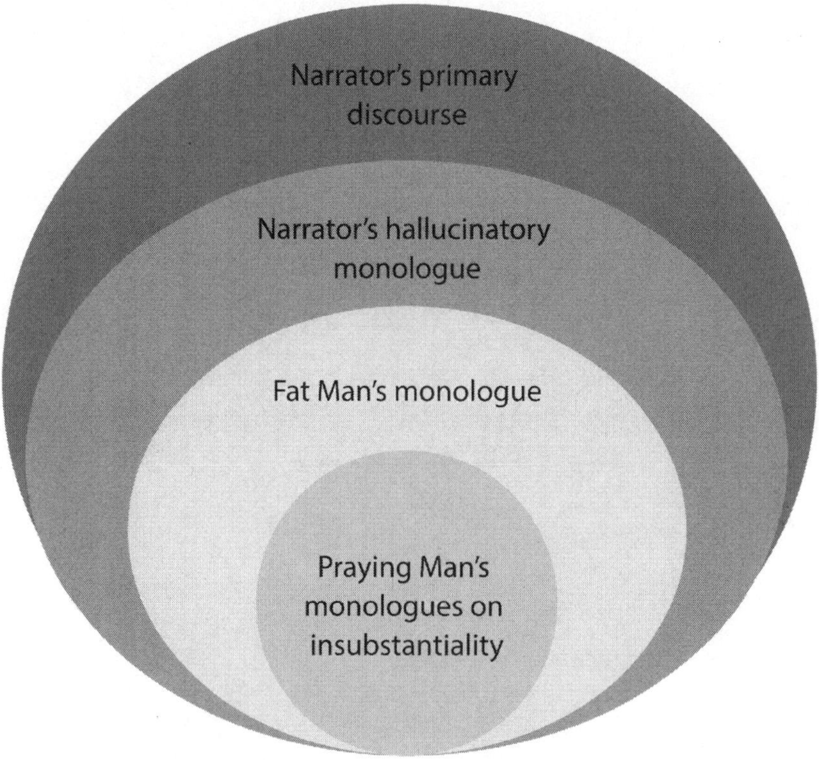

Organization of layers for majority of second section.

wardly directed, second-person exclamation. What used to be an inner monologue now resounds in an outdoor space. Now, the narrator is speaking in the present-tense imperative to a crowd of unnamed passersby, presumably on a city street. But even in this jarring jump out of the narrative frame, the theme of insubstantiality continues to radiate outward. The phrase "passersby," or "vorübergehende Leute," which conjures up the image of pedestrians, also can be read as meaning "provisional" people, people who are ephemeral and finite. And so, the implied audience for this phrase, the collective subject addressed here, flickers in and out of existence, lacking enduring substance like all the other characters so far. Here, "Description of a Struggle" offers virtual interface with a reader, gesturing to include one of "us" outside the text into this brittle community of solitary vacuum-beings.[54] This radical turn in the text can be illustrated in terms of a rearrangement of discursive layers, which are thrown into disarray as the narrator attempts to return to the familiar outside world of Prague. The arrangement of layers that endures for most of section 2 is pictured in the above diagram. The final, unsettling arrangement of layers is pictured in the diagram on the next page.

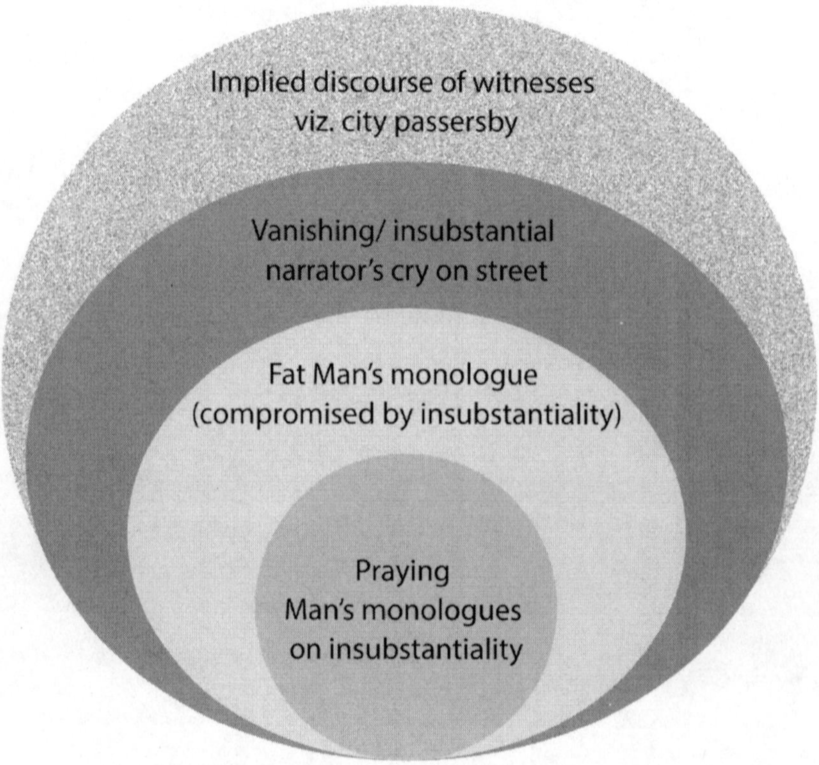

(Dis)organization of layers at end of second section.

Kafka's handwritten draft of the story underscores the strangeness of this structural explosion. It is clear from the punctuation, and subsequent correction, that the author grappled with how to demarcate and locate this last cry of the narrator. A close-quotation mark punctuates his request, which Kafka later crossed out in pencil on his ink draft. This close-quotation mark is problematic, because it doesn't correspond an open-quotation mark anywhere else in the text. It would technically identify the narrative discourse of the entire story as a monumental block of uninterrupted, direct speech whose transcription began *in medias res*. As of the moment that this quotation mark appears, the entire story has been the unbroken speech of someone or something screaming in the street, who claims he will gain corporeality only through the intervention of an anonymous bystander. The entirety of "Description of a Struggle" has been the monologue of a vacuous alien. The text is not a story at all but rather a *plea* for some minimal connection or kinship with strangers. This minimal "kinship," which would be improvised in the crowd scene through a transfer of words from mouth to the ear, now becomes the aim of the entire text. If "Description of a Struggle" has a plot, then its climax arrives in this moment of ontological redefinition, where the theme of insubstantiality flows out into the street.

The Praying Man's Teaching of Insubstantiality

The quotation mark, and Kafka's crossing out of it, suggest that the text has reached a moment where its internal boundaries are being renegotiated. The story is at its outermost threshold. Through this tenuous piece of punctuation, the safe distance between the reader and the deformed narrator is eliminated. As I have said, the conclusion of section 2 has a didactic function: the "lesson" learned regards that experience of insubstantiality described by the Praying Man, which has now permeated all layers of the text. This insubstantiality is something held in common; it conjures a collectivity in the face of a void, a collectivity of *vorübergehende Leute* in the sense of provisional, ephemeral figures. This is indicated already in the Praying Man's speech about the disappearance of the city around him, which is spoken in the first-person plural: "when everything stands still without our knowing it, since *we* are not looking at it, and then disappears" (DS, 43, translation modified, my emphasis). These lines inaugurate a collective subject that will encircle more and more voices as the section concludes. So it makes sense that the narrator cries out here directly to someone outside the bounds of the text; the only thing to keep him from disappearing completely would be the expansion of this "we" by embedding his voice within the voice of another. The narrator's question needs to reappear within the answer of someone in the crowd on the street. The street, as a site of anarchic movement through which people are provisionally passing, is the empty space where community can take shape and silence can be broken. The quotation mark that finishes this section, this sole marking that Kafka crossed out in pencil on his pen-ink draft, is a seed of sociality. The quotation mark is the basic template for the embedding of one voice within another; it is a basic building block for vocal community.

The middle section of "Description of a Struggle," as this chapter has shown, resists simple summary. However, with the theme of insubstantiality in mind, the story's middle section can be summarized in a way that illuminates the articulation of insubstantial/impossible community: in a volatile landscape, the narrator hears the Fat Man's monologue (section 2.1, 2.2, 2.3a). The Fat Man tells of how he heard the Praying Man's teachings of insubstantiality, after confessing his own doubts about language (section 2.3b). The Praying Man has been spreading this teaching to strangers in the city streets (section 2.3c). The Praying Man demonstrates the truth of this insubstantiality of existence to the Fat Man by showing that his mere breath can blow away the clouds above them (section 2.3d). As the Fat Man's monologue finishes and the world around him and his listener dissolves, the narrator imbibes this teaching of insubstantiality as the landscape around him dissolves. The narrator then jumps out of his own story and cries out for listeners outside, carrying this teaching of insubstantiality past the outermost frame of the story into the unmarked space beyond (section 2.4). The teaching of insubstantiality crosses from one monologue to the next and finally crosses (virtually) out of the story itself into the voice of a spectral "other," who is needed for the narrator to not vanish. The irony is that, just as the narrator enacts his own self-erasure, a community emerges. This community is not defined by common origins, kinship ties, or even by a shared spatial-material context. Rather, it is made through a chain of vocal interdependence. Each ephemeral voice rescues the next from fading away by embedding that voice within itself.

As a model of relationality, Kafka's early vision of vocal community resembles Brian McHale's account of the metaleptic relations that define much postmodernist fiction: texts abolish the partitions between ontological levels that are supposed to remain distinct (such as fiction and reality, or intratextual speaker and extratextual reader).[55] McHale speculates that metalepsis, as a relation between beings who inhabit different planes of reality, is in fact an allegory for what literature as a whole does: readers are affected by characters and narrators as if they were real people, readers fall in love with or despise characters, transporting themselves into a reality incompatible with their own.[56] Fiction allows us to set up relationships across the uncrossable boundaries between worlds. Following McHale, we could say that the relationship between the distinct figures in Kafka's novella (the Praying Man, the Fat Man, the narrator, and the passersby) is metaleptic in a similar sense: all the disappearing characters *share* something across ontological boundaries. The delivery of monologue has a metamorphic effect on the one who hears it and embeds it in their own discourse. By delivering and quoting the monologues of others, the characters enter into existential interdependence with one another. By passing on the teaching of insubstantiality, they confirm their own disappearance but also connect outward to another disappearing character. Their insubstantial realities are conjoined through the continual embedding of speech. Metalepsis, which stages an impossible relationship between isolated subject-positions, emerges as the very form of community in "Description of a Struggle." An open, progressively expanding community encompasses the Praying Man, the Fat Man, the narrator, his acquaintance, and the nameless passersby beyond the text. What literature allows, then, is the conjunction of solitudes. All these alienated figures, although they are stranded within their own separate worlds, can appear together, in the absence of any stable circumstances that could unite them.

What "Description of a Struggle" offers us, then, is the idea of a *binding* alienation that differs from the banal alienation of the contemporary workplace. The intimate interdependence of alienated subjects, as envisioned in Kafka's text, offers an alternative to the indifferent social relations of economic life, as described by the narrator with the words, "All day in the office, evenings at a party, at night in the streets," (den Tag über im Amt, abends in der Gesellschaft, in der Nacht auf den Gassen) (DS, 12, translation modified; *BK*, 25). This automatized routine, which is about to restart at the story's beginning, minimizes the unexpected and only allows for a very circumscribed form of "acquaintance" between isolated individuals. Such routine acquaintance must be contained within the prescribed hours between the end of work and the end of the night. By the story's third and final section, new possibilities of kinship and togetherness become possible in the "real" nighttime Prague where the narrator and acquaintance have been aimlessly walking all along. The influence of the Praying Man's vacuum-community is evident, even now that the strange section II has been ostensibly terminated through a page break and a new numeral heading. For instance, the narrator's acquaintance impulsively stabs himself in the arm on a park bench, and the narrator puts his mouth on the wound and sucks in his blood, improvising a kind of blood bond out of nowhere (DS, 50). Blood, if we recall Tönnies, is traditionally considered to be the most basic grounding for human community. With Kafka, this "grounding" can be conjured out of nowhere, between acquaintances who are nearly strangers. In the same scene, the narrator improvises the news that he is "engaged" (verlobt), again conjuring a familial bond out of nowhere (*BK*, 95; DS, 50). The story does not find a happy or satisfying closure; the narrator and the acquaintance do not arrive at a common understanding, and they seem to be talking past one another until the last page. Still, the final section sees a proliferation of baseless yet intimate attachments that are founded on nothing and yet cause the characters to stick tightly together: "We sat high up on the mountain as in a small room. . . . We sat close together despite not liking one another at all, but we couldn't move far apart because the walls were firmly and definitely drawn" ([Wir] saßen oben auf dem Berg, wie in einem kleinen Zimmer. . . . Wir waren nahe beisammen, trotzdem wir einander nicht gerne hatten, aber wir konnten uns nicht weit von einander entfernen, denn die Wände waren förmlich und fest gezogen) (DS, 50; *BK*, 96). A structure of relations emerges that is both insubstantial and rigid. The "room" that entraps the pair is nonexistent, sheer metaphor. Nevertheless, it guarantees a baseless intimacy between two mutually alienated characters. The strange insights of the story's middle section, with its interframe community of nobodies, seem to have precipitated a subtle mood shift. The narrator's words and actions now suggest an inclination to an indiscriminate sociality, which does not adhere to norms regarding the foundation and termination of human relationships. In this way, he continues to be the formless alien on the street who appeared at the end of section 2.

Although Kafka's first story is ostensibly apolitical, particularly when compared to his later narratives of opaque and violent institutions, its treatment of community nevertheless dovetails with political and social philosophy.

Like Landauer, Kafka was interested in how the voids of nihilism could engender a form of collective identification outside prevailing institutions, and beyond the concrete possibilities of the world as we know and accept it. For this reason, each author espouses an unworldly anarchism that depends on extremities of fiction as an imaginative medium. Their discontent with prevailing institutions is not, however, identical: Landauer, circa 1893, was more transparently a romantic anticapitalist of his time, who was opposed to the solidarities created by party, the nation-state, and an impermeable notion of social class—as well as those of ethnicity and religion, as evidenced in the disturbing anti-Semitic episode of the *Death Preacher*, which shows how far the young Landauer was from avowing his own Jewish heritage.[57] Kafka, circa 1907, betrayed a discomfort with other modes of collective identity and social authority. "Description of a Struggle" ironizes the social habits of the urban bourgeoisie and the everyday rhythms of office work. The story expresses anxiety toward the appendages of state power, as represented by an oblivious policeman, who, "two hundred feet from an imminent murder, saw and heard only himself" (dieser Polizeimann, der zweihundert Schritte von einem baldigen Mord nur sich selbst sah und hörte), while whistling and holding his sword in the air (DS, 17; *BK*, 108). The authorities are not there for "us," but only for themselves. Along with the state, the story ironizes the patriarchal family: the final scene on the park bench indicates an aversion to the imperative of marriage as a cornerstone institution of bourgeois coming-of-age. There is, however, no pretense that the "community of nobodies" imagined in the story marks a world-historical turning point, as in *Death Preacher*, which Landauer imagined would have a real propagandistic purpose. However, the unworldly anarchisms of both Kafka and Landauer *do* converge in their privileging of masculinity. The voiding voice, whether that of the Death Preacher or the Praying Man, belongs in both cases to a man. Unworldly anarchism, however much it diverges from normative models of community, is in the end a mode of male homosociality.

While "Description of a Struggle" does not transgress every possible social norm, it joins Landauer in repurposing the monologues of nihilism in a surprising way. The "verbal epitome of loneliness and isolation" acquires a new positive meaning, diametrically opposed to its expected, negative meaning.[58] Unlike the Underground Man, the Praying Man performs a form of verbal nihilism that—even as it erases self and world—expresses *generosity* and *gratitude*. When the Praying Man announces to his listener at a party that all humans are fated to an unreal shadow-existence of being "cut out of tissue paper, like silhouettes" (aus gelbem Seidenpapier, so silhuettenartig, herausgeschnitten) (DS, 38; *BK*, 80), he offers this insight—which is nothing short of a revocation of humanity's existence—as a way of giving thanks (zum Dank) (*BK*, 80). Entrusting the world with his incessant verbal nihilism, the Praying Man gives the gift of emptiness to whatever listeners would care to stand by him. A comparison can be made here with Dostoevsky's Underground Man, who voids the world as "corrective punishment" (*NU*, 129). Rather than punishing the world, the Praying Man gives thanks to the world by generously verbalizing an abyss, in which the context of the surrounding universe is cancelled out.

Did Kafka remain true to his youthful vision of groundless community? By one account, he outgrew it. At age twenty-seven, Kafka himself acknowledged that he had experimented during his early years with a certain domesticated version of nihilism, which embraced nothingness alongside the rhythms of everyday existence. In a diary entry from February 1920, which scholars have seen as a gloss on "Description of a Struggle,"[59] Kafka described how he had aspired in his youth to fashion a "view of life" in which life could simultaneously retain its "natural rising and falling, but at the same time be recognized with no less clarity as a Nothing, a dream, a floating."[60] Kafka's hoped-for view of life might be understood as a kind of "soft nihilism," which evokes the duality of Schopenhauer's asceticism: the world is real, *and* it is nothing. "Description of a Struggle" would seem to epitomize the "soft nihilism" that Kafka had embraced in his younger years. In Kafka's diary entry, he implies that he had since outgrown this version of nihilism. Yet the simultaneity of substantial reality and insubstantial nothingness does return within Kafka's most famous prose works. The novels *The Trial* and *The Castle* are narratives of baseless hierarchies that are conjured out of thin air but nevertheless become coextensive with the entire world: wherever K. turns, the mechanisms of the institution materialize out of nowhere. What Kafka seems to have been saying, in so many of his later works, is that the most powerful institutions are themselves *societies of nobodies*; they are anarchic and unworldly even though they make up our world. In this view, Kafka did not abandon the vision of community in "Description of a Struggle." Rather, he came to understand it as an inescapable norm and not a liberating alternative. His later works depict forms of oppression and powerlessness that *should not* be possible but *are*. "Description of a Struggle" remains hopeful by comparison. Impossible forms of community can become possible when we step through the portal opened by literary fiction.

Chapter 4

✦

Monologue Overgrown

The Language of Hypertrophy in Thomas Bernhard's *Leichtlebig*

The phrase "unworldly anarchism" names an unexpected swerve in the tradition of nihilism that takes place around the start of the twentieth century and becomes manifest within experimental fiction. Written on both sides of the turn of the century, Landauer's 1893 novel *Death Preacher* and Kafka's 1907 story "Description of a Struggle" employ the medium of monologue to erase the world and expose a void that is held in common. This void becomes the basis for the creation of a community that assumes no other shared origins and does not take for granted any preexisting institutional framework. The conceit of Landauer's and Kafka's early fiction is that the assumed, given world is marked by false distinctions and distances, which monologue qua verbal nihilism shows to be insubstantial, "there but not there."[1] With their subversive appropriations of literary nihilism, Kafka and Landauer fit neatly into the discourses of decadence, secession, and rupture that defined the central European fin de siècle, when pessimism was fashionable and Schopenhauer's influence was ubiquitous. In looking to postwar German-language literature, we might expect that such playful sympathy for nihilism would fade away completely, given that National Socialism was frequently labeled as an instance of radical nihilism that had created its own catastrophic void through the murder of millions and the desolations of war. A later chapter of Thomas Mann's novel *Doctor Faustus*, published in 1947, refers to Hitler's Germany as a "regime sworn from the start to nothingness" (von Anbeginn dem Nichts verschworene Herrschaft).[2] Clearly, in the postwar context, a free play with the trope of the "void" becomes questionable.

In the postwar era, then, the stakes of nihilism hinge on *what kind* of void is embraced and what the ethical implications of this void are. Indeed, sympathy for the antisocial nihilist, or "underground" character did endure into postwar literature, as some writers portrayed nihilist refusal as an appropriate reaction to fascism, war, and genocide. German-language literature of the 1950s and 1960s saw a number of works that espoused radical solitude as the only ethical response to the Second World War and to the new global threats of the Cold War. Both Arno Schmidt's 1951 science fiction novel *Black Mirrors* (*Schwarze Spiegel*) and Ernst Jünger's essay *The Forest Passage* (*Der Waldgang*) from 1952 identified the depopulated natural landscape as the only proper home for the individual in light of the political violence of the twentieth century.[3] Both texts can be categorized as conservative expressions of anticollectivism that draw on ideologies of libertarianism (Jünger) and anti-Americanism (Schmidt) to oppose the Nazi legacy (rather than espousing an explicitly antifascist agenda). However, similar sympathies for the antisocial outsider also appear in Marlen Haushofer's ecological feminist novel *The Wall*, published in 1963. In this text, an absolute, misanthropic solitude is the only ethical option in the wake of the destruction wrought by industrial civilization.[4]

Of all the writers of the postwar decades who embraced the underground posture, the Austrian novelist and dramatist Thomas Bernhard stands out as a practitioner of the unworldly anarchism imagined by Kafka and Landauer, with its odd blend of solitude and solidarity. Like those turn-of-the century antecedents, Bernhard deploys monologue and metalepsis as the devices of a "strange new communality," making verbal voiding into a means of relating to others.[5] In Bernhard's prose, monologue brings about a verbal eclipse of the world: the mundane bleakness of postwar industrial society is overwhelmed by the excessive bleakness of incessant nihilist monologue, which darkens the world and opens up a new space for relations. Whereas Jünger's and Schmidt's misanthropic texts hold up something like a practical code of conduct for contemporary outsiders in *this* world, Bernhard's narrative is otherworldly in a way that recalls both Landauer and Kafka.

Bernhard's novels of the early 1960s pretended, in their opening pages, to be realist works providing an authentic picture of rural life in Austria of the 1950s and 1960s. Both *Frost* (1963) and the unpublished *Leichtlebig* (concluded 1961) concretely portray the reconstruction of industrial society after the desolations of the Second World War. Bernhard offers his readers a panorama of the Austrian industrial order with its workers, infrastructural networks, and political organizations. As these novels progress, their façade of realist verisimilitude crumbles: certain outsider characters negate this concrete world in its entirety, voiding it with incessant monologues that take over the text and eclipse the known world. The conceit of Bernhard's earliest novelistic writing is that a forceful prose of nihilism could serve as an antidote to the emotional and social vacancy of the industrial order. Against the official languages of both Austrian and Soviet socialism, Bernhard's outsiders spout an artful language of negation that conjures a metaphysical vacuum that is coextensive with all of nature. Against a concrete vision of a shared material world, Bernhard presents characters who incessantly insist that there is *nothing* between themselves and others.[6] Following these eruptions of verbal nihilism, new relations between alienated individuals become possible. By spouting speech that strips away every abstract, sentimental, idealistic notion of human togetherness, Bernhard's characters bond over a shared sense of meaninglessness and futility. As with Kafka, monologue is a way both of making the world disappear and of connecting outward to others. As with Kafka, this connection occurs across ontological boundaries, outside the limits of the concrete social world depicted by the text. For Bernhard as for Kafka, literature is a medium of negative togetherness.

One basic idea imparted by Bernhard's early fiction is that *solitude is not solitude.* This is relayed through the anarchic, "unhierarchized" juxtaposition of plural realities, which allows characters to be utterly alone and deeply connected at the same time.[7] As in Kafka's "Description of a Struggle," Bernhard's *Leichtlebig* approaches the relationship between solitude and community through a pairing of two formal devices. Solitude is signified by monologue, by the ongoing and unidirectional discourse that a speaker projects out into a world, without ever establishing a firm attachment to it. Instead of implying that community would arise through the emergence of a multilateral dialogue where the monologue would come to an end, Bernhard envisions community as something that emerges at the point where solitude turns inside out. The furthest depths of isolation offer a connection to others. This moment of turning inside out, where one's solitary voice transforms into a node of sociality and relationality, is signified by metalepsis: the speaker's active voiding and replacement of the frame in which the monologue is embedded. The moments of metalepsis, where the world becomes un-worlded, transforms the meaning of solitude. Michael Clune, writing of Bernhard's 1985 novel *Woodcutters*, has described this inverted solitude in terms of a "non-relational 'I'" that becomes "boundaryless" in such a way as to permit the self to merge with whatever is other to or outside of the self.[8] In short, the "I" forges a relation of nonrelation to others. Clune shows that Bernhard's late prose creates this sort of nonrelational "I" through a form of first-person narration indebted to Samuel Beckett's "unrecognizable" narrators of the *Molloy* trilogy.[9] However, Beckett is not the primary source for Bernhard's model of negative sociality. As with Kafka and Landauer, Bernhard connects back to nineteenth-century discourses of nihilism and anarchism.

Bernhard's inversions of solitude can be related to his enduring fascination with "anarchy" and "radicality." He is known for his (and his fictional characters') persistent refusals of every political ideology that might promise a stable model of social coexistence. This oppositional literary stance was foundational for Bernhard's literary life, according to his autobiographical work *The Cold* (*Die Kälte*). Here, Bernhard recalls being first immersed in literature by the "insatiability and radicality" of Dostoevsky's novel

Demons.[10] Bernhard is attracted to Dostoevsky's fictionalized account of how anarchy erupts in a small Russian town through the workings of several radical conspirators who are "possessed" by an anarchist-nihilist ideology. But rather than following Dostoevsky's moralistic critique of these nihilists, it was the subversive, dangerous "radicality" of the novel that inspired Bernhard to immerse himself further in literature. Literature would offer a safe space in which to experiment with radical ideas, outside the realm of practical action. The *Demons*, in other words, are the departure point for Bernhard's private embrace of anarchy as the basic substance of any literary undertaking. Such an embrace of anarchy is evident already in Bernhard's first novel *Frost*, where the monologues of the Painter Strauch represent an "anarchy" introduced into the "state structure" of the brain.[11] No fixed structures, whether they are a matter of mental or social life, are left untouched by this "anarchy," which "makes everything fluid" (119). This "poetics of anarchy"[12] is reprised in Bernhard's 1978 novel *Yes*, the motto of which reads: "Society, no matter which society, must always be overturned and abolished."[13] Such overturning and abolishing is, for the narrator of *Yes* and for so many of Bernhard's other outsider characters, located first of all in verbal activity. Debate has persisted among Bernhard scholars as to whether all these references to anarchy add up to a coherent political ideology that might place the author someplace on the left-right spectrum. Already in his earliest prose fiction from around the 1960s, Bernhard experimented with visions of anarchy that staked out a distance from the concrete political possibilities available in the world of the Cold War. At a time when the political map of central Europe was divided into the monumental systems of democratic capitalism and communism, with democratic Austria poised at border between the two, Bernhard fashioned a subversive vision of togetherness that had more in common with Landauer's "unworldly anarchism" than with these official political systems. Whereas the "real existing" socialism of the postwar era involved collectivization of land and the means of production, Bernhard's experimental prose performed a highly eccentric collectivization of *solitude*. The process of collectivization is not a narrative in the familiar sense that would allow us to say that a character has been "changed" because of an impactful external occurrence (such as a war, a marriage, or a rebellion). Rather, this collectivization plays out as transformation of the solitary voice into a node of sociality. This transformation does not so much "take place" as it "takes away place," rupturing the spatial-temporal fabric of the surrounding narrative. Through the verbal nihilism of antisocial monologue, the character in question voids and replaces the frame in which he exists. It is in the unpublished novel-fragment *Leichtlebig* that Bernhard most clearly performs this operation, flaunting its antimimetic, antirealist consequences.

Contrasting Modes of Solitude in *Leichtlebig*

Leichtlebig is actually only an arbitrary (though logical) title given to the attempted novel that Bernhard abandoned and cannibalized into the 1963 novel *Frost*. I proceed from the heuristic assumption that the four separate portfolios preserved in the Thomas Bernhard Archive (formerly in Gmunden, Austria), all comprise distinct parts of that single attempted novel, featuring a protagonist with the surname Leichtlebig.[14] These drafts and convolutes refer consistently to the same constellation of characters, and all take place during Leichtlebig's convalescent holiday in a mountain village near Schwarzach in Upper Austria. As of 2013, the shorter two of the four archival portfolios containing this novel are available in print through the Suhrkamp publishing house under the title *Arguments of a Winter Walker* (*Argumente eines Winterspaziergängers*). That title is taken from the heading of a nineteen-page manuscript that Bernhard apparently culled from this same *Leichtlebig*-project and prepared for separate publication in the journal *Wort in der Zeit* (though the text never actually appeared in print).[15] Although readers can now read a fragment entitled "Leichtlebig" in the 2013 volume, the majority of the preserved pages belonging to the novel are scattered across a large convolute, which became intermixed with later drafts of *Frost* and underwent heavy corrections and deletions through the author's pencil. As Raimund Fellinger and Martin Huber have noted, it would be virtually impossible to reconstruct a readable edition of these drafts, as the editors have done for the shortest preserved portfolios.[16] Though the novel is fragmented and unfinished, crucial sequences remain intact, which stage a metaleptic eclipse of the world through monologue––a formal and thematic complex that became characteristic throughout Bernhard's oeuvre. My goal, in this chapter, is to reconstruct the narrative trajectories of this lost novel, as well as its remarkable experimentation with forms and ideas.

The early folios of *Leichtlebig* vividly capture the austere world of early postwar Austrian industrial society. Within this world, the reader witnesses the chance meeting of two characters separated by class, age, education, and profession, who are linked only by loneliness: a young railroad worker named Leichtlebig, and an elder, vocally misanthropic "Doctor" of law from Vienna, who has no other name. The two characters meet by chance in the small village of Schwarzach in Upper Austria, where Leichtlebig is taking a short convalescent holiday, and where Doctor intends to live out his last days. The basic scenario is culturally specific to Austria, with its tradition of the *Kur*, an extended visit to a health resort, typically in the Alps, to avail oneself of the cold, fresh mountain air and mineral baths. In *Leichtlebig*, the transformative "cure" comes not from the familiar fluids of air or water but from the Doctor's dark monologues, which is its own kind of metamorphic fluid.

As the two become acquainted, each character's solitude is explicated against the backdrop of different narrative contexts. These two contexts are each presented through a stylistically distinct narrative thread. Whereas the vocal Doctor presents his life through breathless and chaotic monologue, the quieter Leichtlebig has his life story visualized through the close third-person narrator, who reveals the basic chronology of his upbringing and career. This exposition of Leichtlebig's life comes at the beginning of the manuscript, in a set of passages that adhere to a degree of documentary realism. These sequences perform an authenticating function, as they establish a narrative scenario rooted in a particular provincial locale that has seen the devastation of the Second World War, since followed by rapid industrial reconstruction. As the narrator describes Leichtlebig's position as a rail-switcher in the junction town of Attnang, the reader is given glimpses of the constraints and possibilities of the industrial working class in Austria during the postwar era of economic reconstruction, following the founding of the Austrian Second Republic in 1955. Bernhard's choice of Attnang-Puchheim as Leichtlebig's hometown is historically significant: the city served as a major rail junction for the Nazis, and during the war its facilities were constructed and repaired by concentration camp prisoners.[17] As mentioned in Bernhard's novel, the junction was heavily bombed by Allied forces on April 21, 1945. Days before the end of the war, concentration camp prisoners were forced to clear the rubble; many of them were shot. Alongside this history of violence and destruction, Attnang-Puchheim was also a significant site for the Austrian resistance against Nazism, as a group of railroad workers formed an underground group there that was affiliated with a group of resistance fighters operating in secret in Salzburg.[18] By making his protagonist Leichtlebig a railroad worker in Attnang who identifies as a socialist but sympathizes with communists, Bernhard gestures toward this violent history of war, forced labor, and resistance—a history that around 1960 is quickly fading underneath a massive wave of reconstruction and further modernization.

The institutions, buildings, and people of Leichtlebig's working-class world are all profoundly shaped by the wave of industrial growth that accompanied the founding of the Second Republic of Austria, following the withdrawal of Allied and Soviet forces. As a railroad worker who touts his position at "one of the most modern train stations in the federal rail districts" (einer der modernsten Bahnhöfe aller Bundesbahndistrike), recently rebuilt after its destruction by American bombers, Leichtlebig can claim for himself a crucial role in the nation's economic rebirth (*LL*, 53). Ostensibly, this would be a source of pride for Leichtlebig, and both he and his interlocutor the Doctor refer—listlessly, and as if automatically—to the "very important assignment" (sehr verantwortungsvolle Aufgabe) that Leichtlebig has been given within the system (53). Leichtlebig is neither happy nor unhappy about his responsibility: it is important to him insofar as gives him a privileged position from which to survey the magnitude and complexity of the new industrial system emerging in Austria following its extrication from the economy of Germany after 1945.[19] As such, he stands within and above this system at the same time. Elevated physically above the ground all day in a switching tower, seated at a "metal board" on which he can survey the "entire string of tracks," Leichtlebig oversees the infrastructure that enables exchange between the centers of production (*LL*, 53). His own life has vanished into the density of this network. In the opening lines of *Leichtlebig*, he thinks "of the great black undergrowth of tracks that had become his fate" (an das große schwarze Gestrüpp von Geleisen, die ihm zum Schicksal geworden sind) (47). The reconstructed industrial system is only a few years old, yet the technological social vision that accompanies it has already become second nature, as suggested by this botanical metaphor of undergrowth. Wherever Leichtlebig goes, he is "on track," functionalized within a vast system. It is in this reality that Leichtlebig's particular form of solitude emerges. It is a socially conditioned solitude, necessitated by the material conditions of his work.

The defining feature of the industrial life presented in *Leichtlebig* is uniformity, as symbolized by the uniform that Leichtlebig himself wears on and off his job. The uniformity of industry covers all bodily movements, mental processes, and social relations. Any element of surprise is removed from all interactions: just as he must wake up at five o'clock sharp every morning, Leichtlebig "react[s] to everything, at least externally, just as all others reac[t] to it" (er reagier[t], wenigstens rein äußerlich auf alles so wie auch die andern darauf reagier[en]) (47). The narrator implies that the disciplinary mechanism of the work schedule is sufficient to impose a total uniformity on the workers' expressive capacities, and that routine has purged emotion from social life. This uniformity is further intensified by the generic nature of the narration that provides all this data on Leichtlebig's everyday life. No particular moments are recounted, and nearly everything recounted (including the statement "he reacted") is an account of what *typically* or *always* happens. What has "happened" in Leichtlebig's life is always the repeatable operation of a system that is never turned off.

Certain moments within Leichtlebig's routine of regimented solitude do suggest the possibility of a future transformation through political-intellectual engagement, which might liberate the protagonist. However, even these exceptions are part of an overarching uniformity. Leichtlebig's work is punctuated with nominal involvement with an unnamed political party, which a contemporary reader might have inferred to be the Social Democratic Party of Austria (Sozialdemokratische Partei Österreichs), as this is the inference made by the workers that Leichtlebig meets in the village (*LL*, 96). Nevertheless, when the narrator reports Leichtlebig's thoughts, it is always "the" party yet *not any party in particular*; it is clearly leftist but ultimately nameless. The narrator's withholding of the actual party name underscores the anonymity and formality of Leichtlebig's political involvement; in these descriptions of party membership, any pathos of resistance is lacking, and there is initially no hint of the radical history of the communist railroad workers in Attnang who actively resisted Nazism. Leichtlebig's party membership functions like a brace that holds his solitude in place, limiting possibilities for unexpected social contact: "Most of the time he talked only with himself, now and then he went to the inn, twice a week he went to the meeting of the party to which he belonged" (Die meiste Zeit unterhielt er sich mit sich selber, ab und zu ging er in die Gaststätte, zweimal in der Woche traf er sich mit zwei Arbeitskollegen auf einer Versammlung der Partei, der er angehörte) (48). Party meetings are punctuation marks that interrupt Leichtlebig's ongoing conversation with himself, providing boundaries that assure a life of tolerable isolation. In other words, the party keeps Leichtlebig's internal monologue in check. The meetings are "more or less a matter of diversion" (mehr oder weniger eine Sache der Abwechslung), assuring the stability of his routine (48).

When Leichtlebig takes his convalescent vacation in the mountains (the trip that begins at the outset of the novel), he begins to think more deeply about this isolating uniformity of his life. He realizes that he has never actually been closely connected to another human being: "He had certainly never had a real friendship, one could place all of [his] relations under the heading of 'more intense acquaintances.' . . . In general railroad employees are not people who tend toward great, intense friendships. That wouldn't suit their sort of work" (Eine wirkliche Freundschaft hat er wohl niemals gehabt, man könnte diese Verbindungen alle mit intensiveren Bekanntschaften überschreiben) (*LL*, 73). Friendships are a distant abstraction because the constraints of the worker's life have prevented Leichtlebig from forming any emotional ties. All conventional language describing close ties is empty, lacking any concrete referent for Leichtlebig. The same is true of heterosexual romantic relationships, which remain for Leichtlebig a total abstraction (*LL*, 103). His family relations, too, have been entirely subsumed into the necessities of working-class economic life. Leichtlebig's father was also a railroad worker, and it is suggested that emotional expression within his family was hampered by material conditions. Even the overt mourning of the dead is stifled by the work routines of the railroad: when Leichtlebig's mother dies, his father only has time for a short meal at an inn before rushing off to the night shift. Even the choice of dinner entrée, smoked cold cuts, suggests a need for speed. The father sheds no tears and says nothing during this time that might otherwise have been set aside for mourning, and the surviving family members speak only to discuss practical issues, such as which belongings his stepsister will inherit (100). Extended, openly expressive mourning is a luxury not afforded by the circumstances, as his father is perpetually locked into a schedule. Leichtlebig himself will share this fate when his father dies. The sequence following his father's funeral is nearly identical to the one following his mother's, as Leichtlebig goes to the same inn for dinner, and like his father before him rushes off to the night shift (100). An unbroken routine governs both life and death, so that when Leichtlebig's father dies, events unfold with hyperbolic uniformity: he eats the same meal of smoked cold cuts, and he does not cry or speak, although he himself can hardly tolerate his own inexpressiveness. It is not just that Leichtlebig has followed in the footsteps of his father as a railroad worker: his life story is told in nearly identical sentences and reenacts nearly identical scenes to those in his father's life, but without once pronouncing a sense of comfort, familiarity, or filial love.

The only space that seems to offer Leichtlebig a meaningful form of autonomy is a small personal library that he has created in his private room. He has collected books inherited from a relative, along with ones of a "political nature that he had purchased personally, history books, books with rules of conduct that he had acquired at the suggestion of the party newspaper" (zum Teil selber angeschaffte politischer Natur, Geschichtenbücher, Bücher mit Verhaltungsmaßregeln, die er sich auf Vorschlag der Parteizeitung besorgt hatte) (49–50). In the more rarified solitude of his small, neat room, Leichtlebig can experiment with language and construct a political voice for himself. He can creatively appropriate the texts at his disposal, drawing on existing transcribed histories, ideologies, and procedures. Two of his favorite writers evoke moments of rebellion and revolution in the early twentieth century: T. E. Lawrence (whose *Seven Pillars of Wisdom* Leichtlebig owns, a book recounting the Arab Revolt of 1916–18) and Vladimir Lenin (*LL*, 34).[20] While Leichtlebig's everyday world is characterized by a certain bleak placidity and regimentation, he can meditate on political confrontation and revolution in the privacy of his small room.

In his room, Leichtlebig cultivates inward radicality. Outside his room, he experiences what we could call *institutional density*. His solitary life is situated in the midst of the interconnected institutions of his employer (the Austrian federal rail company), his trade union (the union of rail workers), his party, and the state. His individual biography exemplifies the intersection and overlap of large blocks of political power. In political-theoretical terms, one might say that Leichtlebig is incorporated into several "leviathans." As a fictional character, Leichtlebig serves as an image of the emerging corporatist structure of Austrian society in the postwar era, which in the 1960s became formalized in the concept of the "Social Partnership" (a form of postwar corporatism that should not be confused with the Austrian fascist-Catholic *Ständestaat* of the interwar period, a self-described corporate state). Jakob Norberg has summarized the workings of Austrian postwar corporatism as the cooperation of "large interest groups—trade unions, chambers of commerce, industrialist associations, and so on," in order to arrive at "mutually beneficial agreements concerning, for example, prices and wages."[21] Postwar Austrian corporatism, as it emerged during the occupation era of 1945–55, created conditions for a "peaceful and affluent society," but as historian Jill Lewis has argued, "this system of economic decision-making concentrated power in the hands of the peak interest groups and was run by an intricate network of committees and sub-committees," constituting in essence "an oligarchy."[22] When Leichtlebig sees his social "environment" as an unmanageable "undergrowth," he is presumably thinking among other things of the institutions of corporatism, including the "Paritätische Kommission," known in in English as the "Joint Commission on Prices and Wages," an unofficial collaboration between employers' and employees' associations. Indeed, in a long list of political injunctions that Leichtlebig compiles for the article he is writing during his *Kur*-holiday in the mountains, he explicitly mentions that there is a "wealth of unsettled questions before the commission."[23] As a skilled worker and as a convinced Leninist, Leichtlebig is both a critical observer of and a passive participant in the corporatist system. If Bernhard's novel had been published (instead of being cannibalized into *Frost* in 1963), Austrian readers of the time could well have understood the text as a provocative commentary on the economic and political institutions of the postwar era. The novel is not simply about modern alienation but about a specific system of administration that arose in postwar Austria. The common literary theme of social alienation is mediated through a vision of Austrian political economy in the early days of the Second Republic. As such, it is useful to reconstruct what was specifically contentious about the institutions of Leichtlebig's mechanized and automated world.

During the occupation period of 1945–55, American diplomatic observers of Austrian price and wage negotiations around 1950 saw the emerging political system there as a threat to the free market and to democratic decision-making in general; the chambers of government that might otherwise only render "technical services" (for example, the Chamber of Agriculture, the Chamber of Labor) gained "direct political and administrative influence."[24] From the pro-free market perspective, corporatism is a potentially authoritarian model that limits the power of individuals to freely compete in an open market. Because government bodies represent the particular interests of producers and employees, the workings of the state have become infused with particular economic agendas put forth by employers or workers. This is not the only possible critique of corporatism; Marxist critics of corporatism have focused on how it precludes any confrontational or revolutionary politics. This is the position taken by the Italian Marxist Antonio Gramsci, who critiqued corporatism in his prison writings. Jan Rehmann paraphrases Gramsci's critical definition of corporatism as "a social group's limitation to its immediate economic goals, cut off from any wider perspective of social emancipation and transformation."[25] In other words, corporatism makes permanent the mistake that revolutionary Marxists found in the workings of trade unions, which pursue the economic interests of particular groups of workers instead of the seizure of political power. There is no question that Austro-Corporatism was intended to do precisely this: the "Social Partnership" was supposed to ameliorate the overt antagonisms that had led to the Austrian civil war in 1934.[26] With the emergence in the postwar era of "a highly organized working class with institutionalized interests," the chances of a spontaneous eruption of violent class conflict were lessened, as the representation of workers' interests became an integral part of the political system.[27] The drawback of such a conflict-averse "social total system" was, as historian Oliver Rathkolb writes, its "strongly authoritarian, obedient-coercive character."[28] These "authoritarian traditions" originated in the Habsburg monarchy and were subsequently cultivated in the Austrofascism of the early 1930s and then utilized by the Nazis. To live amid this total political-economic system, as Leichtlebig does, is to live under the shadows of multiple authoritarian regimes of the distant and recent past. Leichtlebig does not explicitly or directly oppose the authoritarian character of the world around him, even if he did pen an article entitled "The System Is Guilty" (Das System ist schuld) when intervening in the debate over wage parity (*LL*, 81). However, Bernhard includes subtle clues that place Leichtlebig at the outermost margins of the social system and later affirm Leichtlebig's entanglement with the communist groups that had actively resisted Nazism. However, this affirmation of resistance does not occur until Leichtlebig has been exposed to the radical language of the Doctor, who explodes the boundaries of Leichtlebig's everyday existence in the industrial order.

When Leichtlebig encounters the terminally ill Doctor near the mountain inn where he is spending his holiday, he encounters a mode of solitude that resembles, yet radically reframes, his own condition of being "always alone." The Doctor is "always alone" in a way that does not result from entrapment in a particular web of political-economic institutions. Rather, this radical solitude entails an *otherworldly* perspective that has already grasped the negativity of the world in its entirety and is now located *beyond* the world itself. This is where the discourse of classical nihilism enters the novel: for the Doctor, as for Schopenhauer's saint, the world in its entirety is *Nothing*. He is alone because he has seen "everything," having gained panoramic knowledge of both natural and human history: he has written a doctoral dissertation in paleontology,[29] fought on the fronts of World War I and sustained a brain injury,[30] worked in the Austrian state tobacco monopoly,[31] traveled to America, Africa, Australia, and China,[32] and witnessed the end of World War II from a countryside hut. The implication of this panoramic, global education is that the Doctor has "done everything" and "been everywhere." If Leichtlebig's environment is a dense constraining web of institutional strictures that obscure the totality of the world, the Doctor claims to have gained knowledge of this totality in all its darkness. As such, the meeting of the main characters in *Leichtlebig* is a meeting of two kinds of isolation, which correspond to two visions of density. Leichtlebig dwells within a thick weave of social structures, a limited and localized web of density in postwar Austria. The Doctor has suffered through the whole world and now, at the end of his life, is in a position to verbalize the essential density of the world's suffering. In an incessant, densely structured monologue, the Doctor mimics the universe in its inexhaustible negativity.

As the Doctor delivers these monologues with Leichtlebig at his side while the two men walk around the mountain valley surrounding Schwarzach, he presents a vision of "everything" that radically exceeds the dimensions of the systemic totality of corporate postwar Austria. This total reality is an "overgrown" or "hypertrophic" conglomerate that dwarfs any of the industrial conglomerates in Leichtlebig's own world. The Doctor's "everything" is unmoored from temporal and spatial location. In what perhaps sounds like the ravings of a madman, the Doctor claims to be a visitor from another dimension: "Hypertrophies, timeless horror. I have to endure spans of time that human history has not yet seen!" (Hypertrophien, zeitloses Entsetzen. Ich habe Zeitspannen auszuhalten, die die Menschengeschichte noch nicht gesehen hat!).[33] The Doctor's otherworldly perspective involves a radical compression of time into the shortest moments; he claims to suffer from a kind of hypermnesia, or excessive memory, where the progress of cosmic time flashes before his eyes: "In my head I have continual sunsets and sunrises" (In meinem Kopf habe ich dauernde Sonnenuntergänge und dauernde Sonnenaufgänge und wieder Sonnenuntergänge).[34] When the Doctor describes his mental experience as "hypertrophies, timeless horror," he is asserting the sovereignty of his mental condition, claiming for himself a negative authority that derives its power from its lack of a particular location in known time and space. With his purported hyperconsciousness of the universe, he harbors an inner "darkness" that "achieves a degree of density that escalates into insanity."[35] Even if it is insanity, it is also revelatory. All of this darkness has a function within the narrative context of *Leichtlebig*. Through the verbalization of this darkness, the Doctor eclipses the postwar social and material world inhabited by the protagonist Leichtlebig. More so than the outsiders of Schopenhauer and Dostoevsky, Bernhard's ontological outsider produces a rant that blankets the given world in darkness.

As shown above, *Leichtlebig* details the many overlapping forms of social authority that characterize postwar industrial society. The Doctor negates these particular authorities of the present through an unworldly authority beyond all authority. Having retired from his own worldly position of the state tobacco company (*Tabakregie*), the Doctor is now deputized with the (negative) authority of what he calls "darkness," that is, the essentially suffering nature of the universe that permeates, predates, and postdates human history. As the voice of "monstrous universality" (ungeheuere Allgemeinheit [AEW, 11]) the Doctor both symptomatizes and diagnoses the "timeless horror" (zeitloses Entsetzen)[36] of existence and has purportedly transcended all worldly political ideologies. A contrast emerges: the reality of Leichtlebig's postwar Austria is systemic and corporate, defined by the conflicting yet tightly incorporated agendas of different interest groups. Meanwhile, the Doctor's universe, as presented in his monologues, is characterized by a wholly different kind of incorporation, as he claims that all the suffering of nature is concentrated in the darkness of his head. When this unworldly authority is introduced into the everyday reality of postwar Austria, it has an anarchic effect in the novel. In claiming for himself a sovereign and omniscient perspective on the world's darkness, the Doctor's consciousness becomes a kind of black hole into which all localized and contextual manifestations of authority vanish. Indeed, when Doctor himself speaks of the hypertrophies in his head, he boasts that his head is so heavy that, "If I let my head go for just a moment, this head would pull me down through the earth's surface and through the entire globe into the universe [*illegible text*] under the Earth" (Würde ich mich auch nur einen Augenblick lang gehen lassen, dieser Kopf zöge mich durch die Erdoberfläche hinunter und durch den ganzen Erdball in das unter der Erde [*illegible text*] Universum!).[37] From these statements, Bernhard's novel swerves in a blatantly unnatural direction, as these "fantastic thoughts" achieve the status of reality.[38] In other words, they jump from the level of embedded *discourse* and become part of the *story*, or fabula.

The anarchy verbalized by the Doctor's discourse would appear at first to be simply the by-product of madness, which could be disqualified and contained within a clinical diagnosis of the character. However, this is where *Leichtlebig* turns out to have an unnatural narrative structure, with an audaciously "unhierarchized" organization of discursive layers.[39] At first, the novel appears to be neatly layered into a hierarchy of levels, with:

> (1) a primary narrator, who imparts
> (2) Leichtlebig's thoughts and experiences through indirect and free indirect speech, and as a subset of this
> (3) embeds as one facet of Leichtlebig's experiences the direct speech of the Doctor.

If we assume this hierarchy holds throughout the text, then the Doctor's monologues would be contained before the fact as "only" speech, having the same status as the drunken talk of the workers that Leichtlebig overhears in the Schwarzach inn. The monologues about hypertrophies of time would be just one more piece of sonic data that Leichtlebig took in during his stay in the mountains. Yet, as I will show, this hierarchy is subsequently subverted in ways that forbid the assumption of a single, stable fictional ontology. In short, *Leichtlebig* displays the sort of narrative "anarchism" discussed by Brian McHale in the context of postmodernist fiction, where a text presents different ontological orders without deciding between them. In *Leichtlebig*, these plural "orders" are the distinct worlds of Leichtlebig and the Doctor, with their different visions of incorporation and density.[40] The emergence of the Doctor's second order occurs gradually: at the beginning, the narrative is marked as Leichtlebig's story; everything is clearly focalized through him, and he provides the eyes and ears on the world of Schwarzach and its environs. Yet as Leichtlebig listens at length to the Doctor's monologue, the partitions between discourses, and between characters, become permeable. Leichtlebig's worldly solitude becomes conjoined, and compatible, with the Doctor's unworldly solitude.

Connection through Overgrowth

Despite a pervasive vocabulary of bleakness and the seeming hopelessness of the two characters' respective worlds, the outcome of their colliding solitudes is a strange new idea of community. The meaning of Leichtlebig's life story and the Doctor's monologues arises out of the anarchic discursive relation *between* these two solitudes. The text of *Leichtlebig* performs an intermingling and collectivization of solitude, making literature into a site for the declaration of togetherness *amid* the different negativities of the universe. The emergence of this anarchic community can be traced through the journey of a single motif, which wanders between the inner monologues of Leichtlebig and the direct speech of the Doctor. This key motif is *undergrowth*, in German, *Gestrüpp*.[41] This translation is imperfect; the English word "undergrowth," though technically referring to the same "confused, wild" growth, places emphasis on lowness to the ground, whereas the German *Gestrüpp* is built around the root of *Strupp*, meaning "bush." *Strupp* is (as the Grimms noted) "als simplex nicht sehr häufig" (as a simplex not very common) and is more commonly encountered in the "collektivbildung [*sic*]" (collective formation) of *Gestrüpp*, which could be translated as a *bundle of roots, strands, branches.* Unlike "undergrowth," *Gestrüpp* suggests multiple bushes overlapping, whose branches have grown together to become indistinguishable and impenetrable. *Gestrüpp* serves both as a descriptive term for the complex environments surrounding the characters but also for the emergent structure of the text itself, as it is increasingly dominated and densified by the chaotic intergrowth of two narrative contextures (Leichtlebig's and the Doctor's).

The word *Gestrüpp* first appears in the context of Leichtlebig's personal story, as a metaphor for the complex interwoven developments of material and social reality that become identical with the individual. At the start of his story, Leichtlebig thinks of "the great black undergrowth of tracks that have become his fate" (das große schwarze Gestrüpp von Geleisen, die ihm zum Schicksal geworden sind) (*LL*, 47). As a rail-switcher, Leichtlebig has memorized all the combinations of possibilities of this "labyrinth," which he and his coworkers could now navigate "in their sleep"; industry has become second nature (74). Leichtlebig's job is to *tame* this nature, to manage and oversee its complexity, to discern distinctions between different courses of movement so that trains reach their destination without colliding.

From here, "undergrowth" (*Gestrüpp*) mutates from a descriptor of industrial infrastructure into a name for the collective overarching superstructures of the social and political world. As a nascent intellectual and writer, Leichtlebig deploys the word again in an inner monologue as he reflects on the possibility of coming to terms with his environment in all its intimidating complexity. The writings of the communist Vladimir Lenin make it possible to map and manage this greater undergrowth:

> Lenin, he thought, is a quarry for one who wants to deal with the environment, for one who wants to have done with this environment. The entire book consists, at bottom, only of rules of conduct, of entirely simple sentences, which allow the undergrowth sprawling before one like a primeval forest to be cleared up step by step.
>
> Lenin, dachte er, ist eine Fundgrube für einen sich mit der Umwelt auseinandersetzen wollenden Menchen, für einen, der mit dieser Umwelt fertig werden will. Das ganze Buch besteht um Grunde genommen nur aus Verhaltungsmassregeln, aus ganz einfachen Sätzen, die einen das Gestrüpp, das vor einem urwaldgleich wuchert, lichten lässt Schritt für Schritt. (*LL*, 82)

With Lenin's help, Leichtlebig can navigate, interpret, and document the density of the world order. In Marxist terms, Lenin's book allows Leichtlebig to pierce through the surface level of immediate reality and uncover underlying forces that determine it. In other words, Lenin gives Leichtlebig a theoretical tool for understanding the alienation of his own, specific labor as a railroad worker from the interests represented within the political superstructure.

The two contrasting uses of the trope of "undergrowth" capture the thematic core of Leichtlebig's narrative: the problem of the world's opacity. Both as a worker and as a writer, Leichtlebig recognizes the need to navigate the complexity of a massive system that has itself overgrown into a kind of second nature. In both cases, he confronts this neo-organic complexity by focusing on a single line or branch: one track-line within the interwoven rail system or a particular "clear sentence" in Lenin's text. However, as Leichtlebig's story progresses, he discovers the limits of such systematic thinking. The cognitive models of the technician, and of the revolutionary Lenin, cannot fully illuminate the darkness and density of the world around him.

New forms of darkness and density appear on Leichtlebig's horizon when he begins to develop proficiency as a writer, contributing political articles to the "railroad workers' union newspaper" (15). In attempting to give voice to the everyday concerns of workers like himself, Leichtlebig begins to gain a sense of how reality can be constructed anew with language. As Leichtlebig learns to emulate the style of the books that come into his possession, studies the "ways of expression" used in various newspapers, and expands his vocabulary to include words such as "subaltern" and "vehemence," he eventually becomes a successful writer of political commentary (17). However, this new acquisition of vocabulary is not only liberating. It also makes Leichtlebig aware that language is not a transparent but an *opaque* medium that can obscure as much as it reveals. Once he has arrived in the mountains and tries to begin writing a new article, Leichtlebig is suddenly troubled by the clichés inherent in all descriptions and conceptions of the world. Here, he is poised to develop his own form of "language skepticism" that arises organically from his own attempts to grasp his perceived environment, rather than from the Austrian intellectual tradition including Hugo von Hofmannsthal and Ludwig Wittgenstein:

> He looks over to the mountains, they are black and craggy. Actually, he thinks, one has clichéd conceptions of nearly everything, and these clichéd conceptions are all true, one can rotate and turn them however one likes: the mountains are craggy, black, hyperbolically one can also say silent besides that, but that is dangerous. Wherever one looks, everything corresponds completely to the hundreds and thousands of clichéd conceptions.

> Er schaut zu den Bergen hinüber, die sind schwarz und schroff. Überhaupt, denkt er, man hat von beinahe allen Dingen eine Klischeevorstellung, und diese Klischeevorstellungen sind alle wahr, man kann sie drehen und wenden, wie man will: die Berge sind schroff, schwarz, übertrieben kann man auch noch schweigsam dazu sagen, aber das ist gefährlich. Wohin man schaut, alles entspricht vollkommen den hunderten und tausenden und zehntausenden von Klischeevorstellungen. (*LL*, 62)

Leichtlebig is troubled by clichés, not because he perceives them to be inaccurate or misleading, but because he feels that an awareness of the guiding power of these clichés would not only disrupt and discontinue speaking and writing but also entirely revoke his existence. When he thinks to himself that every spoken and written word is a prescripted "phrase," he cautions himself: "But one must not think about that: don't think about it, he says to himself, otherwise everything will stop. Right, then it would be the end" (62). But Leichtlebig cannot stop himself. In the next sentence, he looks over to a mountain and thinks: "That's all like on postcard, like one made by a man without a trace of artistry, painted but true!" (Das alles ist wie auf einer Postkarte, wie von einem Mann ohne jedes Künstlertum, gemalt doch wahr!) (62–63). The threatening potential of this train of thought appears when Leichtlebig turns to himself: "And I myself? Let's not talk about that" (Und ich selber? Reden wir lieber nicht darüber) (63). Leichtlebig begins to suspect that the world in which he exists is constructed of clichéd conceptions that nevertheless have substance: true fictions. He suspects that he will only ever apprehend the world as a tangle of representations whose underlying reality cannot be determined. It is at this juncture that Leichtlebig develops a sense that critical, reflective thought itself can be fatal. A complete theoretical illumination of the world would expose Leichtlebig's own insubstantiality and fictionality. With this passage, Bernhard's novel begins to display the ontological uncertainty and "flickering" of postmodernist, or unnatural, fiction. In wondering whether he himself is a cliché, the text takes a metaphysical turn and calls attention to the tenuous substantiality of its storyworld, which is "there but not there."[42] Leichtlebig's metalinguistic thoughts lead him closer to an epistemological anarchy, in which language has the power to create and negate different realities, and where there is no possibility of ever establishing a stable and unified "world." With the onset of these ontological doubts, Leichtlebig's surname acquires additional meaning. If "leichtlebig" usually means "easygoing," implying a free existence of enjoyment and relaxation, Leichtlebig as a character resonates with another semantic possibility inscribed within the conjunction of *leicht* (light/easy) and *lebig* (living). Leichtlebig is someone who *lives lightly* in the sense of being only *slightly* present in the world, alienated from his environment through his sense of the arbitrariness of his identity as a proletarian, as a technician, and as a communist. He is those things, but he is only *barely* those things, as a flickering figment.

It is in the context of this self-alienation, with Leichtlebig feeling lost in the labyrinth of reality, that his own story intersects with the Doctor's. Once Leichtlebig is walking around the snowy environs of Schwarzach with the Doctor, he takes the opportunity to vent his existential uncertainty regarding the impenetrability and arbitrariness of his reality:

> I often break my head over the question of why I am so and so and that and that and not otherwise and something else, why I have gone this path and not another. To me nearly everything is inexplicable.
>
> Ich zerbreche mir oft den Kopf, warum ich so und so und das und das bin und nicht anders und etwas anderes, warum ich diesen und nicht einen anderen Weg gegangen bin. Mir ist beinahe alles unerklärlich. (*LL*, 85)

Such a statement could be taken as a *captatio benevolentiae*, intended to prompt a refutation (where the Doctor insists that Leichtlebig *does* understand some things in the world). Instead, this enunciation of doubt serves as a rite of passage, welcoming the protagonist into the Doctor's nihilist universe. The Doctor takes Leichtlebig's existential lament as an indication that he is a "more ripe thinking person" ([ein] reifere[r] denkende[r] Mensch) since it is pure philistinism to believe that one has "seen through something completely" (in irgend einer Sache vollkommene Klarheit) (85). The undergrowth-metaphor quietly echoes in this passage. We recall that there was once a time Leichtlebig maintained hope that it would be possible "to have done with the environment" and to "make a clearing" with Lenin's help, but now he finds himself floating. The Doctor's affirmation of Leichtlebig's despair seals the convergence of the two men's very different life paths. As the Doctor responds to Leichtlebig, a crucial word first incubated as a productive metaphor inside of Leichtlebig's head now reappears in the Doctor's mouth. This word, again used to signify the impenetrability of the world, is *Urwald* (jungle), that *urwaldgleiches Gestrüpp* (jungle-like undergrowth) that Leichtlebig once braved with Lenin as his guide. Here, the overgrowth acquires a new level of opacity:

> Leichtlebig, said the Doctor, I understand as little of the world as one can understand, and I also have no clue about all other things, everything disintegrates when I try to touch it, . . . and the older I have become, the more inextricable everything presented itself to me, with time the jungle became thicker and crueler and the air more dreadful.
>
> Leichtlebig, sagte der Doktor, ich verstehe so wenig von der Welt, als man nur verstehen kann, und auch von allen anderen Dingen habe ich überhaupt keine Ahnung, alles zerfällt, wenn ich versuche, es anzugreifen, . . . und je älter ich geworden bin, desto unentwirrbarer stellte sich mir alles dar, mit der Zeit wurde der Urwald dichter und grausamer und die Luft beklemmender. (85–86)

Whereas Leichtlebig's internal monologues contained some preliminary meditations on the opacity of reality as an impenetrable "undergrowth," the Doctor's oral monologues present a perspective where this density and impenetrability has overtaken all aspects of existence. Any firm sense of individuality has been replaced with an image of the self as one node of an endless continuum. Language ceases to function as a means of locating oneself in time and space and instead becomes the incessant illustration of an incommunicable state of darkness, which he calls elsewhere "a monstrous universality" (AEW, 11). The Doctor speaks from a social vacuum that is saturated with the sinister substance of "nature." He thus presents a negative monist vision that insists on the equal distribution of darkness that unifies subject and object.

As hubristic as they sound with their claims to universal knowledge, the Doctor's monologues are not straightforward evidence of a simple egocentrism. They are "selfless," in the sense that they do not purport to express the feelings and beliefs of an essential self but rather reveal the speaking individual to be a nonperson, a node of sheer nullity that functions as hypothetical black holes do in works of science fiction: what the Doctor says in his monologues allegedly does not emit from "inside" him, but rather his own mouth is a vanishing point for our world, and potentially the entryway into another universe. He proclaims access to an anarchic plurality of universes, or a "multiverse" that relativizes the fixity of any given world. It is not, then, an example of familiar egocentrism when the Doctor speaks of the "gravity" of his head and claims that it "is so heavy that a dozen strong men could not carry it" (mein Kopf allein aber ist so schwer, dass ihn ein Dutzend kräftiger Männer gar nicht tragen könnten).[43] The gravity of his head is not a marker of his own greatness or genius. Rather, it is important because it has the potential to crash through the entire sphere of the earth and into another universe below, as noted earlier.[44] If we understand these claims on their own terms, rather than as mad ravings, then we can extract an unusual cosmology where the interior of each mind functions as a black hole giving onto a parallel universe. This cosmology is akin to the "anarchic landscape of worlds in the plural" explored by postmodernist fiction.[45] Interpersonal relations reach *across* realities; to coexist with another person, in this "landscape," is to live and speak across an ontological boundary between separate realities. The Doctor establishes his monologue as an engine of *metalepsis* that cuts through the boundaries of this world. His speech provides a gateway between incompatible universes.[46]

Early in the novel, we learned that the thicket or undergrowth of railroad tracks had become Leichtlebig's fate. As the monologues of the Doctor overtake the pages of *Leichtlebig* and eclipse the world of the novel, a different "thicket" of fate is presented that does not restrict the individual life story to a particular inflexible "track." The Doctor affirms Leichtlebig's lament regarding the opacity and senselessness of fate but goes on to elaborate a vision of fate in which all the determining structures ("tracks") of life vanish into a formless darkness. In his flood of verbal nihilism that incessantly condemns, refutes, and obscures the world, the institutions of family, party, and employer lose their power. The Doctor describes his own fate not as a developmental track but as a process of erasure, disappearance and loss. He speaks of how his sense of a firmly bounded self is progressively engulfed by "the jungle" (der Urwald), which is synonymous with the terms "darkness" and "nature" that he employs elsewhere (*LL*, 86). Such nature imagery has a function analogous to the *abysses* and *vacuums* posited by classical nihilism: it is the imagined space of disappearance, where time, space, and individuality dissipate. The Doctor sets up an alternative notion of biography, which begins with distinction and individuality and leads into a terminal state of indistinction. Fate is an infinitely dense thicket *into which* all distinct tracks disappear, a darkness that engulfs every fixed and distinct identity.

In this narrative context, where his voice has nearly overtaken the novel, the Doctor argues that all differences between human lives are superficial, and thus he seeks to close the gap between his own biography and that of his listener: "Your life, Leichtlebig, is just as interesting as my life. There is, at bottom, no life that would be more interesting than all lives, and there would be none that would be less interesting. All lives have the same meaning, said the Doctor" (Alle Leben haben die gleiche Bedeutung, sagte der Doktor) (*LL*, 84). Their paths have not crossed incidentally; rather, they are fundamentally identical: "You have the paths in front of you that I have behind me" (Sie haben den Weg vor sich, den ich hinter mir habe).[47] Following a continuous associative impulse, the Doctor finds parallels and mirrorings everywhere that cut through the differences between himself and the other. He nullifies the social division of labor that would separate him from Leichtlebig, equating his own work in finance with Leichtlebig's work in heavy industry: "I would like to designate your employment in the switching-works as the counterpart to my position at the bank."[48] Leichtlebig resists these assertions of identity and remains conscious of the social and material circumstances that have shaped their respective fates. He points out that whereas the Doctor was able to travel the entire world, from East Asia to North America, he himself is only given ten days of vacation each year, including the time of commuting to and from each destination. Class differences remain. The Doctor had the privilege of a formal education, having studied law and later had the opportunity to conduct independent research as a "paleontologist."[49] Academic training has allowed him to investigate natural history and search the depths of the earth. His universal knowledge was, in part, purchased with inherited privilege. By contrast, as an autodidact of the working class, Leichtlebig has had to pursue his intellectual interests within strict material constraints; the acquisition of single book has required great effort and patience. The Doctor, however, fails to see a difference; both characters have hit upon the same basic knowledge in their own way. He speaks from a conglomerated perspective allegedly beyond any individuation, where all human lives are entangled into an impenetrable yet permanently unified "jungle." As a morbid monist, the Doctor insists that all apparent separation is actually connection.

The Metaleptic Moment of *Leichtlebig*

As noted above, *Leichtlebig* initially establishes a hierarchy of narrative layers, which positions a (1) primary disembodied narrator over (2) Leichtlebig's thoughts and experiences, which include (3) a record of his meeting with the Doctor. At first, the Doctor is a function of Leichtlebig's own story. However, this hierarchy is permeable, and it undergoes a jarring revision halfway through the novel. Anarchy becomes a fact of the novel's form. In this way, the discursive structure of the novel itself comes to reflect the dense "fatal darkness" that the Doctor has verbalized through his monologues. Carefully assembled textual layers cross in a way that, from the perspective of a biographical realism, makes no sense. One scene in particular marks an unnatural shift, where the text becomes a "thicket" that mirrors the monist nihilism described by the Doctor. This shift occurs during one of the pair's many walks through the snowy forests around Schwarzach, when the Doctor goads Leichtlebig to tell the story of his childhood.

> Leichtlebig, allow me the pleasure, and tell about your childhood. I basically know everything, begin as you like, I know how you will begin, but begin: my childhood, you say, was morose. My father worked for the railroad and my mother often said to him: you disgust me! Is that true? Leichtlebig, is that true? Tell me if that's true! That is an order, Leichtlebig! And then after primary school? After the move? Because your father was transferred to another station, is that not right? To a larger station, because he did no wrong and so he could be properly promoted again and again. . . . Leichtlebig! . . . Leichtlebig, said the Doctor, you must know what the bed you slept in as a child looked like. How your mother looked. How you tried to get close to her. I know you failed in that, Leichtlebig. And your father, the alcoholic![50]

> Leichtlebig, machen Sie mir das Vergnügen und erzählen Sie mir Ihre Kindheit! Im Grunde genommen weiss ich alles, fangen Sie an, wie Sie wollen, ich weiss, wie Sie anfangen, aber fangen Sie an: meine Kindheit, sagen Sie, war grämlich. Mein Vater war bei der Eisenbahn und meine Mutter hat öfters zu ihm gesagt: du bist mir widerwärtig! Ist das wahr? Leichtlebig, ist das wahr? Sagen Sie mir, ob das

> wahr ist! Das ist ein Befehl, Leichtlebig! Und dann nach der Volksschule? Nach der Übersiedlung? Denn Ihr Vater ist doch auf einen anderen Bahnhof versetzt worden, nicht wahr? Auf einen grösseren Bahnhof, denn er hat sich nichts zuschulden kommen lassen und ist dadurch regelrecht und immer weiter aufgestiegen. . . . Leichtlebig! . . . Leichtlebig, sagte der Doktor, Sie müssen doch wissen, wie das Bett ausgeschaut hat, in dem Sie als Kind geschlafen haben. Wie Ihre Mutter ausgeschaut hat. Wie Sie sich ihr zu nähern versucht haben. Ich weiss, dass das misglückt ist, Leichtlebig. Und Ihr Vater, der Alkoholiker!

Initially, the Doctor's claim of *knowing everything* sounds like rhetorical flourish, a reiteration of the idea that "all lives have the same meaning" (*LL*, 84). Yet as he goes on, the Doctor overwhelms Leichtlebig with precise details that corroborate his own knowledge of his interlocutor's childhood. Now the Doctor is an impossibly omniscient character, possessing as much knowledge as—or more knowledge than—the novel's primary narrator. Although the two men were perfect strangers when they first met, the Doctor is now able to recount all the private details of Leichtlebig's childhood, having somehow slipped into a position of authorial authority that permits him to overstep the barriers of time and space. This jarring passage crystallizes, in the text's narrative form, the Doctor's purported knowledge of the "timeless" darkness of the universe.[51] He can access and perceive the universe from any vantage point, including that of Leichtlebig's childhood experience. Therefore, the Doctor's language now collapses the established hierarchy of subject-positions that initially enabled the narration of Leichtlebig's life story. For much of the novel, the outermost layer is provided by the disembodied third-person narrator, whose discourse is focalized through Leichtlebig (see diagram on p. 152). Yet the metaleptic shift, triggered by the Doctor's uncanny omniscience, implicitly replaces that outermost frame with what is supposed to be in the innermost frame (see diagram on p. 153).

The epic third-person reporting by the narrator—which has documented Leichtlebig's youth through a series of flashbacks—is now swallowed up by the second-person imperative statements of the Doctor's monologue. "He did this" becomes "Say you did this!" This narrative coup, which usurps the position of the primary narrator, as well as Leichtlebig's position, has several important consequences. The Doctor's coup instantly nullifies the realist edifice of the novel, with its concretely historical vision of postwar Austrian society, upsetting the established fictional ontology. This is an instance of metalepsis because an intradiegetic character has managed to break through the internal boundaries of the narrative. As in Kafka, the verbal eraser of the world is a *nobody* (the Doctor even refers to himself as a "nobody").[52] As a nobody, the Doctor elevates the "darkness" and "density" of his head, which

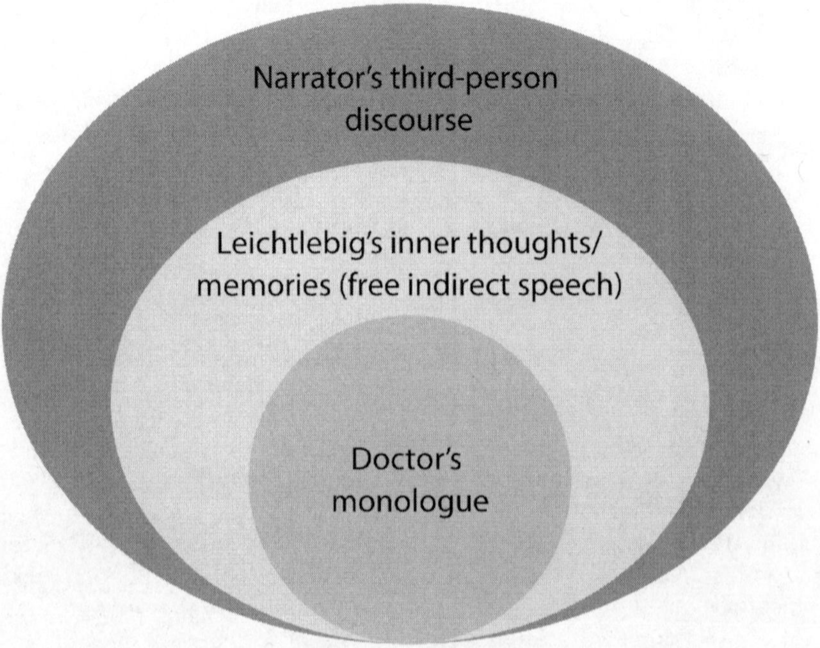

Initial hierarchy of layers.

transcend time and space, to the level of fictional reality and in the same moment exposes a trove of impossible knowledge. His unnatural gesture opens up an entire range of untold stories that belong to Leichtlebig's fate, which he himself (along with the narrator) had not deigned to tell.

> Yes. Yes. Leichtlebig said: my mother, yes. . . . You see, Leichtlebig, said the Doctor, your bed was too short for you and you had to sleep on the floor. You were afraid of rats. You were afraid of bedbugs. Your white face was covered in bites every morning. On Sunday you finally got white bread instead of black bread with your coffee and then your parents took a trip out of the city and went for a walk. And if you had known where they were, you would have gotten up and run away, right? Yes, said Leichtlebig.

> Ja. Ja. Leichtlebig sagte: meine Mutter, ja. . . . Sehen Sie, Leichtlebig, sagte der Doktor, Ihnen war das Bett schon bald zu kurz und da haben Sie eine zeitlang auf dem Fussboden geschlafen. Sie haben sich vor Ratten gefürchtet. Vor Wanzen haben Sie Angst gehabt. Ihr weisses Gesicht ist jeden Morgen zerbissen gewesen. Am Sonntag

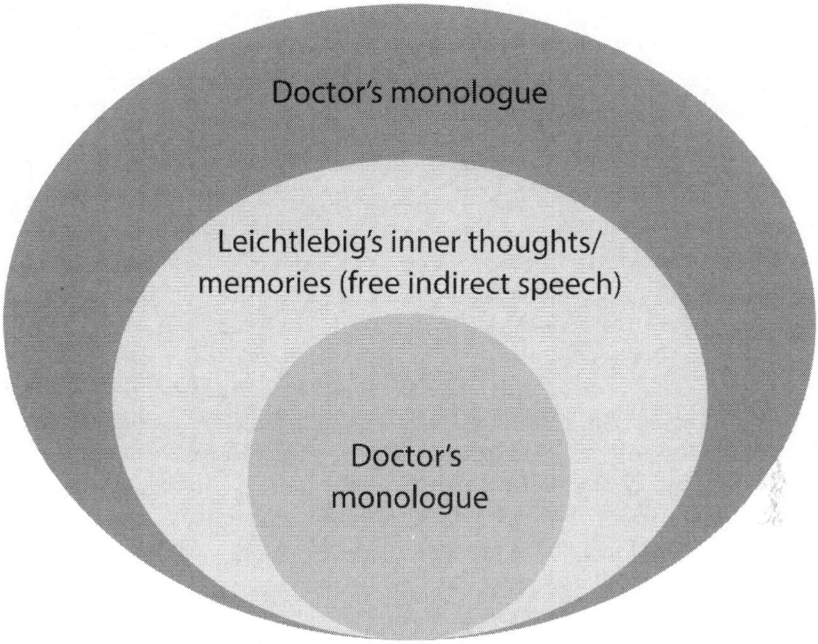

Subsequent hierarchy of layers

> haben Sie zuerst anstatt Schwarzbrot Weissbrot zum Kaffee bekommen und dann sind Sie mit Ihren Eltern aus der Stadt hinausgefahren und haben einen Spaziergang gemacht. Und wenn Sie gewusst hätten, wohin, wären Sie auf und davongelaufen, ja? Ja, sagte Leichtlebig.[53]

These sentences do not only collapse the distinction between authorial narration and character monologue; they also collapse the intimate third-person "he" of the narrator into the second-person "you" of the Doctor, so that a personal pronoun denoting *exterior* experience ("your" father) becomes as intimately revealing as a confessional "I." It is here that we learn the extent of Leichtlebig's emotional pain and material deprivation; the Doctor says more than the narrator was ready to say. What is so unnatural, if not downright fantastic, about this passage, is that Leichtlebig corroborates the authority of the Doctor's "you": "How do you know this? It's true, the bit about the white bread on Sunday. And the trips, that's true too. And about the bugs" (Woher wissen Sie das? Das stimmt, das mit dem Weissbrot am Sonntag. Und der Ausflug stimmt auch. Und auch das mit den Wanzen).[54] With these corroborations, Leichtlebig confirms that Bernhard's text has performed an act of ontological crossing, a metalepsis that nullifies the distinction between the embedd*ing* discourse of the narrator and the embed*ded* speech of a character. This scene is therefore the locus of what Brian McHale calls a narrative "anarchism," which cannot decide between different ontological orders.[55] The first, commonsensical ontological order is structured as a world of individual characters whose separate fates cross yet remain distinct; simply put, it is the plausible fictional ontology of a novel set in postwar Upper Austria. The second, alogical and nihilistic ontological order is that of the Doctor's mental "darkness," in which time, space, and the principle of individuation are cancelled out; distinct positions bleed together into an opaque oneness. This order is encapsulated by the Doctor's response to Leichtlebig after the latter expresses his disbelief at the Doctor's otherworldly access to worldly information: "You see, Leichtlebig, everything is true. Everything is always true" (Sehen Sie, Leichtlebig, sagte der Doktor, alles stimmt, immer stimmt alles).[56] His statements about Leichtlebig's childhood are true because *everything* is true. With this sentence, the Doctor opens a portal into which the entire rest of the text is pulled. The manuscript *Leichtlebig* is one of an infinite array of potential statements, all of which would be equally true.

As skeptical readers, we would have good reason to invalidate such statements for being logically incoherent, or simply insane. Interestingly, this is precisely where *Leichtlebig* opens room for debate over the validity of the Doctor's nihilist claims to capturing a "monstrous universality" (AEW, 11) Leichtlebig speaks up and talks back. Having witnessed the Doctor's strange feat of omniscience, Leichtlebig calls out the obvious inequality of their relationship and points to the epistemological hierarchy that has emerged in the past scene: "It is easy for you to talk like this. A person like you, who knows everything, and who can say everything that he thinks to himself. I cannot say what I think to myself" (Es ist ja für Sie einfach, so zu reden. Ein Mensch wie Sie, der alles weiss, und der auch alles sagen kann, wie er es sich denkt. Ich kann nicht sagen, was ich mir denke).[57] Leichtlebig resists the Doctor's newly revealed access to private information, suggesting that such a transcendent, omniscient perspective is the concretization of past privileges and that the "monstrous universality" contained in the Doctor's speech is the product of power relations. It is only through Leichtlebig's *contestation* of the Doctor's nihilistic authority that Bernhard's novel turns into a bona fide case of narrative anarchy. A vacuum of narrative authority opens up as Leichtlebig and the Doctor engage in a debate about where the power of authentication is to be located, and why. Leichtlebig, in other words, also has the opportunity to contest and revoke the substance of the Doctor's claims, placing them, too, under erasure. Such is the paradoxical, anarchic nature of the text: there is no authority anywhere in the text that could guarantee the substantiality of any particular ontology. Perpetual inversion is the norm. Once this anarchy emerges, it can be revised but not revoked. Both characters are stuck together in it.

The narrative anarchy of *Leichtlebig* is not, however, entirely aimless. The chaotic thicket of fates in the manuscript's pages has a marked purpose, providing the reader with an occasion to rethink the relations that make community. In the moment that the Doctor reveals his intimate knowledge of Leichtlebig's life, the two coexist within an impossible community, which is as unsettling for Leichtlebig as it is for a reader of the text. They contradict each other's existence and cancel out each other's fate, but *this contradiction and cancellation is their common ground.* It is precisely in this unnatural scene that the themes of political community (and conspiracy) come to the forefront. While detailing Leichtlebig's upbringing, the Doctor calls up an intergenerational conflict between socialism and communism that played out in Leichtlebig's family:

> Your father was a socialist, wasn't he? You became a communist. . . . You visited illegal meetings in the railroad quarter, even had the courage to say something. . . . Yes, yes, you don't have to [say], I won't force you! I can't force you! I don't want to force you!

> Ihr Vater war Sozialist, nicht wahr? Sie sind Kommunist geworden. . . . Sie haben die illegalen Versammlungen im Eisenbahnviertel besucht, haben sich sogar etwas zu sagen getraut, Leichtlebig. . . . Jaja, Sie müssen nicht, ich zwinge Sie nicht! ich kann Sie nicht zwingen! ich will Sie nicht zwingen![58]

This strange set of statements wavers between a respect for Leichtlebig's autonomy ("I won't force you") and a determination to expose an untold story about Leichtlebig's political involvement. Ironically, it is precisely by speaking *for* Leichtlebig that the Doctor reveals a secret history of covert agency and voice: Leichtlebig went to communist meetings, where he felt empowered to actively voice his views. Moreover, this talk of secret communist meetings connects Leichtlebig's story to the underground resistance group of railroad workers that formed in Attnang-Puchheim during the Second World War; the communists, after all, were one of the few political groups in Austria involved in armed resistance against the Nazis.[59] When the Doctor oversteps the limitations of time and space and accesses a hidden cache of information on Leichtlebig, he excavates a whole range of new subtexts and semantic possibilities for the novel as a whole. In other words, the Doctor's metaleptic clairvoyance has pierced the surface of the fictional reality established thus far in the novel, exposing a second story that is immediately more conflicted and perilous than the one handed to the reader in the opening passages of *Leichtlebig*. In this story, the radical son grapples with the political legacy of his socialist father, devoting his moments alone to the study of Marxist-Leninism, privately harboring revolutionary thoughts about how the social and political world around him might be transformed. Narrative anarchy brings to light hidden political struggle.

The covert sympathy for communism, which puts Leichtlebig at odds with his father, also places him in closer proximity to the political positions of the Doctor, who elsewhere calls for the collectivization of Austrian countryside through a Soviet-style *kolkhoz* system in which private landholding is abolished.[60] Without referencing the machinations of a historical-materialist dialectic, the Doctor himself declares the obsolescence of socialism and the futurity of communism. One assumes that Leichtlebig would quietly agree at the point in the Doctor's monologue that veers into such sloganeering: "Socialism is dead. The future belongs to communism" (Der Sozialismus ist tot. Die Zukunft gehört dem Kommunismus).[61] A historicist aside is appropriate here: through these communist sympathies, both characters are marked as political outsiders within Austria of the immediate postwar era, which was characterized by a widespread hostility to anything that could be labeled as "communist." The 1950 general strikes inspired by the Austrian Communist Party, even if they never achieved a scale necessary for a seizure of political power, fueled a new flurry of anticommunist discourse that later shaped the political climate of the Second Republic. As the historian Jill Lewis has shown, the 1950 strikes were important not because they represented a real *putsch* that would have aligned Austria with the USSR, but because the strikes prompted politicians to *speak* of an imminent communist takeover as an actual danger to the stabilization of Austrian society.[62] The imagination of conspiracy, rather than an actual immanent conspiracy, shaped the terms of Austrian political discourse.

Bernhard's *Leichtlebig* responds to this trend in Austrian politics by inserting its main characters into an "unreal" communist conspiracy of a very different kind. It is not that Bernhard dramatizes a *putsch* in his novel. The meeting of Leichtlebig and the Doctor, as two communist sympathizers from drastically different socioeconomic backgrounds, does not properly "take place" or "happen" in any conventional sense. Rather, the communist community arises as an anarchic, interframe relation within the text of *Leichtlebig*. The boundaries between their respective solitudes become permeable in a way that unsettles the parameters of time and space previously established in the story. The conspiracy (breathing-together) of the two characters occurs as a *fracture* in the fabric of reality, under the auspices of a major (and patently unnatural) "plot hole" that allows the Doctor to know things he cannot know and allows Leichtlebig to share things that he cannot share. The opening of this plot hole is the center of the novel. Again, it is not that two "communists" meet and fashion a plan about how to seize political power in the future. Rather, the fates of these two radically solitary characters collide in the tangled verbal thicket of Bernhard's text, which permits chaotic shortcuts across temporal and spatial divides. *Leichtlebig* does not narrate the formation of an immanent political community that could be described by an identity such as "*we, the communists.*" The collectivity of the Doctor and Leichtlebig is better captured by the following statement, which I make on their behalf: "*The two of us are speaking between across the gap between our two respective worlds, both of which are equally bleak and equally false. Each of us has the ability to cancel out the other's world using the power of speech, exposing its falsity and fragility.*" It is as if, with the stream of breath that accompanies a speech, each character is capable of swallowing the other character's world. Leichtlebig and the Doctor become a collective of unworldly communists simply by virtue of this common project of continual abolition, which never allows any reality to become frozen in a fixed set of circumstances.

In this way, Bernhard's text recalls the idea of "literary communism" that Jean-Luc Nancy developed to describe the form of togetherness enabled by literature in general. Literary communism is not a political system but rather the "compearance" (appearing-together) of distinct solitudes, separated by chasms of time and space.[63] Literature involves the exposure of a singular, solitary voice to nobody in particular, yet never only to oneself. Speaking to nobody in particular, the solitary voice exposes itself alongside other solitary voices and exists solely *for* these other voices. Nothing else exists "between" these voices. As such, Nancy's conception of community adheres to a familiar postmodernist strain of ontological uncertainty, imagining how community is at once "there but not there," a present absence or absent presence.[64] We exist together by virtue of the abyss that separates us. This is a communal circumstance that, for Nancy, cannot be represented directly through a positive assertion of identity (for example, "We the People," "Workers of the World") but becomes evident *through* the self-exposure of a linguistic subject (the "singular being") that lets itself appear through literature, which for Nancy is a medium that withdraws foundations rather than providing them. In short, Nancy leaves intact an idea of "communism," and of "community," which involves candid acknowledgment that each of us is teetering over the threshold of the void. Each of us is finite, mortal, close to death, almost not here, or lightly, light-living, or *leichtlebig*.

What separates Bernhard's vision of community from Nancy's, however, is the former's anarchic overtones, which surround the entire project with a mood of danger and revolt. The common void in *Leichtlebig* is not exposed (as it is for Nancy) through *any* act of "sharing voices."[65] Rather, in Bernhard's novel, the common void must be exposed through an incessant monologue of refusal and revocation, which actively calls everything around it into question. The negative force of Schopenhauer's pessimism, combined with the Underground Man's act of "pouring from empty into void," provide Bernhard's characters with a vision of community that aggressively subverts the available social and political positions of the postwar era (*NU*, 18). Drawing on those literary resources, *Leichtlebig* insists that implausible, not to say impossible, alternatives are the only ones worth writing about.

Chapter 5

✦

Nobody's Friends

Outside Community in Wolfgang Hilbig's Prose

Even though it has continually connected back to nineteenth-century nihilism, the story of private anarchy told in the previous chapters of this book has borrowed generously from the theoretical and literary resources of postmodernism. The verbal voiding of the world performed by fictional characters is readily describable in terms developed by Brian McHale, who shows how postmodernist fiction tends to foreground ontological problems.[1] McHale discusses metalepsis as a device that plays with the boundaries of distinct worlds, testing their volatility. In the fictions of Landauer, Kafka, and Bernhard, metalepsis has the same role. Their texts display the postmodern tendency to play with the boundary between fiction and reality, creating a "paradoxical continuity between nested narrative and primary narrative."[2] Such stories are literally everywhere in the latter half of the twentieth century, whether in postmodernist literature or pop culture: a film within a novel becomes reality; a film character steps into the television show they are watching; a map becomes coextensive with the whole world. This explosion of metaleptic fictions, for McHale, is tied to the emergence of a new "ontological" dominant in postmodernist art.[3] Such art is concerned with how different media (literature, film, television shows, advertising, computer simulations) create distinct worlds and how contemporary readers and/or consumers must navigate between numerous incompatible worlds and realities. The question therefore arises: at what point, and from what perspective, does the postnihilist tradition of private anarchy lose its literary specificity? When is it valid to subsume the metaleptic fictions of these German-language authors into the genealogy of transnational postmodernism?

The question is particularly salient since these authors explore ideas of community that are describable in terms provided by poststructuralist theorists of community—works that are themselves a facet of global postmodernism's interrogation of essences, immanent presence, and universal truths. For instance, the theories of "inoperative community" and "literary communism" developed by Jean-Luc Nancy, because they dismantle a strict distinction between solitude and collectivity, have been useful in describing the solidarity of isolation found in the works of Landauer, Kafka, and Bernhard. If the literature of private anarchy is so consistently describable in postmodernist terms, then it must be asked whether there is some juncture in literary history at which this fairly obscure stream of German-language literature flows into the wider sea of transnational postmodernism. If we can take recourse to the discourses of postmodernism, can we really insist on the historical particularity, and eccentricity, of private anarchy?

So far, I have managed to avoid this question because of the relative obscurity and prematurity of the texts under consideration: Landauer's *Death Preacher*, Kafka's "Description of a Struggle," and Bernhard's *Leichtlebig* are in each case among the author's earliest and most obscure works. Landauer's novel hardly found any readers at all (as he himself acknowledged in the preface of its second edition) (*DT*, 98). Kafka's and Bernhard's texts were only posthumously published, and even then only with an arbitrary editorial authority that smoothed over the author's many deletions and corrections. These are not the stories that made these authors famous. Indeed, many of the most important passages for my reading of Bernhard's *Leichtlebig* are buried under the author's pencil strikethroughs. As such, it has been possible to understand the eccentric nihilism of these texts apart from broad cultural movements of modernism and postmodernism. As we read ahead in literary history, however, the distinct contours of private anarchy begin to dissolve. Its ideas of community no longer seem out of place; its metaleptic transgressions seem familiar. Initially, unworldly anarchism was a distinct tradition of experimental fiction, but eventually it merges with a dominant aesthetic of the late twentieth century.

In this chapter, I will locate the writings of the East German "outsider" writer Wolfgang Hilbig at this tipping point, between unworldly anarchism and postmodernism. Hilbig's prose shares a number of reference points with the authors of private anarchy. The verbal nihilism of Dostoevsky is evident in Hilbig's "underground language" (Kellersprache),[4] and he directly evokes Kafka's conceit of a "society of nobodies" in his 1991 story "Old Rendering Plant" ("Alte Abdeckerei"), describing a shadowy community of outsiders who are "nobody's friend" (niemandes Freund).[5] These friends of nobody communicate to one another by not communicating: "they did not even seem have contact to their own kind" (sie schienen nicht einmal mit ihresgleichen umzugehen) (AA, 181). Moreover, as with Landauer's and Bernhard's early works, Hilbig develops his vision as a retort to a prevailing form of socialism. His texts respond to the oppressiveness of the East German police state by developing a vision of society bound together through sheer antisociality and nihilist selflessness, carrying the norms of the "closed society" of the German Democratic Republic (GDR) to perverse extremes (180). In short, the most alienating aspects of GDR life become a blueprint for a shared world that is radically opposed to and ontologically distinct from it. In imagining this radically alienated society of nobodies existing below the surface of "this" world of the GDR, Hilbig intersects with the postnihilist tradition that I have identified in the last three chapters. Yet just as Hilbig joins with this postnihilist tradition, his prose also closely mirrors postmodernist norms of virtual or spectral community—even if he himself vehemently took distance from postmodernism in public statements (which have in turn impacted critical and scholarly reception of his works).[6] The shadowy collectives of outsiders imagined by Hilbig are classically nihilist: grotesque, antisocial, and inhuman to a downright supernatural extent. Yet these nihilist collectives also exemplify an idea of being "alone together" that is readily familiar to us from the Internet age and resonates with Giorgio Agamben's obviously postmodern notion of a "coming community," which will take shape in our fully mediatized world, where a "we" comes together as a huddle of weightless avatars, defined by sheer exteriority qua superficiality.[7] Hilbig, too, imagines that, once "we" are reduced to total superficiality, a new community of nullified selves will emerge. As such, Hilbig's prose is an interesting conduit between the nineteenth-century nihilist underground and the collective isolation of our twenty-first-century social media world. His novels are rooted in the comparatively classical art of verbal nihilism, yet they point into our own mediatized (and postmodern) present, in which the distinction between virtual and real community is, if not erased, then at least rendered insignificant within so many aspects of social life.

Literature as Monologue

To begin to understand the ways in which Hilbig oversees a convergence of classical verbal nihilism and postmodernist virtual community, it is helpful to turn to a speech he delivered to the German Academy of Language and Literature in 2002, when he was awarded the Georg Büchner Prize. This speech, entitled "Literature Is Monologue" ("Literatur ist Monolog"), recapitulates a vision of literature that the author had already repeatedly expressed through his narrative prose.[8] Bracketing out any discussion of aesthetics, Hilbig explains that literature is important because it as a medium permits the practice of solitude, which is everywhere forbidden in the course of social life. Literature categorically evades all forms of social and political control since it can only be produced and consumed in perfect isolation from the institutions that force people together into unequal power relations (the state, the media, and presumably also the family). Conversely, according to Hilbig, the literary relation that emerges between reader and writer escapes the manifold and ubiquitous coercions of social life because it does not involve a staged interaction between identifiable subjects. Rather, the literary relation emerges between anonymous nobodies who share nothing but the language of solitude. Monologue is literature, but it is also sociability *contra* the world.

In Hilbig's theory of unworldly sociability, literature is essentially identical to freedom. This freedom, since it can be expressed and practiced nowhere in society, is preserved in an entirely private language: not private in the sense of "exclusively owned" but in the sense of what I would call an "untapped channel" (the model of unfreedom for Hilbig is often the "tapped channel," the speech that is overhead by authorities in order to inculpate one or another individual). When Hilbig writes that "the place of literature is monologue" (der Platz der Literatur ist Monolog), he means that "monologue" is the protected vessel that houses literary expression, a language that is not only secret but also absolutely anonymous.[9] Literature qua freedom can only exist as such on terms of anonymity, by providing contact between two points of complete solitude: the solitary writer who produces the text without thinking of any particular reader, and a reader who reads without thinking of any particular writer. The only factor that unites author and reader before the fact is their nominal solitude. The "strange partnership" (sonderbar[e] Zweierbeziehung) between writer and reader consists in a common solitude that releases them both from social control.[10] The process begins, Hilbig states, when a writer

> oversteps the prohibition on solitude and brings his thoughts to paper. He may well be thinking of a reader, but he doesn't know this reader. If a text or a book comes out of that, it arrives through the detours of marketing to an equally solitary reader, who reads the monologue, he may think of the writer of the monologue, but he does not know him, he knows perhaps only very little about this writer, and if things go well, then a monologue develops in the head of the reader as well. This is how literature works, and it can only work in this way.

> den Verbot des Alleinseins übertritt und seine Gedanken zu Papier bringt. Er mag dabei wohl an einen Leser denken, aber er kennt den Leser nicht. Wenn daraus ein Text oder ein Buch wird, so gelangt dies über die Umwege des Vertriebs an einen ebenso einsamen Leser, der den Monolog liest, er mag dabei wohl an den Schreiber des Monologs denken, aber er kennt ihn nicht wirklich, er kennt vielleicht nur sehr wenig von diesem Schreiber, und wenn die Sache gut geht, dann entwickelt sich im Kopf des Lesers ebenfalls ein Monolog.—Auf diese Art funktioniert Literatur, und sie kann nur auf diese Art funktionieren.[11]

Literature exists through the sharing of monologues. In this vision, it is a foregone conclusion that both solitude (not being with others) and anonymity (not being known by others) are inherently intolerable to both the state and the market, according to Hilbig. As such, literature (as Hilbig defines it) loses none of its subversive force under the altered political landscape after the disappearance of the GDR in 1990. The mass media perform actions that, as described by Hilbig, are parallel to those of the East German Secret Police. It is an infinite array of "tapped channels" permitting no privacy:

> The mass media are apparatuses for airing every secret, and they are thus apparatuses that serve forgetting. It seems to me that in the palaces of the mass media there exists no other intention but to rip everything new, everything that appears new, no matter at all what these novelties might be, into the light of the public sphere, to lend it the appearance of being up-to-date through habitual language use, in order to hawk it for sale.
>
> Die Massenmedien sind Apparate zur Lüftung jedweden Geheimnisses, und sie sind damit Apparate, die dem Vergessen dienen. Mir scheint, in den Palästen der Massenmedien existiert gar keine andere Absicht, als alles Neue, alles was neu erscheint, ganz gleichgültig, wie alt dieses Neue sein mag, an das Licht der Öffentlichkeit zu reißen, es mit dem Sprachgebrauch der Aktualität zu verkleiden, um es danach dem Verkauf feilzubieten.[12]

The implicit metaphor at work in Hilbig's account of social control is that of industrial processing: both the secret police and the mass media harvest the raw material of human interiority and process it into a form that can be accessed and consumed on a massive scale. Against these systems of control, Hilbig posits literature as a kind of private network that cannot be accessed by the powers that be, and where complete freedom is possible on the conditions of total anonymity. Literature is a kind of remote counterculture, a second world beyond the world.

Hilbig's remarks have a subversive agenda, but the form of community he described was arguably akin to the dominant postmodernist model of community. Around the same time that Hilbig was receiving wider recognition in the 1990s, the Australian sociologist Michele Willson (writing in 1997) gave a general account of this new model. Willson noted a parallel between approaches to community in the works of poststructuralist thinkers such as Jean-Luc Nancy and those that arose in new discourses of virtual community on the Internet. Willson described how "theorists of both technological and non-technological orientation have *removed community from a tangible, embodied or concrete possibility*, relegating it either to the sphere of ontological, pre-political, pre-historical existence; or to an experiential existence within the nodes of a computer network system."[13] Both in theory and online, community ceases to be a practical, immanent involvement with others and becomes a mode of *appearing* and *withdrawing* at the same time. Nancy refutes the commonplace notion that community consists in a shared identity and argues that community is instead the "*play* of the articulations" of singular beings, who appear differently each time to one another.[14] Where does this "play" occur? Nancy makes clear that *literature* is the proper site for such appearing-together, where singular qua solitary voices can be shared. Literature is *the* social media. Nancy's 1973 *Inoperative Community* began to circulate widely in the 1980s, contemporary to the creation of the first "communities" on the emergent Internet, which were built on the promise that virtual togetherness would allow an unprecedented "play of articulations" that would be based (unlike in Nancy's theory) on disembodied self-presentation through freely chosen avatars.[15] In both cases, "community" turns into the name for a *networked solitude* facilitated by electronic or print media. Hilbig, too, imagined communities of solitude in several of his best-known stories.

Hilbig's Pathways from "I" to "We"

Wolfgang Hilbig's notable stories "Old Rendering Plant" ("Alte Abdeckerei," 1991) and "The Lore of the Trees" ("Die Kunde von den Bäumen," 1992) appeared in print around the same time as this convergence between poststructuralist theory and electronic social media. Both of these texts, which describe the oppression and alienation of life in the GDR, are built around the idea of literature as monologue that Hilbig articulated so succinctly in 2002. Each text repeatedly plays through process of setting up a networked solitude where one alien's monologue becomes a medium for reaching other aliens. The protagonist of each text drops out of social life, refuses work, and wanders into the geographical and cultural peripheries of industrial society. This protagonist is initiated into a community of antisocial outsiders who do not communicate directly with one another but rather establish bonds by performing an evasion of communication. Hilbig's stories are quite confusing to read because this arc of initiation involves the disorienting mutation of monologue into chorus. A radically solitary "I" turns into a choral "we" by telling its story of rejection and communion. This transformative arc is so consistent across and within Hilbig's texts that it becomes generic, that is, it becomes a convention of Hilbig's own private genre of storytelling. In this genre, the conversion of the "I" into a "we" is sealed at a point of metalepsis, where distinct voices bleed into one another. The narrator's voice is possessed by the language of the other alien characters, and he becomes a medium for the announcement of their community. Metalepsis is the seal of community.

In Hilbig's fiction, the metaleptic rupture of the narrator's monologue is continually represented as the moment where literature as such comes into its own. Literature is not properly literature until the narrator has undergone a ritual dissolution where his voice melts into those of the underground community. The ritual is the same across Hilbig's different texts: the monologic narrator tells of how he breaks off contact from his usual social circles and goes to walk among the despoiled landscapes outside of the industrial city where he lives. Having crossed into this wasteland, he intuits the presence of a shadowy community that has collectively followed this same path of dejection before him. Having picked up signals from these shadowy others, the narrator is converted into "one of them" and begins to speak in chorus, on behalf of this community but not as the result of a tangible meeting between the "I" and these shadowy others. Rather, the "we" is spoken in the wake of what appears to be a *possession* of the one by the many. It is as if the protagonist has, by breathing in the polluted air of the wasteland, also taken a multitude of other voices into himself, so that he now contains an entire chorus of outsiders.

The "punch line" of this strange process is that this chorus of outsiders is nothing other than literature. The narrator joins this collective of nobodies, whom he refers to collectively as "nobody's friend" (niemandes Freund) (AA, 181). In affirming his kinship with these nobodies, the narrator also underscores his fidelity to literary tradition; he articulates this kinship by quoting the anarchic and experimental language of James Joyce's *Finnegans Wake* (in "Old Rendering Plant") or by replicating the demonic narrative of Fyodor Dostoevsky's *Demons* (in "The Lore of the Trees").[16] These intertextual allusions function almost like passwords, necessary for execution of the initiation process. However strange this biographical sequence sounds, it is ultimately a process of naturalization, which installs an idea of what literary narrative is and who is authorized to pronounce it. Literature is a subculture of (always male) misanthropes who have been rejected by the world and have in turn rejected it, and who through the absorption of a secret vernacular are recruited into its underground community.

Hilbig constructs his idea of literature on the basis of a particular image of the outsider as an unworldly being. The Hungarian novelist László Krasznahorkai, a sympathetic reader and critic of Hilbig's works, shows how Hilbig's idea of the "alien" is embedded within the author's cosmology (consistent across his works) that strictly distinguishes between those in charge and the ones who are not even allowed to exist:

> This world really does have its own rules, and there are those who realize and maintain its organization structures, since this is their world, a world in which the aggressive, mean-spirited, cowardly, servile . . . is the lord, pursuing at his pleasure those who are alien

> in his world, which he creates again and again; the alien, those who don't belong there, whose existence cannot be legitimated—indeed, the unfortunates who cannot legitimate themselves.[17]

The protagonists of Hilbig's stories are, in each case, members of the outsider class that Krasznahorkai calls "the alien." Their native language is, by necessity, monologue, because they are incapable of any form of social self-legitimation. Only speech that *nobody* hears could grant them any degree of autonomy or agency. Their monologues are consequently otherworldly, announcing their foreignness from *this* world and their attachment to a space beyond the world. The alien's monologues establish a community, but not one that is located in this world. Instead, community appears and reappears as the violation of spatial and temporal boundaries. The metaleptic transgressions associated with the alien's monologue confirm that the alien is *not here* with the rest of humanity but is *over there* in the otherworldly community of literature.

As such, it makes some sense to speak of a "utopian" side of Hilbig's works, and technically this is a fitting description because of how his community of outsiders coalesces in a *nowhere*, beyond the world. However, the communities envisioned in Hilbig's prose are consistently abject, morbid, and disgusting, located at the peripheries of the material world where fixed forms dissolve into slime and junk. His characters join these communities by following the same routes travelled by industrial runoff, consumer waste, and destroyed nature. To be initiated into the circle of nobodies, the outsider must re-create the "disappearing act" performed by garbage and dying nature. Hilbig's visions of environmental catastrophe and degradation squarely locate his texts within the "era of ecology" that began around 1970, and that also found expression among dissident intellectuals in socialist East Germany.[18] Yet Hilbig's fictional outsider communities do not exhibit a familiar solidarity with nature, in the manner of environmental activist groups of the time on either side of the Iron Curtain. These outsider communities do not come together in celebration of beautiful, threatened nature.

Instead, Hilbig's negative communities are always adorned with grotesque material remains of nature that has been nullified by human industry—celebrating precisely the images that environmentalists used as warning signs. Hilbig's stories experiment with the unsettling idea that living as a mass of talking slime, or underneath a pile of garbage, would be preferable to the status quo of the "false environment" of socialist East Germany.[19] Taking on the avatars of ash and slime, the community marks the boundaries of its secret and forbidden realm, where the world has become *nothing* in the material sense, and where *nobody* would want to go. Whereas Kafka's "Description of a Struggle" created an image of nihilist communion through images of thin air, voids, and abysses, Hilbig's texts derive their vision of "nowhere" from a catastrophic ecological consciousness that only began to circulate widely in the late twentieth century. The narrators of "Old Rendering Plant" and "The Lore of the Trees," perversely, claim ownership *of* and kinship *with* pollution. Each narrator fashions out of pollution a separate world, into which he can escape and where he can properly belong. Perversely, Hilbig's earlier stories fabulate communities decorated with the icons of environmental disaster.

From a critical distance, we can identify this model of community as Hilbig's morbid, and in my view, highly problematic attempt to come to terms with the German past. His texts create multistable images, where images of industrial pollution immediately remind readers of the horrors of the Holocaust (for instance, through the trope of ash). The outsiders in "Old Rendering Plant" openly acknowledge the Holocaust when declaring that they are "stumbling over mass graves" (stolpernd über Massengräbern) (175). Their own identification with dead matter is, then, not only a mirror of environmental destruction but a way of accessing the history of mass murder. Their "underground" existence is supposed to be a way of dwelling closer to the remains of the dead. This unsettling way of invoking the victims of National Socialism should raise ethical concerns about Hilbig's prose, which fashions ambiguous grotesques that recall the dehumanization perpetrated by the Nazi regime but without recuperating the humanity of those who were dehumanized. As distasteful and unsettling as Hilbig's visions may be, I will attempt to reconstruct the narrative logic that creates them and upholds them as an alternative to prevailing models of social solidarity.

In terms of genre, both "Old Rendering Plant" and "The Lore of the Trees" can be categorized as narrative monologues, which hold together through the insistent and incessant act of telling by the protagonist—and not so much through a coherent, consistent sequence of events that can be clearly reconstructed by the reader. Each work is thematically but not chronologically or ontologically consistent. The question of what is "real" retreats behind different articulations of the same basic story of alienation, which takes place in multiple simultaneous storyworlds. "The Lore of the Trees" is presented as the transcribed speech of a man named Waller, who describes repeatedly how he came to be initiated into a circle of outsiders. These outsiders dwell among the debris of GDR society, and also apparently outside the known world. What is important about Waller's monologue is not its credibility but rather its performative effect. It is effectively a disappearing act, staging the vanishing of Waller's individual voice into the collective of the garbageman, which happens "right before the eyes" of the reader (who is reading the transcription of an unnamed narrator). Likewise, "Old Rendering Plant" is a single stream of prose that does not present a unified, linear biographical plot that could be easily reconstructed in terms of the protagonist's start- and endpoint. Rather, the monologue presents a multitude of similar arcs, playing through different stages of the same initiation ritual several times. What the protagonist calls his "path to the margin of society" (Weg zum Rand der Gesellschaft) is modeled multiple times, with increasing intensity, until the text terminates in a de-individuated voice that lacks both an "I" and a "we" (AA, 77). The narrator sheds his individual identity to speak in the collective voice of the "nobodies" who are sequestered in their underground world. The text bears witness to a process of disappearance, initiation, and possession.

Outsider Community in "Old Rendering Plant"

The first steps toward this initiation occur early on in "Old Rendering Plant," when the protagonist recalls how in his youth he sensed the existence of an alternate world of abject persons. He recalls how as a young man he first heard his family speak of the "*vanished ones*" (*Verschwundenen*), who had stepped "out of our circle" (aus unserem Umkreis) (131, 129). If we read historically, it is obvious where this discourse comes from: this abstract category of "disappeared people" is easily recognizable as the part of the population that fled the GDR in the years after its founding, and whose departures eventually triggered the construction of the Berlin Wall. However, instead of pointing the protagonist to the possibility of escaping to the West, his connection to the vanished ones gives him the promise of another reality: he imagines a second version of himself "in another territory, within another condition, within an unknown reality" (in einem anderen Territorium, innerhalb eines anderen Zustands, innerhalb einer unbekannten Realität) (131).

A decisive step in the narrator's movement into this unknown reality is his identification of himself as a "vanished" person. During his youth, he listens to state radio broadcasts announcing the names of the "vanished ones" in alphabetical order, and he imagines that his own name will be read from this list one day (155). Eventually, the crossing into the realm of the vanished is represented as a matter of heritage, as the narrator begins to think that his own family's origin marks him and his kin as "exiles" (162). His kind are not exiles from a particular place who have lost some particular identity; rather, they belong to a certain subclass that never belonged to this world in the first place:

> We were not exiles on the basis of a tidy idea that would enable resistance, but out of instability . . . out of simplemindedness, ignorance, asociality, we had not been torn from our roots, we were exiled because we had never had roots, we did not even try to find these, perhaps we look continually for the worst of all world regions in

order to rest in our rootlessness; like a gray vegetation . . . we settled in the desolate provinces, which were the refuge of malice, where we could proliferate lustfully and without struggle.

> So waren wir nicht Exilanten auf Grund einer sauberen widerstandsfähigen Idee, sondern solche aus Haltlosigkeit . . . aus Unbedarftheit, Unwissen, Asozialität, wir waren nicht von den Wurzeln gerissen worden, wir hatten nicht unsere Rechte verloren, wir waren exiliert, weil wir Wurzeln und Rechte nie gehabt hatten, wir suchten diese nicht einmal zu finden, vielleicht suchten wir andauernd nach der übelsten aller Weltgegenden, um in unserer Wurzellosigkeit auszuruhen; wie eine graue Vegetation . . . siedelten wir in den öden Provinzen, die der Hort der Bosheit waren, siedelten uns an zwischen Abraum und Schutt, wo wir geil und kampflos wuchern konnten. (166)

With this speculation, which may or may not be completely fabulated, the narrator establishes the predestination of his trajectory of escape. The "we" that he will seek out in the trashed margins of industrial society already exists; it is his heritage, both origin and destination. Despite the claims to familial identity put forth here, the narrator does not subsequently discover new connections to the cohabitants of his youthful home. Rather, he increasingly seeks out markers of a marginal status that will confirm his membership in the collective of exiles from this world. At school, he declares to his teacher and classmates his intention to go to work at the titular old rendering plant Germania II, an industrial site at the far edge of the city that pollutes the surrounding swampland with the acrid remains of slaughtered livestock (168). With this career choice, the protagonist retraces the first rebellions of his earlier youth, when he would wander out of the city into the polluted wasteland in the periphery. It is among the stigmatized workers of Germania II, who by the plant's name are associated with the darkest moments of the Nazi past, that the narrator will begin his initiation into underground community. He does not, however, begin this initiation by speaking directly to one of these workingmen, whom he repeatedly encounters in bars outside of town. Rather, he takes up contact with them by drinking alongside them, so that *initiation* is identical to *intoxication*, in the sense of letting a poison into oneself (177). Rather than communicating with them, he becomes one of them by letting himself be "polluted" alongside them, until his own sense of identity begins to dissipate. Intoxication leads gradually to a moment where individuality turns to indistinction, so that the narrator can claim ambiguously that "My conceptions of these men were primarily conceptions of myself" (Meine Vorstellungen von diesen Männern waren hauptsächlich Vorstellungen von mir selbst) (179). They are he, and he is them.

Language acquisition is a decisive element of the narrator's initiation into the outsider community. Drinking alongside these men, the narrator encounters a form of anticommunicative communication that renders dialogue impossible yet also establishes a solidarity between the men. For instance, while at the pub with the rendering plant workers, the narrator looks over their shoulders as they compose letters in the pubs, which contain "incomprehensible constructions" (unverständlichen Fügungen) transcribed in an "antiquated script" (antiquierten Schrift) (175). It is a language framed by natural decay, on the verge of being overrun by insects: "Ants crawled on the grubby sheet between the clueless blue words, which were nothing but curses" (Ameisen jagten sich auf dem schmuddligen Blatt zwischen den ratlos blauen Wörtern, die nichts als Flüche waren) (175). The theme of apocalypse is implicit in these descriptions of the rendering plant workers: they seem to dwell in a world that exists after the collapse of society and the atrophy of the earth itself, among the last survivors cursing their fate (in fiction of the Cold War era, it is often only the insects that survive). Apart from this written language of curses, the narrator is a witness to meaningless gestures and vocalizations by the same shadowy characters. Their gestures are "lost" and "uninterpretable," and their vocalizations are drawn from "animal languages," and so it as if the workers were "fleeing before their own language" (175). The narrator's attestations regarding this antilanguage do not build toward some discrete and revelatory event (for instance, where the narrator is approached by one of the men and drawn into their circle). All narrative information is, in these scenes, generic: it applies not to some particular scene but rather captures the consistency of ongoing and uneventful experience.

The confirmation of the narrator's transformation into "one of them" arrives in the form of a narrative metalepsis, as the narrator's telling *about* the "men of Germania II" and their language turns without transition into a ventriloquizing *of* their voices, which seem to have suddenly possessed him. The turning point of the text can be called, with Juri Lotman, an "explosion" of the narrator's established language, which has been triggered by the "intrusion" of a "discourse in non-existent language" into his own discourse.[20] Polluted by their anticommunicative practices, he acquires a new voice. Although their curses, cryptic gestures, and animal sounds have *not* been comprehended by the narrator, he nonetheless becomes a medium for the further dissemination of their antilanguage, which he relays directly to Hilbig's readers through his monologue. Without having engaged in any direct dialogue with the workers, the narrator telepathically transmits the "sentences in their heads" (Sätze im Kopf) without commentary (AA, 176). This ventriloquizing, consequently, affirms the narrator's successful initiation into the outsiders' community.

To mark the completion of his initiation, the narrator's voice is befallen by a sudden dystaxia, with conventional subject-object syntax vanishing into a paratactic stream. This stream appears as a conduit to a nonhuman sphere of existence, which allies the narrator's community to the degraded nature outside the cities. A crucial turning point arrives as the narrator begins to incant the language contained in the "letters" of his fellow rendering plant workers. Although he was describing their antilanguage externally a moment ago, now he reproduces it from within: "Letters to the meadows the elms the poplars the waters, O trees O tree of trees, O great tree grown from the graves for all trees, O great tree with the name *taboo*" (Briefe an die Weiden die Ulmen die Pappeln die Wasser, oh Bäume oh Baum von Bäumen, oh großer Baum gewachsen aus den Gräbern für alle Bäume, oh großer Baum mit dem Namen *Tabu*) (177). This nonexistent language is, for us as readers, also *poetic* language, which identifies the underground community of outsiders as a specifically *literary* grouping. This grouping, in turn, preserves the purity of artistic language against the dogmas of official socialist culture. This is evident from the polemical reference to Bertolt Brecht's antifascist poem "To Those Born After" ("An die Nachgeborenen"), which mentions how a "conversation about trees" is "almost a crime" because it takes attention away from human suffering.[21] The inhuman language of the "nobodies" in Hilbig's "Old Rendering Plant" breaks the alleged "taboo" set up by Brecht as a literary socialist. This polemical reading of Brecht's poem, in my view, is unfair, but it echoes a common retort to Brecht's critique of the "conversation about trees" among literary environmentalists in both the GDR and the Federal Republic of Germany (FRG).[22] Contra Brecht, Hilbig's outsiders "dare" to speak not only about trees, but *to* them. In ventriloquizing their apostrophe to the trees, the narrator proves both that he has acquired the native language of nobodies and that *he* does not exist as such any longer. He has imbibed their language of erasure and has successfully erased himself. This erasure is confirmed, formally speaking, by the elimination of the narrative's outermost discursive frame. At first, it is the narrator who cites and embeds the workers' voices (see diagram on p. 172).

In the wake of this citation, however, the reader cannot return to the reliable discourse of the same first-person narrator. From this point until the end of the text, a second structure of embedding asserts itself and culminates in the erasure of the narrator's individuality. His voice is only a function of the collective (see diagram on p. 173).

This metaleptic displacement of the narrator's individual voice by the choral voice of the workers is not the final step of initiation into the community of nobodies. For all their abjection and stigmatization, the "men of Germania II" are still a group with a determinate social identity, and they are known by that name within the social world in which the narrator grows up (AA, 179). It is only in the final moments of "Old Rendering Plant," which are devoid of human characters or perspectives, that the community of nobodies properly takes shape. In the story's final moments, which

Initial hierarchy of layers.

narrate the apocalyptic explosion and collapse of Germania II into a watery sinkhole, the narrating subject of "Old Rendering Plant" (both its grammatical subject and the subject who speaks) is established as a plural *nobody.* The nobodies are the narrator. The concluding experiences of the story are mediated entirely in this nonexistent language spoken by the "nobodies," so that the text itself becomes their testament:

> Nobody knew well enough what one was allowed to know, and nobody knew well enough to know, waters knew better what covered them, white fogs knew what they were doing, owls, ravens, spiders, rats knew—but nobody's clan knew nothing of the knowledge of the all the world.
>
> Niemand wußte gut genug, was man wissen durfte, und niemand wußte gut genug zu wissen. Wasser wußte besser, was sie bedeckten, weiße Nebel wußten, was sie trieben, Eulen, Dohlen, Spinnen, Ratten wußten. . . . Niemands Sippe aber wußte nichts vom Wissen aller Welt. (199)

This passage prompts two interpretations. It can be read as a statement on knowledge that is possessed by nobody *but* natural entities and is simply a

Eventual hierarchy of layers.

set of negative statements excluding all humans from a privileged knowledge of nature. On the other hand, as Ingo Schulze points out, the passage can be read as a set of statements about an entity called Nobody, and the group to which this Nobody belongs. In this case, "Nobody" is a "proper name" (Eigenname).[23] This interpretation is supported by the capitalized "N" of "Niemand," which implies it is not a pronoun but the avatar of a group. This group is radically inaccessible to those who participate in the human world—except through the form of the text we are reading.[24] In its final moments, the previously asserted narrative identities are folded into a new outermost frame, the subject of which is "nobody."

The concluding passage of "Old Rendering Plant" makes Hilbig's text into a direct descendent of "Description of a Struggle," establishing kinship with Kafka through a reiteration of the "society of nobodies." Not only through this intertextual allusion but also through its Joycean style, the passage seems to revive literary modernism: the free semiotic stream (or "stream of consciousness") represents the modernist hope for a new language through which the experience could be known and represented in totality. Yet while Hilbig's text is clearly indebted to the "nonexistent language" of high modernism, its relation to this tradition plays out in terms familiar to postmodernist fiction. The final pages of "Old Rendering Plant" create a pastiche of Joyce's and Kafka's nonexistent languages in a way that stresses their *ontological* dimension, their world-making capacity.[25] The literary pastiche shows how such language conjures and constitutes a separate fictional world—one that, in this case, is walled off from the everyday reality of East German society. More so than his literary antecedents, Hilbig verges on conventions of fantastic and speculative fiction, engaging in the business of building distinct worlds and setting up transit between them. "Old Rendering Plant" shares in what Brian McHale calls "the general diffusion of fantastic 'charge' throughout postmodernist writing," whereby "dialogue springs up between different ontological realms or levels."[26] In Hilbig's story, this dialogue takes the form of a perpetual metalepsis that becomes a structural norm of the text: we can always expect thoughts and words from the alien underworld to jump into that of the narrator, and via him, into the projected world of the reader. Our narrator, in "Old Rendering Plant," has crossed the boundary to the underworld and been utterly transformed, and his monologue has been sent back across that boundary to us, testifying to the underworld's existence. When a coherent grammatical subject falls out of this monologue, it appears as the language of an alien being with its own native territory and "clan" (AA, 199). Literature—as so often happens in postmodernist fiction—is ontologized as an alien world with its own autonomous existence.

Outsider Community in "The Lore of the Trees"

Hilbig's story "The Lore of the Trees," written around the time that "Old Rendering Plant" was published, continues the experiments of world-building undertaken in the latter. Both the form and content of this story are familiar from "Old Rendering Plant": a man named Waller delivers a narrative monologue that repeatedly loops through similar sequences of events, without adding up to an entirely coherent chronology. As in "Old Rendering Plant," this monologue testifies to a process of alienation, with Waller taking distance from his upbringing in an industrial town in East Germany and escaping into the wastelands at the urban periphery, where he makes contact with an otherworldly community of "garbagemen" (Müllmänner).[27] Eventually, he too is transfigured by this encounter, and his monologue becomes a chorus representing the outsider community, his "I" turning into a mysterious "we." As in "Old Rendering Plant," the process of initiation involves rituals of self-isolation that begin in the protagonist's youth and culminate in a bizarre communion in the wasteland. Even more clearly than in the previous story, the destruction of the natural environment is the defining feature of the East German society that Waller is trying to escape. He recalls his deep bond with a grove of cherry trees as a child, which subsequently were killed by air pollution and then cut down to make room for industrial development. Later in life, while walking around the former cherry grove, he discovers a garbage dump that soon becomes a refuge for his solitary existence, and where he tries to write a text in honor of the dead trees. This writing project fails, but Waller finds his way into the world of literature in another way, as he is gradually inducted into a circle of the anonymous "garbagemen" who work at the site when Waller is not around. These garbagemen, like the rendering plant workers, turn out to be the unlikely guardians of literature within the hostile environment of the GDR. Through the strange antics of these unseen men, the narrator of "The Lore of the Trees" establishes a connection to the work of Fyodor Dostoevsky and, by extension, to literary discourses of nihilism.

Waller sets up a writing desk in a hut next to the garbage dump where the cherry trees once stood and attempts to compose an ode to the trees. However, suffering from writer's block, he initiates a nonverbal "dialogue" with the garbagemen using discarded objects (DKB, 242). This dialogue of garbage takes on greater significance than Waller's attempted writing. He finds that the men have positioned several discarded mannequins in a circle, and the two parties begin to communicate by placing the figures into different poses, which are by turns expressive and vulgar. When Waller sets a mannequin at a writing desk with a pen in his hand, the garbagemen overturn it and place the pen in its rear end. This "dialogue" initially seems like pure parody, mocking both the possibility of writerly expression as well as any attempt to create literary community. Yet the relations that take shape through the mannequins also have a serious purpose. The bizarre garbage-dialogue ultimately grants Waller access to a world of literature that has been hidden from him until now. In this way, his individual voice will be subsumed into the chorus of outsiders. This process begins as a discarded novel appears in the hands of one of the effigies:

> Now the dialogue found no continuation for a few days, one changed nothing on the arrangement . . . until one set a book into the hands of my figure, which were sitting in its lap: she was a reader or a lecturer with a considerable audience. The book was a tattered prewar edition of the Demons by Dostoevsky.–The doorkeeper had not been changed, but now he was more of a warning figure: with an arm stretched out he pointed past the forest . . . and it was as if, from over there, the bell-ringing of the church in W. had rolled in. Underneath this sound, though, was suddenly something that resembled the shrill screeching of a herd of swine, which plunged itself into abysses . . . it was the squeaking and screeching of the bulldozers that were ripping into the village of W. In all excess, the noise of a storm's rolling thunder set in over this sound. What a ghostly scene!

> I thought.–Eventually I developed the conviction—and this was just as ghostly–, that it was only the garbagemen who in this age were capable of realizing a poetic thought.
>
> Nun fand der Dialog für einige Tage keine Fortsetzung, man veränderte nichts an dem Arrangement . . . bis man meiner sitzenden Figur ein Buch in die im Schoß liegenden Hände gedrückt hatte: sie war ein Leser oder ein Vorleser mit beträchtlichem Publikum. Das Buch war eine zwefledderte Vorkriegsausgabe der Dämonen von Dostojewski.–Den Torwächter hatte man nicht verändert, doch war er jetzt eher eine warnende Gestalt: mit ausgestrecktem Arm deutete er über den Wald hinweg . . . und es war, als sei von dort gerade das Glockenbimmeln der Kirche von W. herangedrungen. Unter dem Geläut aber war plötzlich etwas, das dem gellenden Kreischen einer Sauherde glich, die sich in Abgründe stürzte . . . es war das Quietschen und Kreischen der Bagger, die auf das Dörfchen W. losgingen. Zu allem Überfluß setzte über diesem Lärm das Donnerrollen eines Gewitters ein. Was für eine gespenstische Szene! dachte ich.–Nach und nach gewann ich die Überzeugung—und diese war ebenso gespenstisch–, es seien allein noch die Müllmänner, die in dieser Zeit einen poetischen Gedanken zu verwirklichen vermochten. (242–43)

This communication closely resembles the communion that Hilbig would later describe in his 2002 speech "Literature Is Monologue." Without ever meeting his new friends, Waller is connected to the garbagemen through Dostoevsky's book. The presence of the discarded novel triggers a set of fantastic qua metaleptic effects, collapsing spatial and temporal distances and opening a portal into the world of literature. As thunder rolls and bulldozers rumble in the distance, Waller is visited—without ever picking up the book to read it—by a vision of the swine presented in the biblical epigraph of Dostoevsky's *Demons*, from Luke 8:32–36.[28] The contents of the novel have literally jumped from the tattered cover of the book and created an "abyss" in the midst of Waller's world that will provide a subsequent escape route from the oppressive strictures of everyday life. As it turns out, the metaleptic transit triggered by the appearance of the *Demons* is demonic, remaining faithful to key themes of Dostoevsky's novel.

The *Demons* becomes a conduit for Hilbig's own renegotiation of the legacy of nihilism. We recall Thomas Bernhard identified the novel as a watershed for his own "radical" prose.[29] As it happens, Bernhard was not unique in this respect. The novel's polemics against nihilism have become canonical reference points for understanding the conspiratorial operations of modern radical politics, and this is also true of Hilbig.[30] The novel's classic story of conspiracy and violence is neatly encapsulated in Dostoevsky's brief biblical epigraph. A man, possessed by demons, allows them to pass out of him and enter a herd of pigs, "and the herd rushed down the steep bank into the lake and were drowned."[31] The "demons" in Dostoevsky's novel are, first of all, the (radical, atheist, anarchist) nihilist ideas of the charismatic and enigmatic Nikolai Stavrogin, which are absorbed in turn by a set of radical, "underground" characters like Alexei Kirillov and Pyotr Verkhovensky. Radicalism is an evil demon that jumps from one body to the next. All these characters allow themselves to be infected by the Stavrogin's nihilism, they are the the tools of an ideology, just as the herd of swine became the medium for demons. These characters are infected by the (for Dostoevsky) antisocial impulses of atheism and anarcho-nihilism, and are eventually driven to suicide and terrorism. The conspiratorial activities that unsettle a provincial Russian town are, following the epigraph, part of an ongoing process of transference where "evil thoughts" are passed from one person to the next, where the last recipient of these ideas brings about his own swift annihilation. Those who adopt revolutionary political ideas are, in this view, suicidal pigs who delude themselves into believing they are serving a higher purpose, when in fact they are only hastening their own destruction by carrying out the will of evil spirits. The downward plunge of the swine off the edge of a cliff already prefigures a downward movement back to hell. At the outset of Dostoevsky's novel, the message seems to be: nihilism needs company, it is an insatiable herd mentality that carries humanity to hell.

There are several ways to interpret the appearance of Dostoevsky's novel in "The Lore of the Trees" and its significance within the East German reality depicted in the story. One possible historical interpretation would go as follows: the demonic and metaleptic movement of the biblical pigs across time and space (from the Bible, into Dostoevsky's novel, into the garbage dump in Hilbig's story) establishes a straightforward continuity of nihilism as an evil that recurs throughout history. Waller and the garbagemen have rescued the "prewar edition" of the *Demons* in order to point to the "demonic possession" qua nihilism that has triggered the catastrophe of National Socialism and, afterward, the socialist GDR. In this way, Hilbig's text would be establishing a questionable, because homogenizing, explanation for the course of modern German history. What complicates this interpretation is that Hilbig's text (unlike Dostoevsky's novel) does not only invoke the trope of possession in order to condemn particular people's possession by radical politics. Rather, like the other authors studied in this book, Hilbig's characters actually *affirm* some of the heretical postures that Dostoevsky meant to condemn. The narrator Waller becomes *aligned* with the demonic nihilism of the swine, who signify not only radical evil but also the transhistorical power of literature.

"The Lore of the Trees" derives from the *Demons* a fascination with the possibilities of possession. Waller himself becomes "possessed" by the spirit of literature (the squeal of the pigs leaps from the book into him), and he himself seeks to become a kind of "nihilist scum" (the subhuman class of nihilists against whom Dostoevsky wrote).[32] The demonically possessed pigs, which metaleptically leap out of the tattered book and into the atmosphere above Waller, are mascots of literary communication, which enables contact across massive gaps in time and space. The biblical pigs, which for Dostoevsky could signify the radical underground of Russian life, are once again resurrected to signify the industrial nightmare of the twentieth century, and Hilbig folds their plunge into the abyss into an all-encompassing storm that has raged from antiquity to the immediate present. As such, the pigs signify the transhistorical transmission that is uniquely enabled by literature. Hilbig pursued a similar thought in his speech "Literature Is Monologue," where literary communication only ever takes place between a solitary-anonymous writer and a solitary-anonymous reader. A monologue is written down, exported, and sent off, then picked up and turned into another monologue in the head of the recipient. So it is with the pigs, who squeal for one reader in one era, then another, and then yet another.

The garbagemen complement the pigs, as they too are involved in the resurrection of the voices of the discarded worlds of the past. They are the protectors of literary community because their labor of garbage-picking ensures the continued transmission of messages across the chasms of history. Hilbig's text, then, makes an immodest and openly hyperbolic claim on behalf of literature even in its most paltry materializations (that is, a tattered old paperback). Literature conjures a possible world of unity and coherence that goes unrealized during the reproduction of everyday life. In this other world, the regimen of productive labor (where nature is converted into finished products) is overtaken and reversed as the discarded by-products of industry come to life again in a way that is either antimaterialist or hypermaterialist; the first and best example for this resurrection of lost material is the discarded copy of Dostoevsky's *Demons*, which ceases to be one lost thing among others and begins to actively reshape the atmosphere above and around the narrator once it has been placed into the hands of the mannequin. It is as if, were we to reassemble discrete pieces of garbage in just the right way, they would come to life and replace the world that threw them away with one where there is free traffic between past and present, and where nothing discarded is lost.

The demonic power of Dostoevsky's novel in "The Lore of the Trees" permits the protagonist a perspective that is unrestricted to any single position in time and space. In the "ghostly scene" curated by the garbage workers, Waller gains a perspective on an impending "storm" that unsettles the established narrative world. The storm is not merely meteorological; it is an all-encompassing oblivion that engulfs and encompasses the very fabric of reality, upsetting the relations of past and present, cause and effect, dead and living, narrator and narrated. One example of this oblivion is the cluster of dark clouds that resculpts and repopulates the landscape below as it passes overhead. The clouds actually seem to *contain* the past and can conjure lost objects and beings. The cherry trees, those mourned objects to which Waller has dedicated his entire monologue, suddenly and impossibly reappear out of the clouds:

> Full of black melancholy I looked to the place where they had once stood . . . there they had at their disposition a previously untold episode, they hung there as a shadow on the sky: out of ever-darkening clouds there dripped a few forked branches of shadows, like streams of water coming from above, which were washed in a burnt-yellow light.
>
> Voll schwarzer Melancholie blickte ich zu ihrem einstigen Ort hinüber . . . sie hatten dort noch eine bisher verschwiegene Episode parat, sie hingen dort als Schatten am Himmel: aus immer dunkler gewordenen Wolken träuften dort einige seltsam gegabelte Zweige von Schatten herab, wie von oben kommende Wasserstränge, die von einem brandgelben Licht umspült waren. (243)

An absurd order of things emerges, as the insubstantial turns substantial. This unnatural occurrence, as described by Waller, confirms the perpetual metalepsis of Hilbig's "Lore of the Trees," whereby linguistic entities and fantasies are constantly being ontologized, jumping from the world of memory into "this" world. The vanished cherry trees descend from the clouds as shadows, taking on form and color despite their definitively established absence. The lightning of the storm, too, exhibits a similarly fantastic conjuring-effect: "and suddenly I thought I saw in the light of the first lightning flashes the trees of the cherry alley, once or twice their grotesque figures emerged from the darkness, they strove with the haste of storm-hunted wanderers to the edge of the forest" (und plötzlich glaubte ich im Licht der ersten Blitze die Bäume der Kirschallee zu sehen, ein-, zweimal traten ihre grotesken Gestalten aus der Finsternis hervor, sie strebten mit der Hast von sturmgejagten Wanderern auf den Rand des Waldes zu) (245). The trees are resurrected under the flash of lightning like refugees fleeing their removal by woodcutters, which (again, has been established) already happened years earlier. The "ghostly scene" that Waller recognized first when seeing the *Demons* continues here, as the dead trees reappear to reenact the moments preceding their destruction. With these unnatural reversals of time, it becomes clear that the storm pictured by Waller is a storm of history, a disaster that unites disparate moments of time and tosses up the debris of the past before Waller's eyes.

It is no coincidence that such a history of disaster and decay recalls the writings of Walter Benjamin; Hilbig borrows the epigraph of "The Lore of the Trees" from Benjamin, where the latter laments the collective loss of the "ability to tell a tale properly" (83). The unifying mode of "poetic thought" expressed in the "ghostly scene" of the storm immediately recalls the way of seeing associated with Walter Benjamin's "angel of history," as described in his 1940 *Theses on the Philosophy of History*. The angel of history, like the garbage workers and Waller after them, perceives progress in its totality as a storm. The angel sees not a "chain of events" but rather "one single catastrophe which keeps piling wreckage upon wreckage."[33] It is not possible, from the angel's vantage point, to narrate history in terms of discrete occurrences. The sheer violence of historical progress forces everything into a destructive totality, disallowing any simple linear account. Indeed, the reason the garbage workers have been able to preserve something akin to poetic storytelling is because they already see *everything* as debris. Like the angel of history, the garbage workers consider all things in relation to the catastrophe that nullifies and degrades them to the status of wreckage: "before the garbage workers the things had removed the limitations of their usefulness and began to tell stories . . . and so in our eyes they reached out past their perishing" (DKB, 243). Waller, we recall, saw the cherry trees return amid the storm. When he is possessed by "poetic thought," which sees personal and collective history *as* a storm, Waller can restore a vision of the world's unity. This unity is located by Hilbig's writing (in classic postmodernist fashion) in an ontologically separate realm, a shadow world or "world next door," which is created by the imaginative act of storytelling.[34] It is only from within this virtual, unified world that Waller can confirm the existence of a community and change the subject of his monologue from "I" to "we."

Hilbig's fiction, as László Krasznahorkai has suggested, outwardly reflects a "monochromous" world that can only induce disgust and despair.[35] The vantage point opened by the garbage workers would seem to confirm this, since it relies on a monochrome, unifying optic that sees *everything in the world as garbage*. This negative unity has a positive consequence: the garbage workers, by recognizing the absolute negativity of human history, provide Waller with a new possibility of community, specifically a *community of those who see the desolation*. Waller cannot find any one name for this community, calling the garbage workers "my colleagues, my acquaintances, my countrymen, my neighbors, my custodians of literature" (meine Kollegen, meine Bekannten, meine Landsleute, meine Nächsten, die Literaturverwalter) and finally coining the neologism "meine Geseilschaften" (DKB, 253). This untranslatable word, which inserts the noun *Seile* (rope) into the second syllable of the word *Gesellschaft* (society), captures the intimacy and emotional ambivalence of a (literally) tight-knit negative community. In this sense, Hilbig's story takes a drastic step that Benjamin's theories were too sober to take. "The Lore of the Trees" plays with the idea that the melancholic gaze of the angel of history could be shared in such a way as to inaugurate a new negative collectivity, which dwells *intentionally* in the wreckage of history and convenes ritualistically around sites of debris. In other words, Hilbig's story suggests that the angel's unifying view of catastrophe and wreckage could constitute a subculture that would exist against modern society with its insistence on production and use value. Cultivating this perverse hope, Hilbig's shadow-community follows in the footsteps of Enlightenment utopianism, albeit in highly eccentric ways. When Waller recalls his vision of the storm from within the garbage workers' hut, he calls on a familiar repertoire of images from the tradition of utopian writing, imagining himself as a sort of Robinson Crusoe "in a desolate ship cabin, or in a makeshift habitation on an island, or in a desert region" (in einer verwahrlosten Schiffskabine, oder in einer behelfsmäßigen Behausung auf einer Insel, oder in einer Wüstengegend) (244–45). The desert oasis, the sea journey, the island refuge: in Western literature, these adventurous locales have typically served as free spaces for the realization of ideals that would be impossible in present-day society. The hermetic, insular space of the hut shared by Waller and the garbage workers (albeit never at the same time) is a site for the realization of a negative ideal quite different from Crusoe's dream of enlightened self-reliance.

It is true, as László Krasznahorkai claims, that "Hilbig's world is sick and disgusting," as well as "monochromous."[36] For Waller and the garbage workers, however, it becomes possible to *embrace* the monochromous world and make it into the site for the formation of a "we." By imitating and intensifying the desolation of the world as it *is*, these characters conjure a possible alternative world. The "unsure" ground that Waller feels when he is alone in his cabin is a new common ground that becomes for him a new gathering point, where it becomes possible to write down his monologue and prepare it for delivery to the rest of the world. The sort of gothic community presented by Hilbig resembles, in fact, the model of collectivity that Timothy Morton has recently theorized under the heading of "dark ecology." Dark ecology is driven by the "queer idea that we want to stay with a dying world," as it is *our* dying world.[37] Its impulse is not to fight to conserve something called "nature" against the encroachment of humans (that is, to protest the removal of Waller's cherry trees by invoking their naturalness) but instead to "stay with the darkness."[38] This is similar to the otherworldly path that Waller chooses, following the example of the garbage workers. All these characters emphatically identify with the wreckage of the world, fashioning a second world out of it by embracing the most grotesque forms of denaturalized nature. This identification is radical because it cuts through the distances and distinctions that permit functioning in everyday social life, such as those between past and present, between presence and absence, and even between reality and hallucination. Waller and the garbage workers commune through the antisocial practice of *seeing everything as a storm*.

This historical "storm-watching" practiced by Waller and the garbage workers allows for the proliferation of transhistorical connections. Everything can be connected through the storm, and everything is poised over the abyss. Indeed, "storm" and "abyss" become almost interchangeable terms in Hilbig's fiction, where maelstroms of precipitation accompany images of abyssal downward movement. The scene alluding to Dostoevsky's biblical epigraph centers on the opening of an abyss: first, he hears the sound of pigs plunging into an abyss, a sound that becomes retroactively attached to the rolling of bulldozers toward the church tower of the town of W. The pigs' downward plunge may be a metaphor both for the collapse of traditional belief systems (the collapsing church) and the destruction of nature (the felling of trees through industrial progress). The downward plunge into the abyss is repeated later, as Waller thinks he hears the church tower collapsing into the man-made abyss of the nearby surface mine (*Tagebau*). Waller's synthesizing, synesthetic way of hearing and seeing finds everywhere the same trajectory of nihilism first taken by the biblical pigs, who become an allegory for all aspects of social life (it's all going down). Waller cultivates a mode of seeing where it becomes possible to see *all* downward trajectories in tandem, so that the history of humanity becomes reducible to two basic actions: Humanity digs an abyss and jumps into it.

Even if Hilbig's text is polemically opposed to the dialectical materialism officially espoused by the GDR, his text seems to endorse another, unusual form of the Hegelian "negation of the negation." Once Waller and the garbage workers perceive this negative process of digging and falling in its totality, recognizing it as a universal process, they can *negate* this universal negation by mirroring it in the verbal art of the choral monologue. Civilization has created a massive void with its storm of progress. Through such monologue, Hilbig's heroes (for it is by now clear that Hilbig holds an immodestly heroic worldview) can bear witness to this voiding process and declare solidarity with everything that has been voided. By so doing, they map out an escape path into another possible world. Here it is useful to draw a comparison with the experimental fiction of Landauer, Kafka, and Bernhard: whereas those authors adopted various revisionist stances toward the nihilist gesture of "conjuring a void," Hilbig's fiction assumes that this *voiding* is a historical fait accompli. Nihilism is the unifying thread of world history. What remains to be done is to establish a way of writing and thinking *beyond* this nihilist voiding. It is in the literary monologue, which is transcribed and shared anonymously, that Hilbig and his characters place their hope. Monologue signifies the outsiders' complete secession from the course of world history, and his (it is always *his* for Hilbig) intention to make community outside of it. By dropping out of this world, Hilbig's outsiders appraise and appreciate the extent of its destructive "storm" and subsequently fabulate for themselves an alternate world in which the storm has already come to an end.

The solitary community presented in "The Lore of the Trees" is reflected in the text's arrangement of narrative frames. The text withholds any information about who Waller is, to whom he is speaking, or when he is speaking. In terms of context, the first sentence of the story establishes nothing other than the fact that Waller's discourse is a spoken monologue, delivered somewhere at some time with a listener. Over the course of the text, little more will be revealed about this scene of delivery, except that it is interrupted by pauses (denoted by ellipses, " . . . "), as well as Waller's "sour laughter" (meckerndes Gelächter) (211). Other than these discourse markers, the narrator adds nothing to Waller's speech, so that the text appears as antisocial monologue *par excellence*. The narrator quoting Waller is properly anonymous, betraying not a single detail about himself. As such, the outermost frame of the text is conspicuously blank, and it allows for the reader to step into the narrator's position as the anonymous listener of Waller's monologue. This device of the blank frame is closely connected to the content of Waller's monologue. Waller is telling of how he became privy to a secret poetic communication circulating among the garbage workers. By entering anonymously into communication with them, he became initiated into their circle and claimed them as his most essential comrades (for whom he coins the term *Geseilschaften*, the rope-relation that implies a lifeline as well as a mutual entrapment). Through his initiation into this secret countersociety, Waller was able to secure his solitary yet shared perspective on the all-devouring negativity of modern history. By presenting the monologue within a blank frame, Hilbig's texts also beckon to the reader to *join* the company of the garbage workers: readers may let themselves in on the secret and thereby expand the circle of monologic communication that defines literature for Hilbig.

It is easy to dismiss this conceit as an unapologetic overestimation of literature and its subversive power. It is flattering to think that any reader of a literary text is inserted into this ever-widening circle of outsiders, but it also can seem like a very weak form of resistance to social forces. However, at the end of Waller's monologue, it becomes clearer why this strong claim for literature is not just a whim but a necessity. As it turns out, Waller's monologue in its entirety is an account of how and why he decided not to commit suicide, despite a crippling sense of depression and meaninglessness. The community of anonymous outsiders that Waller posits within his monologue (in the guise of the garbage workers) and outside it (in the guise of the anonymous listener) provide Waller with a way of reframing loneliness and depression, so that the most profound unhappiness turns into a way of being-together. A suicidal "I" becomes a "we" determined to survive. In the end, right before Waller removes the noose from his neck and steps down from the tree from which he was going to jump, he is rescued by a sudden resigned insight: "Nothing is left to me anymore but to keep house with the unhappiness and the stagnation . . . and to act as if it could become bright again someday" (Mir bleibt nichts übrig, als hier drinnen mit dem Unglück und mit der Stagnation hauszuhalten . . . und so tun, als könne es einmal wieder hell warden) (277). In other words, Waller resolves to make himself at home in unhappiness and in this way preserves hope for some unspecified future change that is described only as a return of light. This last-minute discovery of hope in despair echoes the unorthodox form of community that emerged earlier in his interactions with the garbage workers. Waller was able to reconstruct a vision of community through the depressive and depressing perspective on human history as a nihilistic downward plunge. At the epitome of despair, Waller's "I" yields to this "we," and his monologue becomes choral. The "we" becomes affixed to a set of slogans that cement this subversive group identification: He claims that "we" are "ceaselessly in the process of remembering all the forgotten things" (ununterbrochen dabei, an all die vergessenen Dinge zu denken) (269). The slogan, "to each his own private revolution, we think" (jedem seine private Revolution, denken wir) captures the fusion of solidarity and solitude inherent in this idea of community. Abysmal, underground life fosters its own inward revolutions, a feeling of collective purpose without the need for coordinated political action.

Hilbig's Perpetual Metalepsis

As in the fictions of Landauer, Kafka, and Bernhard, metalepsis is the condition of community for Hilbig. Waller's "we" is made possible by a perpetual motion of metaleptic transgression. The boundaries between foreground and background, between mental and material existence, as well as between past and present, are exceedingly fluid in Hilbig's text, and each of these moments of "transit" provide brief shocks for Hilbig's reader. More precisely, the reader becomes a witness to the metamorphoses and mutations of Waller's "I" into the "we" of the garbage workers who inhabit a space beyond the end of historical time. The narrator straddles two continuums of time, one biographical and the other eternal. In this sense, Hilbig's text adheres to Brian Richardson's account of unnatural narrative, which constructs "contradictory, and multilinear fabulas."[39] The literary text itself becomes a kind of portal, allowing a kind of "belonging" that crosses uncrossable ontological boundaries. Waller's narrative emits both from an utterly isolated "I" and from a close-knit choral "we," neither of which is "more real" or "more illusory" than the other.

That is not to say that Hilbig creates a community that is immediately appealing as an alternative to the oppressive and unchosen national community of the GDR, or one that avoids coercion and conformity. The complexity of the "we" is that it is, on the one hand, "dirty and ragged," "wasted" and morbid, but, on the other, it enjoys unbreakable solidarity in this abjection.[40] More so than the anarchic communities imagined by Kafka and Bernhard, the outsider community in Hilbig's "Lore of the Trees" is marked by a sanctimonious sense of self-assurance and pride. Waller is proud to melt into this class of outcasts, and his entire monologue can be understood as a kind of oath of loyalty to the underworld; he expresses a sense of fidelity to the others in that separate world. This is clear from an early moment of the story, when Waller is walking around the garbage dump at the edge of town, and hears "a voice . . . out of the nothingness" (eine Stimme . . . aus dem Nichts"), which called out to him: "Do not forget us!" (Vergiß uns nicht!) (217). Waller (much like the narrator of "Old Rendering Plant") answers this call by counting himself among the category of the "vanished" (diese Verschwundenen) who have cried out to him (216). His belonging to the underworld of the vanished is marked by the same sentiments ascribed to the socialist citizenry he is trying to escape: loyalty, pride, and endurance over time. The subcultural pose of Waller's "nobodies" who have dropped out of GDR society nonetheless claims a moral and artistic high ground (since they are the ones still able to "realize a poetic thought") (243). Indeed, Waller's underworld coheres around an idea of eternal communion, and a sense of timeless monumentality that is reminiscent of how an empire represents itself as infinite and immortal. Waller at one point imagines himself as a statue, representing the garbage workers, living "deaf and blind and mythically in the ash" for all eternity (262). When Waller's "I" dissolves into the "we" of the garbage workers, he augments this vision of a timeless monument to a timeless community: "We have always been here. We have always waited here and were always present here . . . since the dawn of human thought we were here and have grinned in anticipation, here at this site" (referring specifically to the garbage dump) (270). The countercultural "we" polemicizes against East German society and the socialist state by claiming an origin beyond the beginning of recorded time. This moral victory against socialism is, of course, won at the price of an ontological schism: the "we" is native to another world, invisible to the authorities and to Waller's family, with its own distinct model of time.

When Waller and the garbage workers pay tribute to Dostoevsky's *Demons*, they uncover a portal into a totally annihilated world, a scorched earth without time that they can see but that is "next door" to the bleak everyday world of the 1980s GDR. In a sense, this second world is the derivative of the philosophies presented in the *Demons*, particularly the ideas of "eternity" explored by its nihilist characters. These ideas are encapsulated in the famous scenes in the chapter "Night" in *The Demons* (sections 5 and 6). These sections recount Nikolai Stavrogin's private conversations with two of his followers, who are implicated in the conspiracy of the local revolutionary

"Society." In section 5, Stavrogin speaks in a secluded backroom with the engineer Kirillov and shares with him a nihilist speculation: that "if one did some villainy, or worse, some shame, that is disgrace," it would be possible to escape one's own implication through suicide: "'One blow to the temple, and there will be nothing.' What do I care then about people and how they'll be spitting for a thousand years, right?"[41] For Stavrogin, then, nothing is eternally bad. His interlocutor, Kirillov, formulates another inverse nihilist insight: "everything is good, everything," including starvation and violence; he claims it is possible to reevaluate everything, to the extent that it is possible for a new kind of human being (the "man-god") to make it so that "time suddenly stops, and will be eternal."[42] The shared goal of both discourses is an overthrow of time itself, violating both the Christian notion of eternity, as well as the rational notion of time as a linear, continuous, and unidirectional medium of existence. Both characters dream of an *anarchy of time*. Nihilism is underpinned by the denial of time as a shared framework of human experience, which then permits the outbreak of amoral, senseless violence.

Hilbig's "Lore of the Trees" reevaluates such temporal anarchy, building it into the narrative structure of the text. Temporal anarchy is no longer (as in *The Demons*) an abstract philosophy contained in the mouths of particular characters. Rather, through Waller's monologue of refusal, temporal anarchy becomes installed as a second reality, integral to the fabula of the text, which allows the protagonist to escape from one world into another. It is as if Kirillov, after claiming on one page that it is possible to conjure eternity, on the next page would *really* stop time and freeze himself and Stavrogin within an everlasting moment affirmed by the narrator. In short, "The Lore of the Trees" is a radical text because Waller's monologue realizes the temporal anarchy that was only theorized in the *Demons*. Certain characters *really* have the ability to "drop out" of the temporal continuum of the world as a matter of will, by entering the underworld of literature. With the appearance of the tattered copy of Dostoevsky's novel, Hilbig's story underwrites a form of verbal nihilism, or monologue, that paints an escape route into another world and therefore into another continuum of time.

There is, as one can see in Waller's case, an affinity between classical articulations of nihilism (à la Dostoevsky's characters) and the sort of transgression performed by postmodernist fiction, with its "ontological poetics," where fictional characters pass into extrafictional reality and vice versa.[43] Both discourses are audaciously solipsistic in their denial of a single objective reality; both discourses make it possible to see a single person's subjective vantage point as a pivot point where one world ends, and another begins—this, indeed, is why Dostoevsky portrays the nihilists as being so dangerous; similar concerns have led critics to see in postmodernist fiction a total loss of reality. Moreover, both classical nihilism and postmodern poetics endorse a form of ontological pluralism in which "parallel worlds or universes" coexist and collide.[44] Hilbig shares this idea that, by overstepping the boundaries of the given world by way of metalepsis, the alienation of our own world can be overcome. Seen in this light, the most important gesture for the imagination of community in Hilbig's text is not actually those sentences in which the protagonist claims to have glimpsed some community of the wasteland. Rather, the most important metaleptic jump occurs in the moment when the solitary narrator invites others (his implied listeners and readers) to join the circle of communication that constitutes the outsiders' community. It is, for instance, the moments of "language acquisition," where Hilbig's narrators begin to explain the vocabulary, syntax, and gestures of the outsiders, and where the monologic "I" becomes a choral "we." Hilbig's readers are invited to identify with the figures lurking in the shadows and margins. As such, his texts evoke horror and hope at the same time. They invite imaginative participation in a homosocial bond with characters who have been ejected or have ejected themselves from the world, paving the way for the sort of solitary companionship that Hilbig imagined when he stated categorically in 2002 that "literature is monologue." For Hilbig, literature is a monologue of the many, inspired by nihilism, which conjures another world.

Conclusion

Telling the story of nihilist community in the past chapters has required a lengthy farewell to a term that long bound together Western conceptions of what verbal art is and where it comes from: *genius*. Monologue, in particular, has traditionally been seen as a habit of the solitary, antisocial genius who must live without peers of his artistic or intellectual stature. Writing in 1985, Ken Frieden staked out the scope of this inheritance when he argued that "Genius is the intellectual obsession of our times, and monologue is one symptom of that disorder."[1] In the story I have told in *Private Anarchy*, monologue remains, but genius vanishes. The sovereignty, the magical inspiration, the preciousness, the rarefaction, and the supreme confidence associated with the idea of "genius" fade away. What remains is a fascination with the experiential possibilities allowed by the "monologue" that was once seen as the exclusive domain of the genius. Already with Schopenhauer, for whom "genius" remained an essential category for any consideration of aesthetics, the word was gradually transforming into a name for a (repeatable, replicable) act of turning away from the world. For the writers that followed Schopenhauer, a different model of eccentricity emerges: what is important is not genius as a spirit or inborn character but as the voluntary verbal act of monologue. With Landauer, as a follower of Schopenhauer, the genius has already vanished behind the character of the unworldly anarchist: the one who wants nothing, who refuses everything, in hope of discovering another, freer world. The unworldly characters depicted in the twentieth-century texts considered here (Kafka, Bernhard, and Hilbig) have already bid farewell to the emphatic notions of genius, retaining only the radical solitude that was once conserved in the name of genius. As Hilbig says, *literature is monologue*, and not genius in particular. If *Private Anarchy* is at all a story of progress, then it is the story of learning to do without the oppressive construct of "genius" and of uncovering unknown languages that were obscured by its dominance. The progress is helped along by the insights of intellectual nihilism.

This story does not end with Hilbig, who passed away in 2007. For instance, the Hungarian novelist László Krasznahorkai, who has been active since the 1980s, continues this tradition of postnihilist experimentation. Krasznahorkai has explicitly avowed affinities to most of the authors studied in this book: he has spoken of Dostoevsky, Nietzsche, Kafka, Bernhard, and Hilbig either as influences or foils.[2] Monologue dominates as the basic narrative medium in nearly every one of Krasznahorkai's novels, especially in his fiction from around the year 2000 and afterward, where the text frequently *is* one transcribed monologue delivered by an eccentric who wants "to leave the earth."[3] Monologue is, at once, an eraser and an exit strategy. The basic verbal scenario that I have uncovered in this book is strongly in evidence in a short story that Krasznahorkai wrote in prewriting for his novel *War and War*, entitled "Isaiah Has Come." This text introduces an eccentric archivist named Korim, who visits a bar in a desolate and nameless bus station, where he delivers an "unstoppable monologue"[4] about how "the world is gone."[5] Just as the story's setting has been established, the narrator retreats behind a character's torrent of words. The primary (extradiegetic) narrator is almost entirely eclipsed by Korim's speech, so that (for both reader and narrator) the objective world surrounding the scene of delivery begins to vanish. This disappearance of the objective world is also tied to the content of Korim's incessant speech. His message, simply put, is that "it's over,"[6] an "over-ness" that Korim expresses elsewhere in the novel *War and War* in terms of an insight that "there was nothing, but *nothing* worthwhile left in the world."[7] In short, the character's speech is a familiar instance of verbal nihilism. What is striking is that this verbal nihilism—as I have shown is the case with Krasznahorkai's experimental predecessors—ultimately becomes a means of *relating outward* and creating a sense of coexistence. The "verbal epitome of loneliness and isolation" is the beginning of a new outward relation.[8] Krasznahorkai himself said of the Korim character: "I wanted to write a book, which is absolutely a fictional work, but I wanted my main character, who is absolutely fictional, to be introduced to reality, and this fact, this desire in me, determined everything."[9] How can any writer possibly accomplish this? Krasznahorkai adopts several creative strategies of framing and de-framing. The effect of Korim's incessant speech is to eclipse not only the narrator but also the boundary between the intratextual fictional world and extratextual reality, so that we as readers are overwhelmed by "this monologue" in which he "talks about the human condition, how the world is gone."[10] His speech acquires a metaleptic function by aggressively denying its framework of utterance (the world itself). There is another, even more extreme way in which Korim, as a character of the novel *War and War*, exists through metalepsis: the novel's ending, where Korim takes his own life, is not located within the boundaries of the novel at all but rather is inscribed on a plaque that can be found to this day outside the art museum in Schaffhausen, Switzerland. Korim's traces are not only in our physical world but also in today's online world: the website on which Korim sought to preserve a manuscript he discovered, warandwar .com, really exists, even if it contains nothing other than an error message stating that all its data have been erased because of a failure to pay for the domain.[11] Krasznahorkai's novel points in different ways on a dead-end search through our own world for its missing protagonist—who himself declared that our *own* world has already gone missing. In this way, we are asked to imagine that we share the void voiced by Korim.

In one of Krasznahorkai's most recent novellas, the idea of a community conjured by nihilist monologue is illustrated even more concisely. The 2009 novella *Az ultosó farkas*, published in English as *The Last Wolf* in 2016, presents an idea of solitary community that—as with *War and War*—both evokes and exceeds the modes of virtual interconnectedness offered by contemporary Internet culture. Its story line begins (as in so many of Krasznahorkai's texts) in a forlorn bar, this one in Berlin-Schöneberg, where a destitute former academic sits alone, apparently in a state of complete nihilism, as he is overcome with laughter fueled by "futility" and "scorn," which is addressed to existence in its entirety:

> The subject was, uniquely, everything, arising from an everything that was everywhere, and, what was more, if indeed it was everything, arising out of everywhere, it would be difficult enough to decide what it was at, arising out of what, and in any case it wouldn't be full-hearted laughter, because futility and scorn were what continually oppressed him, and he was doing nothing, not a damn thing, simply drifting, spending hours sitting in the Sparschwein with his first glass of Sternburg at his side, while everything around him positively dripped with futility, not to mention scorn.[12]

Once this hopeless scene is set, the man delivers a relentless and vehemently detailed monologue about a trip he took to the western Spanish region of Extremadura. His speech is ostensibly delivered for the benefit of the Hungarian bartender, but from the spare information provided by the narrator, it becomes clear that the speaker is beyond caring whether or not anyone in particular is listening: his speech is addressed *to nobody in particular*, or *anyone but himself*. A greater part of his narrative is filled with logistical details, explaining how years after losing his academic reputation (likely due to alcoholism and depression), he was contacted via e-mail by an "unheard-of foundation" in Spain, devoted to the promotion of the western region of Extremadura, who knows of his reputation as a writer.[13] At the time that this e-mail reached him, he was already fully convinced of the nullity of his own individual identity; he was baffled that anyone would remember him for his "few unreadable books full of ponderously negative sentences and depressing logic in claustrophobic prose."[14] As for his academic title, he sees it as a defunct sign that covers over a complete void of personal identity: "yes, there had been someone of that name some time in the past, the name right in that sense, but that there wasn't anyone behind the name now, no 'Herr Professor.'"[15] In other words, he is nobody. He decides to take the trip, he explains, simply in order to not disappoint his kind hosts. Thus, the trip begins as an essentially hopeless, goalless enterprise, which is bound in advance by a nihilist logic; it can lead to nothing. Once he is in Extremadura, while his hosts take him on a tour of the countryside by car, his first suggestion for an initial destination is inspired not by any particular goal but through a whim of his failing memory; he recalls a sentence from an article he had read online about how "it was south of the River Duero in 1983 that the last wolf had perished."[16] This single sentence, which has remained in his memory, spontaneously creates a destination for the man and his hosts, who then go seek out this site where the last wolves had died out from Extremadura. They seek out a particular, man-made void.

The nihilist tone of his monologue—which could accurately be described in the speaker's own words as "negative sentences and depressing logic in claustrophobic prose"—persists throughout the entirety of *The Last Wolf*.[17] However, what this stream of "negative sentences" ultimately adds up to is a remarkable web of interpersonal and interspecies connections. The dramatic and emotional climax of the story arrives in an encounter with a gamekeeper named José Miguel, who tells the heartbreaking story of how, after years of being hunted close to extinction, the last wolf in the region was struck (perhaps deliberately) by a car, having been unable to run away in time because "she was pregnant, because her belly was already too large and so *she could not run* across the road fast enough to escape the accident prepared for her."[18] The moment is relayed through a chain of interconnected and distinct voices, each stricken with a different grief: "Jose Miguel continued speaking piling one sentence on top of another, one Spanish sentence running into the next, the interpreter so full of tears that she couldn't even speak let alone translate, at which point he, he pointed to himself in the Sparschwein, suddenly felt anything but empathy, rather rage, because he couldn't understand why he was being left to his own devices at the most exciting moment of the story."[19] At the precise moment at which communication breaks down under the weight of grief, an entire chain of interdependence is revealed: the man speaking in the Sparschwein voices the frustration of his former self, who was listening to the weeping of the interpreter, who was listening to the sad story of José Miguel, who himself had gathered his own story from the scene of the wolf's death. The breakdown of the communicative chain demonstrates both the fragility and the remarkable reach of this chain, which connects the forlorn scene of the empty bar in Berlin to the sad passing of an already endangered animal. The human speakers and listeners are bound together through grief over the fate of a nonhuman creature and through frustration over the impossibility of properly understanding and conveying this experience of death. As such, Krasznahorkai's text constructs its own vision of a community that emerges unexpectedly through the expression of painful memory. Each person speaks in a voice that is dislocated, emitting from someplace and someone else. The text itself, in its final sentences, is a document of this shared dislocation. We read, at the text's conclusion, that the professor had "locked Extremadura in the depths of his own cold, empty, hollow heart, and that ever since then, day after day, he had been rewriting the end of Jose Miguel's story in his head, and that that's exactly where he was now, at the end."[20]

There is a subtle metaleptic "jump" in this final phrase, as the "here and now" of the text's ending becomes aligned with the professor's inner monologue, which is itself nothing but a continuation of José Miguel's monologue. In this way, each recipient of the narrative blends in with the one who is narrating it, transported in time and space to the "inside" of the narrative they are hearing. The monologue that fills the text is, then, both isolating and binding. The voice of the lonely "I" is committed to preserving a voice that came before it, and it needs to pass this other voice onto somebody, anybody, to keep the chain intact. As with Kafka and Bernhard, monologue matters not because it declares the sovereignty of the self but because it represents the effort to maintain a fragile line (or bridge) that crosses gaps of time and space and connects different instances of isolation. For Krasznahorkai, this nonlocation of monologue offers a chance to recognize forms of loss and suffering that exceed the capacity of human understanding: none of the speakers or listeners in *The Last Wolf* can fathom the death of the animal, but they are connected in this collective incapacity. If there is, then, something special about Krasznahorkai's nihilist protagonist, it is not that he is a "genius" inspired to tell an original story. As someone who has given up on himself entirely, he turns into a conduit for other voices to pass through him, which he then passes on to the reader with exacting fidelity to historical, geographic, and social detail. In other words, the strange afterlife of verbal nihilism in the work of László Krasznahorkai is that it becomes an alternative *documentary* medium—at a time when documentary media are becoming ubiquitous through the proliferation of digital media. In this sense, Krasznahorkai's affinities to Hilbig extend beyond the ones that he himself acknowledged.[21] Both authors find a future for literature in its capacity to make community out of isolated voices.

The story told in this book has cohered in part through a common set of literary influences, a nihilist "heritage" that all of these authors share—along with a tendency to gender the "epitome of loneliness and isolation" as male.[22] Yet the impact of a literary study is limited if it we cannot not distill some concept that can be generalized and applied in comparative studies to other texts outside the tradition in question. In concluding, I would like to suggest that the practices of imagining community that I have studied so far can be understood, in general, with the concept of "nonlocality of voice." Verbal nihilism produces its anarchic narrative effects by scattering the discourse of *one* speaker across disparate positions, and across different worlds. The work of verbal voiding results in a situation where the speaker is more than one thing at once: present and absent, isolated and attached, solitary and solidary. As such, nonlocal voice creates a problem for some of our basic tools of narrative analysis. Usually, the analysis of narrative "voice" requires, at a minimum, knowledge of the identity, as well as the spatial and temporal location of the "narrating instances" featuring in a text—that is, the hypothetical mouth out of which a particular segment of the story is poured.[23] Such temporal and spatial data help readers determine the relationship of the one who is narrating to what they are narrating. However, the texts considered in the preceding chapters all feature voices that exhibit a strange nonlocality. From Landauer to Hilbig, the nihilist monologue, which takes over the narration for a significant portion of the text, locates its speaker in at least two places at once. Kafka's Praying Man is standing on the street *and* floating in a void. Bernhard's Doctor is walking in the mountains with his younger friend Leichtlebig *and* dwelling in the total darkness of another universe. Hilbig's hero Waller is living a lonely life in the GDR *and* communing with his fellow garbagemen in an infinite field of ash. Krasznahorkai's hopeless professor is in the "barren wasteland" of the Sparschwein bar in Berlin *and* dwelling within the story told by the gamekeeper José Miguel. Each text follows a program of productive confusion where the initial context is eclipsed and replaced. If this confusion is taken seriously, then the reader is actually prevented from reconstructing a single, consistent fictional world. Instead, what the text represents is a relationship between two or more mutually exclusive worlds. As I have shown, this expression of nihilism is not as pessimistic as it would appear at first glance. True, these texts put forth a claim that different people inhabit different worlds, thereby endorsing a kind of solipsism that denies certain facts of shared, external reality. Yet the texts are optimistic, in that they remain focused on the *entanglement* of distinct worlds: the world as it is and the world as it could be. Each of these worlds is fragile and unstable and therefore permeable. The reader is presented with the possibility of community by witnessing a traffic that flows between one world and another.

It should be conceded here that it still remains difficult to "find" community in the works of the authors studied in *Private Anarchy*—particularly Kafka, Bernhard, and Hilbig—and it makes sense that so many readers and critics have remained focused on the symptoms of isolation and alienation that characterize their works. Their texts seem too negative to contain any trace of community. The metaleptic relations triggered by verbal nihilism are, often enough, easy to miss. What I hope to have shown in *Private Anarchy* is, however, that even the most misanthropic literature imagines community, often in subtle and nearly invisible ways. This idea did not come from nowhere. Rather, the entire story I have told so far was inspired by the challenging ideas of "literature as utopia" developed by the Austrian writer Ingeborg Bachmann (1926–1973).[24] Bachmann's unique utopianism develops out of sustained reflections on the nonlocality—and negativity—of literary voice. As such, her works provide a powerful lens through which to understand, and reframe, the anarchic tradition I have studied in this book. Bachmann is not usually understood as a "nihilist," but her works provide a compelling idea of how literature can find community in an abyss conjured by verbal negativity.

The strongest expression of Bachmann's literary utopianism may be found in her 1964 poem "Bohemia Lies by the Sea," one of the last poems of her career. Here, Bachmann presents an image of community that begins with an act of complete verbal negation, which first erases and then unexpectedly relocates the speaking subject.

> Ich will nichts mehr für mich. Ich will zugrunde gehen.
>
> I want nothing more for myself. I want to go under.[25]

The poem performs a creative transformation, whereby the act of *wanting nothing* has unexpected consequences. What sounds like an announcement of the speaker's suicide turns into a declaration of hope. The epitome of the speaker's self-willed downfall (going "to the ground," or "zugrunde") suddenly provides buoyancy, as the speaker is displaced onto the fluid surface of the sea: "zugrunde, das heißt zum Meere / dort finde ich Böhmen wieder (under / that means the sea / there I'll find Bohemia again).[26] From here, the speaker turns directly to other lost ones, others with nothing to lose, and invites them to join a community of outcasts ("all you Bohemians, seafarers, dock whores, and ships unanchored").[27] As Nicole Schumacher has shown, Bachmann envisions a "utopian homeland" that is "based on" nothing but "the abandoning of all temporal, geographical, individual and historical laws that have been valid up to this moment.[28] In other words, Bachmann's vision of utopia is a state of baseless anarchy, a togetherness that begins with renouncing both oneself and the world. For Bachmann, literature is the nonexistent place where this anarchy can be verbalized, and where we can imaginatively erase prevailing hierarchies. In short, literature creates a vacuum in order to paint another world, allowing us to momentarily and imaginatively transpose ourselves into this other world.

It is important to note that the mechanism allowing this transposition in "Bohemia Lies by the Sea" is *metalepsis*. Bachmann's utopian metalepsis resonates both with the term's original definition as a rhetorical device and with its postmodern definition as a crossing of ontological boundaries. In my introduction, I showed that metalepsis for Quintilian was the importation of a theme from one statement into another, allowing a passage between distinct discourses; the metaphor deployed within one statement acquires a life of its own within a second statement ("tensions boiled over; my head cooked in the heat").[29] For Quintilian, this sort of transitioning is not especially important, earning only a passing acknowledgment. Yet in Bachmann's poem, the "passage" provided by the use of metalepsis is actually central to the functioning of the entire poem; it is its utopian core. Moreover, Bachmann's use of metalepsis involves the same sort of passage between *worlds* that is associated with the ontological, narrative metalepsis of postmodernist fiction. When Bachmann's speaker says, "Ich will zugrunde gehen" (literally, "I want to go to the ground"), the adverb *zugrunde* seems at first an entirely familiar metaphor for perdition, self-loss, or even death. But through metalepsis, this *zugrunde* is carried into the speaker's next statement, where it acquires new attributes and turns into the "sea," where the speaker will discover a new kind of belonging. The utopian homeland is located on the *other side of a metaleptic jump*, whereby the speaker has been transposed into another world through one word. The idea is that the speaker has entered the world of that one word, *zugrunde*, rather than simply staying with *zugrunde* as a metaphor for something in *this* world (the first, initial world of despair). The poem oversteps the boundary between the level of discourse (the use of *zugrunde* as metaphorical language) and the linguistic reality (story, or fabula) conjured by that discourse.

Insofar as Bachmann's poem is narrative in nature, we could say that it performs a transgression of the boundary between discourse and story. As such, Bachmann employs metalepsis in a way that anticipates the conception of the device that Brian McHale developed in his 1987 study *Postmodernist Fiction* and that the narratologist Monika Fludernik further articulated in 2003, when she speculated on what it would mean to treat metalepsis as a "fairly central instance of narratological theorizing."[30] McHale suggests that metalepsis could be considered to be one of the basic operative principles of imaginative literature, which by definition involves the readers' imaginative transposition of themselves into a fictional world.[31] Fludernik, in parallel to this, suggests that it is possible to stipulate a kind of metaleptic transgression anytime a narrator's voice blends with that of a character (any case of free indirect speech). If literature provides a "passage," or "transit," into someone else's world, it is functioning metaleptically, by way of an "impossible" relation that makes poetic or fictional speech "reality." Bachmann's poem—even though its narrative dimension is perhaps not obvious—clarifies something about metalepsis that remains only implicit in the works of these literary scholars. In "Bohemia Lies at the Sea," metalepsis is the possibility of passage that makes literature both utopian and communal. It enables entry into a nowhere, a nonexistent world in which prevailing norms and institutions no longer hold, and where a new "we" can be created. Utopian metalepsis is not the same thing as political revolution, of course, since it is a passage that remains restricted to the field of literature. But, being limited to literature in this way, it preserves a free space where we can imagine what we are not yet capable of being, or allowed to be. Utopian metalepsis is the reminder of freedom in a condition of unfreedom, a reminder of community in a time of isolation. As such, Bachmann finds in metalepsis a lifesaving quality.

This lifesaving quality of metalepsis becomes clear in one of Bachmann's most critically incisive prose works, an unfinished novel that simultaneously thematizes a variety of the "ways of death" that shape the postwar world: domestic violence and emotional abuse, patriarchal academic institutions, the Holocaust, European imperialism in Africa, and the geopolitical tensions of the Cold War. In the second chapter of *The Book of Franza*, the titular protagonist explains how her experiences in an abusive marriage impacted her ways of thinking and speaking. In an extended monologue delivered to her estranged brother, she explains how her husband's verbal and physical violence against her forced her to flee into the space afforded by her own inner monologue. This flight is by no means properly liberating: it is first of all a symptom of trauma, which makes nearly anything in her environment into a reminder of violence she has experienced. For instance, the sight of a glass of water triggers the memory of a glass that her husband Jordan threw at her, only narrowly missing her head. Her own inner monologue follows this process of triggering, where each word precipitates another word that recalls a past act of violence. Yet as Franza's inner monologue proceeds, this chain of associations eventually leads her thoughts away from the scene of violence and into a space where nobody can harm her:

> then I arrive at my border, a wall, and I stand there and my lament carries through a large space, one like a desert, without onlookers, without confidants, facing no one.[32]

> dann gerat ich an meine Grenze, an eine Mauer, und da stehe ich und mein Lamento hallt durch einen großen Raum, einen wüsthaften, ohne Zuschauer, ohne Vertrauten, niemand zugewendet.[33]

The monologue takes a defensive turn, as Franza locates herself now in an empty space where she is utterly isolated, yet protected from any external coercion. Her sole interlocutor is "nobody." The movement from one image to the next is metaleptic: the metaphorical "border" of the self becomes an insulating "wall," which opens a "space" that is vast and empty as a "desert." Through continuous metalepsis, Franza's monologue has jettisoned the given world and created a space where it is possible to *sing* the suffering she has experienced, which is a step toward recovering her freedom and autonomy. Franza's monologue is first a symptom but finally an active exit strategy. The pattern of escape constructed in these sentences of Franza's monologue are not inconsequential for the plot of the novel: they prefigure Franza's actual escape from her husband's apartment in Vienna and her subsequent flight into the Egyptian desert. In short, this passage in *The Book of Franza* imagines a process of escape comparable to the one performed in the poem "Bohemia Lies by the Sea," where strategic use of metalepsis makes it possible to imagine routes out of a hopeless situation. In *Franza*, that literary utopianism of Bachmann's 1964 poem has been modified by a broad historical consciousness that positions the self with relation to histories of European fascism, patriarchy, and colonialism. As such, the sense of community that Franza eventually gains is markedly different from the "bohemian" one pictured in the poem. In the final passages, preceding the scene of her death in Egypt, Franza's own voice begins to blend in with an recalcitrant voice of the formerly colonized peoples she encounters in Egypt and the Sudan; she begins to speak on behalf of an indeterminate collective of the oppressed, about the curse of "the whites" (Die Weißen), whom she in turn curses.[34] One could say that *The Book of Franza* rewrites the escape routes of "Bohemia Lies by the Sea" for the decade of Frantz Fanon, as an outsider within the continent of the colonizer sheds her individuality in order gain a sense of connection to the colonized.[35]

If the uses of metalepsis in Bachmann's poetry and documentary fiction can shed some light on the fiction studied so far in this book, it is because they perform a markedly different version of a similar process. All the texts studied in *Private Anarchy* enact a process that we could call "voluntary vanishing from the scene of patriarchy," with greater or lesser degrees of self-consciousness. Franza vanishes from this scene because of immanent physical and psychological dangers posed by particular authoritarian men who embody the legacy of fascism. The nihilist characters studied in this book can also be said to "vanish from the scene of patriarchy," but without being fully conscious of doing so and without directly confronting the sort of physical and psychological abuse that is so explicitly represented in Bachmann's late fiction (one must read elsewhere in these authors' works for such direct portrayals of embodied violence).

The outsiders studied in *Private Anarchy* do disown forms of masculine authority that they might have otherwise inherited, yet they never totally shed the mood of exceptionalism that surrounds this authority: they continue to privilege male homosociality in their delineations of alternative community. We might say that their fiction approaches the border of feminism without ever crossing into it. One virtue of private anarchy is its radical remoteness from any embodied experience. This remoteness, however, weakens the sense of resistance that otherwise radiates from these writings. Anarchic community is "there but not there," evident and absent at the same time.[36]

NOTES

Introduction

1. Mieke Bal, *Narratology: Introduction to the Theory of Narrative* (Toronto: University of Toronto Press, 1997), 60.

2. Victor Erlich, "Notes on the Uses of Monologue in Artistic Prose," *International Journal of Slavic Linguistics and Poetics* 1–2 (1959): 229.

3. Ibid.

4. Antony Shaftesbury, "Soliloquy; or, Advice to an Author," in *Characteristics of Men, Manners, Opinions, Times, with a Collection of Letters* (Basil: Tourneisen, 1790), 1:148.

5. Jürgen Wertheimer, *Der Güter Gefährlichstes, die Sprache: Zur Krise des Dialogs zwischen Aufklärung und Romantik* (Munich: Fink, 1990), 77.

6. Jean-Jacques Rousseau, *Reveries of a Solitary Walker*, trans. Russell Goulbourne (Oxford: Oxford University Press, 2011), 3.

7. Erlich, "Notes on the Uses of Monologue," 226.

8. Dina Al-Kassim, *On Pain of Speech: Fantasies of the First Order and the Literary Rant* (Berkeley: University of California Press, 2010), 9.

9. David Riesman, *The Lonely Crowd: A Study of the Changing American Character* (New Haven: Yale University Press, 1950).

10. Erlich, "Notes on the Uses of Monologue," 230.

11. In following a historicism through a history of forms, Erlich's approach prefigures the critical approach advocated by Roland Barthes in his essay "Myth Today": "I shall say that a little formalism turns one away from History, but that a lot brings one back to it" (Roland Barthes, "Myth Today," in *A Barthes Reader*, ed. Susan Sontag [New York: Hill and Wang, 1983], 96–97).

12. Ralph Ellison, *Invisible Man* (New York: Vintage, 1995).

13. Valentin Volosinov, *Marxism and the Philosophy of Language*, trans. Ladislav Matejka and I. R. Titunik (New York: Seminar, 1973), 89.

14. "Das Alleinsein ist ein defizienter Modus des Mitseins" (Solitude is a deficient mode of being-with) (Martin Heidegger, *Sein und Zeit* [Tübingen: Niemeyer, 2006], 120, my translation).

15. Julia Kristeva, *Revolution in Poetic Language*, trans. Leon Roudiez (New York: Columbia University Press, 1984).

16. Nayan Shah, *Stranger Intimacy: Contesting Race, Sexuality, and the Law in the North American West* (Berkeley: University of California Press, 2011).

17. Malcolm Bull, *Anti-Nietzsche* (London: Verso, 2011), 175.

18. See Jean-Luc Nancy, *The Inoperative Community*, trans. Peter Connor (Minneapolis: University of Minnesota Press, 1991); Giorgio Agamben, *The Coming Community*, trans. Michael Hardt (Minneapolis: University of Minne-

sota Press, 1991); and Roberto Esposito, *Terms of the Political* trans. Rhiannon Noel Welch (New York: Fordham University Press, 2012), 15.

19. Nancy, *The Inoperative Community*, 80–81.

20. Gustav Landauer, *Der Todesprediger* (Lucerne: Edition Libertaire, 1990), 98.

21. Ibid.

22. I derive this critical term "anonymous society" from Hans Helms, *Die Ideologie der anonymen Gesellschaft* (Cologne: Verlag M. DuMont Schauberg, 1967).

23. I understand "explosion," with Juri Lotman, to be a contingent yet irreversible structural change triggered by an unplanned interaction between different systems of signification (Juri Lotman, *Culture and Explosion*, trans. Wilma Clark [New York: De Gruyter, 2009]).

24. Gustav Landauer, *Skepsis und Mystik: Versuche im Anschluss an Mauthners Sprachkritik* (Cologne: Marcan-Block-Verlag, 1923), my translation.

25. Johann Wolfgang Goethe, "Prometheus," in *Sämtliche Werke, Briefe, Tagebücher und Gespräche* (Frankfurt: Deutscher Klassiker-Verlag, 1987), 1:203–4.

26. Erlich, "Notes on the Uses of Monologue," 229.

27. Ibid., 226.

28. Ibid.

29. Jan Mukařovský, *The Word and Verbal Art: Selected Essays by Jan Mukařovský*, trans. John Burband (New Haven: Yale University Press, 1977), 88.

30. Erlich, "Notes on the Uses of Monologue," 228.

31. Mukařovský, *The Word and Verbal Art*, 88.

32. Erlich, "Notes on the Uses of Monologue," 230.

33. T. O. Sloane, "From Elocution to New Criticism: An Episode in the History of Rhetoric," *Rhetorica: Journal of the History of Rhetoric* 31, no. 3 (2013): 297–330. For a discussion of vocal projection in Victorian theater, see Emily Allen, "The Victorian Novel and Theater," in *The Oxford Handbook of the Victorian Novel* ed. Lisa Rodensky (Oxford: Oxford University Press, 2013), 571–88.

34. Richardson first used the term "unnatural" in his 2006 book *Unnatural Voices*, the goal of which is to take account of "the many odd, unusual, or impossible speakers" who populate much contemporary fiction (*Unnatural Voices: Extreme Narration in Modern and Contemporary Fiction* [Columbus: Ohio State University Press, 2006], 5). Richardson provides another useful term for understanding my project in his most recent book, *Unnatural Narrative*. The narrators of the texts analyzed in *Private Anarchy* correspond in particular to Richardson's concept of the "permeable narrator," who cedes control of narrated universe (Brian Richardson, *Unnatural Narrative: Theory, History, and Practice* [Columbus: Ohio State University Press, 2015], 95).

35. Quintilian, *Quintilian's Institutes of Oratory; Or, Education of an Orator*, trans. J. S Watson (London: Bell, 1875), 2:133.

36. Ibid.

37. Gérard Genette, *Narrative Discourse: An Essay in Method*, trans. Jane Lewin (Ithaca, NY: Cornell University Press, 1980), 234.

38. Ibid.

39. Robrt Walser, *The Robber*, trans. Susan Bernofsky (Lincoln: University of Nebraska Press, 1986), 101.

40. See, for instance, David Ben-Merre, "Time Travels: Metalepsis and Modern Poetry" (PhD diss., Brown University, 2008).

41. Genette implies that the device necessarily makes trouble within a text, undermining its storytelling project, as it involves a transit that is "if not impossible, at any rate always transgressive" (Genette, *Narrative Discourse*, 234).

42. Ibid., 236.

43. Brian McHale, *Postmodernist Fiction* (London: Routledge, 1989), 223.

44. I take this phrase from Nayan Shah, *Contagious Divides: Epidemics and Race in San Francisco's Chinatown* (Berkeley: University of California Press, 2001), 97.

45. Karl Marx, *Grundrisse: Foundations of the Critique of Political Economy*, trans. Martin Nicolaus (New York: Penguin, 1993), 223.

46. Friedrich Engels, *The Origin of the Family, Private Property, and the State* (New York: Penguin Classics, 2010).

47. Jean-Jacques Rousseau, *Discourse on the Origin of Inequality*, trans. Donald Cress (Indianapolis: Hackett, 1992), 60.

48. Ibid., 57.

49. Marx, *Grundrisse*, 223.

50. Karl Marx, "Alienation and Social Classes," in Karl Marx and Friedrich Engels, *The Marx-Engels Reader*, trans. Robert Tucker (New York: Norton, 1978), 134.

51. Ferdinand Tönnies, *Community and Civil Society*, trans. Margaret Hollis (Cambridge: Cambridge University Press, 2001), 52.

52. Karl Marx and Friedrich Engels, "Manifesto of the Communist Party" in *The Marx-Engels Reader*, 342.

53. Tönnies, *Community and Civil Society*, 52.

54. Émile Durkheim, *Professional Ethics and Civic Morals*, trans. Cornelia Brookfield (Glencoe: Free Press, 1958), 15.

55. Ibid.

56. Ibid.

57. Durkheim, qtd. after Mark Cladis, "Beyond Solidarity? Durkheim and Twenty-First-Century Democracy in a Global Age," in *The Cambridge Companion to Durkheim*, ed. Jeffrey Alexander and Philip Smith (Cambridge: Cambridge University Press, 2005), 396.

58. Helmut Lethen, *Verhaltenslehre der Kälte* (Frankfurt: Suhrkamp, 1994), 52.

59. Hermann Broch, *Die Schlafwandler: Eine Romantrilogie* (Frankfurt: Suhrkamp, 1978), 705.

60. Ibid., 705.

61. Siegfried Kracauer, *The Mass Ornament: Weimar Essays*, trans. Thomas Y. Levin (Cambridge: Harvard University Press, 1995), 130.

62. Ibid., 131.

63. Ibid., 129, 132.

64. Kracauer details a range of types in terms of their relationship to the void: Messianic-revolutionary communists who want to "break out of the vacuum"

(ibid., 133); skeptics who embrace for the void (135); those who embrace new forms of spirituality, who are "refugees from the vacuum" (138); and, finally, "those who wait," a group that is also cut off from the absolute and remains *open* to reality as it currently is.

65. Ibid., 140.

66. Helmuth Plessner, *The Limits of Community: A Critique of Social Radicalism*, trans. Andrew Wallace (New York: Humanity Books, 1999), 65.

67. Ibid.

68. Fritz Stern, *The Politics of Cultural Despair: A Study in the Rise of the Germanic Ideology* (Berkeley: University of California Press, 1961), xvi.

69. For a critical discussion of "immanent" community that is present to itself, see Nancy, *The Inoperative Community*.

70. Gerhard Richter, "Siegfried Kracauer and the Folds of Friendship," *German Quarterly* 70, no. 3 (1997): 233–46.

71. I take this phrase from Ian James, "Naming the Nothing: Nancy and Blanchot on Community," *Culture, Theory and Critique* 51, no. 2 (2010): 171–87.

72. Dieter Arendt, *Nihilismus: Die Anfänge von Jacobi bis Nietzsche* (Cologne: Hegner-Bücherei, 1970), 59.

73. For a brief (Europe-focused) "History of Negation" that shows the metamorphosis of "nihilism" from an accusation to a conscious stance taken by defined groups of people, see Bull, *Anti-Nietzsche*, 7–13.

74. Arthur Schopenhauer, *The World as Will and Representation*, vol. 1, trans. E. F. J. Payne (Mineola, NY: Dover, 1966), 412.

75. Friedrich Nietzsche, *The Will to Power*, trans. Walter Kaufman and R. J. Hollingdale (New York: Vintage, 1968), 35.

76. Ibid., 36.

77. Schopenhauer, *The World as Will and Representation*, vol. 1, 412.

78. Nietzsche, *The Will to Power*, 36.

79. Max Stirner, *The Ego and His Own: The Case of the Individual against Authority*, trans. James Joseph Martin (London: Verso, 2014), xxi.

80. Ibid., xxiii.

81. See Stern, *The Politics of Cultural Despair;* and Georg Lukács, *The Destruction of Reason* (Atlantic Highlands: Humanities Press, 1981); see also Helms, *Die Ideologie der anonymen Gesellschaft*.

82. Stern, *The Politics of Cultural Despair*, xvi.

83. See Marta Petru, *An Infamous Past: E. M. Cioran and the Rise of Fascism in Romania* (Chicago: Dee, 2005), 244.

84. Geoff Eley and David Blackbourn complicated the link between pessimism and Germanic nationalism by showing that "it was not cultural despair as such that was peculiarly German; it was the fact that it was so strikingly conjoined with a continuing affirmation of urban, mechanical life, with all its attendant artefacts and cultural forms" (David Blackbourn and Geoff Eley, *The Peculiarities of German History: Bourgeois Society and Politics in Nineteenth-Century Germany* [Oxford: Oxford University Press, 1984], 217).

85. Shah, *Stranger Intimacy*.

86. Vivian Liska, *When Kafka Says We: Uncommon Communities in German-Jewish Literature* (Bloomington: Indiana University Press, 2009), 15.

87. See Paul Mendes-Flohr, *From Mysticism to Dialogue: Martin Buber's Transformation of German Social Thought* (Detroit: Wayne State University Press, 1989), 102.

88. Timothy Malchow, "Thomas Bernhard's *Frost* and Adalbert Stifter: Literature, Legacy, and National Identity in the Early Austrian Second Republic," *German Studies Review* 28, no. 1 (2005): 65.

89. Paul Cooke, *Speaking the Taboo: A Study of the Work of Wolfgang Hilbig* (Amsterdam: Rodopi, 2000), 2.

90. Caroline Levine, *Forms: Whole, Rhythm, Hierarchy, Network* (Princeton: Princeton University Press, 2015).

91. Richardson, *Unnatural Narrative*, 161.

92. Franz Kafka, *Beschreibung eines Kampfes und andere Schriften aus dem Nachlaß* (Frankfurt: Suhrkamp, 1993), 91, my translation.

Chapter 1

1. Jürgen Wertheimer, *Der Güter Gefährlichstes, die Sprache: Zur Krise des Dialogs zwischen Aufklärung und Romantik* (Munich: Fink, 1990), 77, my translation. Cited in Günter Butzer, *Soliloquium: Theorie und Geschichte des Selbstgesprächs in der europäischen Literatur* (Munich: Fink, 2008), 447.

2. Rousseau, *Reveries of a Solitary Walker*, 7.

3. Kant describes a certain kind of misanthropy, "most improperly so called," which older and experienced individuals will turn to in order "to avoid hating where we cannot love," that is, in order to maintain their love of mankind that been disappointed so many times by the "evils" that humans "inflict upon themselves" (Immanuel Kant, *Critique of Judgement*, trans. James Creed Meredith [Oxford: Oxford University Press, 2008], 106).

4. Ibid.

5. Brian McHale, *The Cambridge Introduction to Postmodernism* (New York: Cambridge University Press, 2015), 42. See also the chapter "Worlds under Erasure" in McHale, *Postmodernist Fiction*, 99–111.

6. For a discussion of how an elevated fear of the void (*horror vacui*) can be related to the emergence of crowded urban space (agoraphobia, claustrophobia), see Anthony Vidler, *Warped Space: Art, Architecture, and Anxiety in Modern Culture* (Cambridge: MIT Press, 2001), 17–24.

7. Erlich, "Notes on the Uses of Monologue," 229.

8. Arthur Schopenhauer, *The World as Will and Representation*, vol. 1, trans. E. F. J Payne (New York: Dover, 1966), 412. This English edition is henceforth cited as *WWR1*.

9. Arthur Schopenhauer, *Die Welt als Wille und Vorstellung I* (Frankfurt: Suhrkamp, 1986), 277. The German edition is henceforth cited as *WWV1*.

10. Ken Frieden, *Genius and Monologue* (Ithaca, NY: Cornell University Press, 1985), 30.

11. This is my own translation of the German; the English translation from the 1969 edition is "inclined to soliloquize" (*WWR1*, 190).

12. The original German is: "demnach ist der Eindruck der Gegenwart auf sie sehr mächtig, reißt sie hin zum Unüberlegten, zum Affekt, zur Leidenschaft" (*WWV1*, 272).

13. Matthew Arnold qtd. after Brian Stock, *Augustine's Inner Dialogue* (Cambridge: Cambridge University Press, 2010), 65.

14. Friedrich Nietzsche, *The Complete Works,* vol. 16, trans. Oscar Levy (New York: Russell and Russell, 1964), 77.

15. My translation.

16. Michael Allen Gillespie, *Nihilism before Nietzsche* (Chicago: University of Chicago Press, 1994), 192.

17. My translation.

18. Gillespie, *Nihilism*, 192.

19. Heinz Gerd Ingenkamp, "Gefühlsfalle oder Intertext? Kritisches zu Schopenhauers Lehren über Leid und Mitleid," in *Schopenhauer im Kontext: Deutsch-polnisches Schopenhauer-Symposium 2000* (Würzburg: Königshausen und Neumann, 2002), 28.

20. Schopenhauer shamelessly makes exactly this plea, with extreme condescension toward the working class, in his chapter "Ueber Lärm und Geräusch," in *Parerga und Paralipomena* (Berlin: A. W. Hayn, 1851), 2:517–19.

21. I derive this term, here as elsewhere, from Brian McHale.

22. For a recent sustained argument for the defensibility of *The Destruction of Reason*, see János Kelemen, *The Rationalism of Georg Lukács* (New York: Palgrave Macmillan, 2014).

23. Lukács, *The Destruction of Reason*, 208.

24. Wertheimer, *Der Güter Gefährlichstes*, 77, my translation. Cited in Günter Butzer, *Soliloquium: Theorie und Geschichte des Selbstgesprächs in der europäischen Literatur* (Munich: Fink, 2008), 447.

25. Erlich, "Notes on the Uses of Monologue," 229.

26. I derive this use of the term "contexture" from Mukařovský, *The Word and Verbal Art*, 87.

27. Lukács, *The Destruction of Reason*, 208.

28. Joseph Frank, "Nihilism and 'Notes from the Underground,'" *Sewanee Review* 69, no. 1 (1961): 35.

29. Wolf Schmid, *Der Textaufbau in den Erzählungen Dostoevskijs* (Munich: Fink, 1973), 255.

30. McHale, *Postmodernist Fiction*, 18.

31. Erlich, *Notes*, 230.

32. Mikhail Bakhtin, *Problems of Dostoevsky's Poetics*, trans. Caryl Emerson (Minneapolis: University of Minnesota Press, 1984), 51.

33. Rado Pribic, *Bonaventura's "Nachtwachen" and Dostoevsky's "Notes from the Underground": A Comparison in Nihilism* (Munich: Sagner, 1974), 137.

34. Victor Erlich, "Two Concepts of the Dostoevsky Novel," *International Journal of Slavic Linguistics and Poetics* 25–26 (1982): 130.

35. Dostoevsky wrote in his notebooks, years after completing *The Double*, that Goliadkin Junior was his "most important underground type." The author suggests that Goliadkin's doppelgänger, the bold usurper who splits off

from the consciousness of the menial bureaucrat Goliadkin Sr., prefigured the underground misanthropes and conspirators who would feature in the author's later fiction (see the introduction by Evelyn Harden in Fyodor Dostoevsky, *The Double: Two Versions* [Ann Arbor: Ardis, 1985], xviii).

36. For further explication of the concept of voice regulation, see Boris Eikhenbaum, "Leskov and Contemporary Prose," *Russian Literature Triquarterly* 11 (1975): 211–24.

37. Erlich, "Notes on the Uses of Monologue," 230.

38. Irina Paperno qtd. in Claudia Verhoeven, *The Odd Man Karakozov: Imperial Russia, Modernity, and the Birth of Terrorism* (Ithaca, NY: Cornell University Press, 2009), 56.

39. Fyodor Dostoevsky, *Notes from Underground*, trans. Richard Pevear and Larissa Volokhonsky (New York: Vintage Classics, 1994), 3ff. Henceforth cited as *NU*.

40. René Girard, *Resurrection from the Underground: Feodor Dostoevsky*, trans. James Williams (East Lansing: Michigan State University Press, 2012), 17.

41. László Földenyi, *Dostojewskij liest in Sibirien Hegel und bricht in Tränen aus*, trans. Hans Skirecki (Berlin: Matthes and Seitz, 2008), 49; English translation my own.

42. See Mikhail Bakhtin, "The Hero's Monologic Discourse and Narrational Discourse in Dostoevsky's Early Novels," in *Modern Critical Views: Fyodor Dostoevsky*, ed. Harold Bloom (New York: Chelsea House, 1989), 17, 20.

43. Fyodor Dostoevsky, *"The Double" and "The Gambler,"* trans. Richard Pevear and Larissa Volokhonsky (New York: Vintage Classics, 2007), 53. Henceforth cited as *TD*.

44. For a discussion of Dostoevsky's critique of rational egoism, see Kenneth Lantz, *The Dostoevsky Encyclopedia* (Westport, CT: Greenwood, 2004), 281.

45. This translation is from Fyodor Dostoevsky, *The Double: Two Versions*, trans. Evelyn Harden (Ann Arbor: Ardis, 1985), 49.

46. I take the translation "hyperconsciousness" from Joseph Frank, *Dostoevsky: A Writer in His Time* (Princeton: Princeton University Press, 2009), 418. In the translation by Pevear and Volokhonsky, it is rendered as "heightened consciousness."

47. Compare to Molly Anne Rothenberg, *The Excessive Subject* (Boston: Polity, 2010).

48. Frank, *Dostoevsky: A Writer in His Time*, 418.

49. Erlich, "Two Concepts of the Dostoevsky Novel," 131.

50. Qtd. in Joseph Frank, *Dostoevsky: The Mantle of the Prophet, 1871–1881* (Princeton: Princeton University Press, 2003), 434.

51. This interpretation was advanced by Assen Ignatov in his essay "Demon and the Übermensch: The Anticipation of Totalitarianism in Dostoevsky and Nietzsche," *Philosophical Alternatives Journal* 20 (2011): 147–61.

52. Erlich, "Two Concepts of the Dostoevsky Novel," 130.

53. Wertheimer, *Der Güter Gefährlichstes*, 148.

54. Ibid., 77.

55. Novalis, *Philosophical Writings*, trans. Margaret Mahony Stoljar (Albany: State University of New York Press, 1997), 34.

56. Ibid.
57. Erlich, "Notes on the Uses of Monologue," 230.
58. Friedrich Nietzsche, *Complete Works XIV: The Will to Power I*, trans. Oscar Levy (New York: Russell and Russell, 1964), 22.
59. Ibid., 21.
60. Friedrich Nietzsche, *Complete Works XVI: Twilight of the Idols*, trans. Oscar Levy (New York: Russell and Russell, 1964), 104.
61. Ibid., 105.
62. Ibid.
63. David Smith, "Nietzsche's Hinduism, Nietzsche's India: Another Look," *Journal of Nietzsche Studies* 28 (2004): 40.
64. Ibid., 52.
65. Ibid., 39.
66. Nietzsche, *Complete Works XVI: Twilight of the Idols*, 105–6.
67. Ibid., 105.
68. Ibid. German original quote is from Friedrich Nietzsche, *Götzen-Dämmerung* in *Nietzsche. Werke: Kritische Gesamtausgabe* pt. 6, vol. 3, ed. Giorgio Colli and Mazzino Montinari (Berlin: De Gruyter, 1969), 141.
69. Paolo Stellino, *Nietzsche and Dostoevsky: On the Verge of Nihilism* (New York: Peter Lang, 2015), 81.
70. Nietzsche, *Complete Works XVI: Twilight of the Idols*, 105.
71. Ibid., 105, translation modified.
72. Ibid., 104.
73. Ibid., 103.
74. Ibid., 105.
75. Ibid.
76. Ibid., 90.
77. Ibid., 103.
78. Ibid.
79. Ibid., 106.
80. Ibid., 104.
81. Ibid., 77.
82. Daniel Cottom, "Futurism, Nietzsche, and the Misanthropy of Art," *Common Knowledge* 13, no. 1 (2007): 91.
83. Daniel Conway, "Whither the 'Good Europeans'? Nietzsche's New World Order," *South Central Review* 66, no. 3 (2009): 40.
84. Friedrich Nietzsche, *Human, All Too Human*, trans. Marion Faber and Stephen Lehmann (London: Penguin Classics, 1994), 16.
85. Cottom, "Futurism, Nietzsche," 91.
86. Alenka Zupancic, *The Shortest Shadow: Nietzsche's Philosophy of the Two* (Boston: MIT Press, 2003), 8.
87. Ibid.
88. Émile Durkheim, *On Suicide*, trans. Robin Buss (London: Penguin Classics, 2007).
89. Lukács, *Destruction of Reason*, 208.

Chapter 2

1. Landauer initially delivered "Durch Absonderung zur Gemeinschaft" as a speech for the founding of the commune Neue Gemeinschaft at Schlachtensee outside Berlin (an important site for the Lebensreform movement around 1900). After Landauer had already parted ways with the Neue Gemeinschaft and fellow founders Julius and Heinrich Hart, he used the speech "Durch Absonderung zur Gemeinschaft" for the opening section of his 1903 book *Skepsis und Mystik* (Berlin: Fleischel, 1903). For more on the Neue Gemeinschaft commune, see Eric Paul Jacobsen, *From Cosmology to Ecology: The Monist World-View in Germany from 1770 to 1930* (New York: Peter Lang, 2005), 247–48.

2. Erlich, "Notes on the Uses of Monologue," 229, 228.

3. Gustav Landauer, "Der Anarchismus in Deutschland," in *Erkenntnis und Befreiung: Ausgewählte Reden und Aufsätze* (Frankfurt: Suhrkamp, 1976), 12, my translation.

4. Friedrich Nietzsche, *Thus Spoke Zarathustra*, trans. R. J. Hollingdale (New York: Penguin Classics, 1961), 71.

5. Arthur Schopenhauer, *The World as Will and Representation*, vol. 2, trans. E. F. J. Payne (Mineola, NY: Dover, 1966), 3. The German original reads: "mit erstarrter, kalter Rinde überzogen sind, auf der ein Schimmelüberzug lebende und erkennende Wesen erzeugt hat" (Arthur Schopenhauer, *Die Welt als Wille und Vorstellung II* [Frankfurt: Suhrkamp, 1986], 13).

6. Gustav Landauer, *Der Todesprediger* (Lucerne: Edition Libertaire, 1990), 3. Henceforth cited as *DT*. All citations are from the 1990 edition. Beyond the 1990 reprint, the most widely available edition is Gustav Landauer, *Der Todesprediger* (Cologne: Marcan-Block-Verlag, 1923), appearing four years after Landauer was murdered in the 1919 revolution. All translations from this work are my own.

7. Stirner, *The Ego and His Own*, xxiii.

8. Nietzsche, *Complete Works XVI: Twilight of the Idols*, 105.

9. George Woodcock, *Anarchism* (Toronto: University of Toronto Press, 2004), 22.

10. Ilija Trojanow, "Freiheit, Skepsis, Totenkopf: Eine kurze Reise durch die glorreiche Vielfalt anarchistischen Denkens und Wirkens," in *Anarchistische Welten* (Hamburg: Edition Nautilus, 2012), Kindle e-book. The original German reads: "Es ist ein lebenslanges Projekt, der zynischen Einsicht in die Notwendigkeit der Not nicht anheimzufallen."

11. See Ulrich Sieg, *Jüdische Intellektuelle im Ersten Weltkrieg: Kriegserfahrungen, weltanschauliche Debatten und kulturelle Neuenwürfe* (Berlin: Akademie, 2001), 148.

12. Landauer, "Der Anarchismus in Deutschland," 13, 17.

13. See Murray Bookchin, *The Spanish Anarchists: The Heroic Years, 1868–1936* (New York: Free Life Editions, 1977).

14. Landauer, "Der Anarchismus in Deutschland," 11–12.

15. Ibid., 12.

16. Ibid.

17. Ibid.

18. Ibid., 16.

19. See Axel Kuhn, *Die deutsche Arbeiterbewegung* (Stuttgart: Reclam, 2004), 92–94.

20. Max Nordau, *Entartung* (Berlin: Duncker, 1896). Available in English as *Degeneration* (New York: H. Fertig, 1968).

21. Peter Cersowsky, *"Mein ganzes Wesen ist auf Literatur gerichtet": Franz Kafka im Kontext der literarischen Dekadenz* (Würzburg: Königshausen and Neumann, 1983), 14.

22. See Nancy, *The Inoperative Community.* See also Roberto Esposito, "Community and Nihilism," *Cosmos and History: The Journal of Natural and Social Philosophy* 5, no. 1 (2009). For a discussion that synthesizes different postmodernist notions of "negative community," see Bull, *Anti-Nietzsche.*

23. Corinna Kaiser, *Gustav Landauer als Schriftsteller* (Berlin: De Gruyter, 2014), 94.

24. Philippe Despoix, "Toward a German-Jewish Construct: Landauer's Arnold Himmelheber," in *Gustav Landauer: Anarchist and Jew*, 121–31 (Berlin: De Gruyter, 2015), 122.

25. Eduard Bernstein, "Etwas Erzählungsliteratur," in *Die Neue Zeit: Revue des geistigen und öffentlichen Lebens* 11, no. 2 (1893): 262.

26. Karl Marx and Frederick Engels, *Selected Correspondence* (Moscow: Foreign Languages Publishing House, 1953), 479. The phrase is explained in Engels's April 1888 letter to Margaret Harkness.

27. Bernstein, "Etwas Erzählungsliteratur," 262–63.

28. See Rosa Luxemburg, "Reform or Revolution," in *The Essential Rosa Luxemburg*, ed. Helen Scott (Chicago: Haymarket, 2008), 41–104.

29. Neither the protagonist nor the narrator reflects at any length on the implicit fictional fact that Starkblom's intellectual solitude is predicated on the exploitation of Haitian labor by German capital, as part of a new wave of investment and immigration to Haiti from Germany in the late nineteenth and early twentieth centuries (see Steeve Coupeau, *The History of Haiti* [Westport, CT: Greenwood, 2007], 66–67).

30. Bernstein, "Etwas Erzählungsliteratur," 263.

31. Ibid., 265.

32. Kaiser, *Gustav Landauer als Schriftsteller*, 135.

33. Eugene Lunn, *Prophet of Community: The Romantic Socialism of Gustav Landauer* (Berkeley: University of California Press, 1973), 338. This is a thirdhand report, relayed from an eyewitness to the writer Ernst Toller, who transcribed it in turn.

34. Stirner, *The Ego and His Own*, 291.

35. Kenneth Lantz, *The Dostoevsky Encyclopedia* (Westport, CT: Greenwood, 2004), 201.

36. Ibid.

37. All five parts of "Zur Entwicklungsgeschichte des Individuums" are compiled in Gustav Landauer, *Signatur: g.l.: Gustav Landauer im "Sozialist," 1892–1899*, ed. Ruth Link-Salinger (Frankfurt: Suhrkamp, 1986), 324–49.

38. Ibid., 325, 334.

39. Ibid., 332.

40. Stirner, *The Ego and His Own*, xxiii.

41. Erlich, "Notes on the Uses of Monologue," 230.

42. Ibid.

43. Schopenhauer, *The World as Will and Representation*, vol. 1, 398.

44. Rolf Kauffeldt, "'Rückkehr in die Großstadt': Bemerkungen zu einem frühexpressionistischen Text Gustav Landauers," in *Literarische Fundstücke: Wiederentdeckungen und Neuentdeckungen: Festschrift für Manfred Windfuhr*, ed. Manfred Windfuhr, Ariane Neuhaus-Koch, and Gertrude Cepl-Kaufmann (Heidelberg: Winter, 2002), 226.

45. Hans Hinterhäuser, *Fin de siècle: Gestalten und Mythen* (Munich: Fink, 1977), 67.

46. Ibid., 68.

47. See Arthur Schopenhauer, *On the Basis of Morality*, trans. E. F. J. Payne (Indianapolis: Hackett, 1999).

48. Yossef Schwartz, "Martin Buber and Gustav Landauer: The Politicization of the Mystical," in *Martin Buber: Neue Perspektiven/New Perspectives*, ed. M. Zank (Tübingen: Mohr Siebeck, 2006), 215.

49. McHale, *The Cambridge Introduction to Postmodernism*, 150.

50. Ibid., 42.

51. Landauer, *Skepsis und Mystik*, 118–19.

52. Ibid., 119.

53. Here I am playing on the name of Food Not Bombs, a self-described anarchist organization active today, which serves free food to the homeless or hungry, and which I first learned of with their operation in Madison, Wisconsin.

54. Landauer, *Skepsis und Mystik*, 17.

Chapter 3

1. My use of the term "antimimetic" is derived from Richardson, *Unnatural Narrative*, 3.

2. Nancy, *The Inoperative Community*, 12.

3. Franz Kafka, "Description of a Struggle" in *The Complete Stories*, trans. Edwin and Willa Muir (New York: Schocken, 1971), 383. This English translation of the story is henceforth cited as DS. Original German is from Franz Kafka, *Beschreibung eines Kampfes und andere Schriften aus dem Nachlaß* (Frankfurt: Fischer, 1994), 113. German original henceforth cited as *BK*. Note that the English translation here is taken from the short text "Excursion into the Mountains," which Kafka also used verbatim in "Beschreibung eines Kampfes" draft B, but which does not appear in the English-language "Description of a Struggle" translated by Tania and James Stern and published in the *Complete Stories*, which is itself a composite of drafts A and B, edited by Max Brod (see "On the Material Included in this Volume" in Kafka, *Complete Stories*, 467–68).

4. Franz Kafka, "The Excursion into the Mountains," in *The Complete Stories*, 383.

5. Franz Kafka, *Letters to Milena*, trans. Philip Boehm (New York: Schocken, 2015), 112.

6. According to Max Brod, Kafka also read Landauer's anthology *Letters from the French Revolution* (*Briefe aus der französischen Revolution*) (Max Brod, *Über Franz Kafka* [Frankfurt: Fischer, 1974], 342–43).

7. See Mark Gelber, *Kafka, Zionism, and Beyond* (Tübingen: Niemeyer, 2004), 115–16.

8. Gustav Janouch, *Conversations with Kafka* (New York: New Directions, 1971).

9. Mijal Levi, *Kafka and Anarchism* (New York: Revisionist, 1972), 2.

10. Ernst Pawel, *The Nightmare of Reason: A Life of Franz Kafka* (New York: Farrar, Straus and Giroux, 1984), 153.

11. Noting Kafka's differences from "liberal and Marxist philosophers," Anderson writes that "Kafka is closer to Max Stirner and other anarchist philosophers who see work and any participation in the *Verkehr* of the socio-economic sphere as a threat to individual identity" (Mark Anderson, *Kafka's Clothes: Ornament and Aestheticism in the Habsburg Fin de Siècle* [Oxford: Clarendon, 1992], 134n15).

12. Joseph Vogl, *Ort der Gewalt: Kafkas literarische Ethik* (Munich: Fink, 1990), 199, 200.

13. See Manfred Engel and Bernd Auerochs, *Kafka-Handbuch: Leben–Werk–Wirkung* (Stuttgart: Metzler, 2010), 216.

14. Michael Löwy, "Franz Kafka and Libertarian Socialism," *New Politics* 6, no. 3 (1997).

15. See Landauer, *Skepsis und Mystik.*

16. Rainer Nägele, *Literarische Vexierbilder: Drei Versuche zu einer Figur* (Eggingen: Edition Isele, 2001), 26.

17. Vivian Liska, *When Kafka Says We: Uncommon Communities in German-Jewish Literature* (Bloomington: Indiana University Press, 2009), 15.

18. Franz Kafka, "Nachts," in *Sämtliche Erzählungen* (Frankfurt: Suhrkamp, 1973), 355. English translation by Tania and James Stern published as "At Night" in *The Complete Stories*, 436.

19. Franz Kafka, *Der Process. Roman in der Fassung der Handschrift* (Frankfurt: Fischer, 1994), 241.

20. McHale, *Postmodernist Fiction*, 106.

21. Ibid.

22. Günther Anders, *Franz Kafka* (London: Bowes and Bowes, 1960), 21.

23. Anders, *Franz Kafka*, 20.

24. Ibid.

25. Ibid.

26. Lubomir Dolezel, *Heterocosmica: Fiction and Possible Worlds* (Baltimore: Johns Hopkins University Press, 1998), 164.

27. For a critique of immanent community (as shared immediate presence of alleged members), see Nancy, *The Inoperative Community.*

28. B. Burssow, "Dostojewski und der Modernismus," *Sowjetwissenschaft: Kunst und Literatur* 14 (1966): 170.

29. Ibid., 171.

30. Ibid.

31. Dostoevsky wrote in his notebooks, years after completing *The Double*, that Goliadkin Junior was his "most important underground type." Goliadkin Sr. might, by extension, be seen as a departure point for all of the author's underground types (see the introduction by Evelyn Harden in Dostoevsky, *The Double: Two Versions*, xviii).

32. See William J. Dodd, *Kafka and Dostoevsky* (New York: St. Martin's, 1992). Dodd's work is the only book-length parallel study of Kafka and Dostoevsky. He argues that "the narrative situation in *Beschreibung eines Kampfes* has certain fundamental features in common with Dostoyevsky's use of first-person narrators, and there is also a certain thematic resonance with the early stories on the theme of the 'Petersburg dreamer'" (198).

33. Patrick Bridgwater points out that the Prague encounter in "Description" shares topographical affinities with Goliadkin's initial encounter with his doppelgänger (Patrick Bridgwater, *Kafka, Gothic and Fairytale* [Amsterdam: Rodopi, 2003], 9).

34. Frank, *Dostoevsky: A Writer in His Time*, 418.

35. McHale, *The Cambridge Introduction to Postmodernism*, 42.

36. McHale, *Postmodernist Fiction*, 32.

37. For a physiological interpretation of section 2 as the consequences of a concussion suffered by the narrator, see J. A. Asher, "Turning Points in Kafka's Stories," *Modern Language Review* 57, no. 1 (1962): 47–59. For a discussion of how the story creates a dichotomy of internal and external experience, permitting Kafka to fuse together materials he had written separately, see Jost Schillemeit, "Kafkas *Beschreibung eines Kampfes:* Ein Beitrag zum Textverständnis und zur Geschichte von Kafkas Schreiben," in *Der junge Kafka,* ed. Gerhard Kurz, 102–32 (Frankfurt: Suhrkamp, 1984).

38. See McHale, *Postmodernist Fiction*, 102.

39. Ibid., 103.

40. See Richardson, *Unnatural Narrative.*

41. Franz Kafka, *Briefe 1902–1924* (Frankfurt: Fischer, 1958), 22. Qtd. after Cersowsky, *"Mein ganzes Wesen ist auf Literatur gerichtet,"* 61.

42. Ibid.

43. Ibid.

44. Benedict Anderson, *Imagined Communities* (New York: Verso, 2006).

45. Jonathan Culler, *The Literary in Theory* (Stanford: Stanford University Press, 2007), 72.

46. Here I am borrowing terms that Schopenhauer used to discuss the "genius," as I showed in chapter 1 of this book.

47. Johann Georg Sulzer, *Allgemeine Theorie der schönen Künste: In einzelnen, nach alphabetischer Ordnung der Kunstwörter aufeinanderfolgenden, Artikeln abgehandelt, IV* (Hildesheim: Olms, 1967), 355.

48. Anders, *Franz Kafka*, 21.

49. Reiner Stach, *Kafka: Die frühen Jahre* (Frankfurt: Fischer, 2014), 319.

50. Lukács describes this universal condition of nonbelonging: "for to be a man in the new world is to be solitary" (Lukács, *Theory of the Novel*, 36).

51. David Herman, "Toward a Formal Description of Narrative Metalepsis," *Journal of Literary Semantics* 6, no. 2 (1997): 148.

52. An ontological metalepsis, as opposed to a rhetorical metalepsis, stipulates the actual boundary-crossing of an entity between discursive frames (i.e., a character who steps out of a movie screen to occupy the world around it). A rhetorical metalepsis is a technique of narrative that suggests interframe relationships but does not actualize them (i.e., when a narrator pretends to be

watching a character in real time but does not claim actual presence in the character's fictional world). For a discussion of the distinction between ontological and rhetorical (or "real" and "metaphorical") metalepses, see Monika Fludernik, "Scene Shift, Metalepsis, and the Metaleptic Mode," *Style* 37, no. 4 (2003): 382–400.

53. A photographic reproduction of the original handwritten draft, showing this elided quotation mark, is provided in Franz Kafka, *Hefte 2: Historisch-kritische Ausgabe sämtlicher Handschriften, Drucke und Typoskripte* (Basel: Stroemfeld/Roter Stern, 1995), 196–99.

54. Clayton Koelb has also noted the ambiguity of the phrase "vorübergehende Leute," suggesting that it might refer to the readers who are "'passing by' [the narrator's] writing" or to the "'transitory people' created by the text" (Clayton Koelb, *Kafka's Rhetoric: The Passion of Reading* [Ithaca, NY: Cornell University Press, 1989], 194).

55. McHale, *Postmodernist Fiction*, 226.

56. Ibid.

57. For discussion of Landauer as a romantic anticapitalist, see Michael Löwy, *Redemption and Utopia.*

58. Erlich, "Notes on the Uses of Monologue," 229.

59. See, for instance, Kári Driscoll, "Copia Nostri: Echoes of a Poetic Self in Kafka's 'Der Ausflug ins Gebirge,'" *German Quarterly* 84, no. 3 (2011).

60. Franz Kafka, *I am a Memory Come Alive: Autobiographical Writings* (New York: Schocken, 1974), 100.

Chapter 4

1. McHale, *Cambridge Introduction to Postmodernism*, 42.

2. Thomas Mann, *Doktor Faustus: Das Leben des deutschen Tonsetzers Adrian Leverkühn, erzählt von einem Freunde*, ed. Ruprecht Wimmer and Stephan Stachorski (Frankfurt: Fischer, 2007), 697.

3. Arno Schmidt, *Brand's Haide: Zwei Erzählungen* (Hamburg: Rowohlt, 1951); Ernst Jünger, *Der Waldgang* (Frankfurt: Klostermann, 1952).

4. Marlen Haushofer, *Die Wand* (Munich: DTV, 1991).

5. Nägele, *Literarische Vexierbilder*, 26. Nägele uses this expression to describe Kafka, but I apply it to Landauer and Bernhard as well.

6. In this sense, Kafka's text is in tune with the general spirit of Jean-Luc Nancy's theorizations of community, in which "nothing" names the missing metaphysical grounding that would assure the existence of community (see Ian James, "Naming the Nothing: Nancy and Blanchot on Community," in *Culture, Theory & Critique* 51, no. 2 [July 2010]: 171–87).

7. Richardson, *Unnatural Narrative*, 45.

8. Michael Clune, "Bernhard's Way," *Nonsite.org* 9 (2013), http://nonsite.org/feature/bernhards-way.

9. Ibid.

10. In his autobiographical work *Die Kälte: Eine Isolation*, the narrator—a highly stylized derivation of the empirical "Thomas Bernhard"—recounts how, while confined in a sanatorium in the Alps, he read *The Demons* (*Die Dämonen*) by Dostoevsky, a book of an "insatiability and radicality" (Unersättlichkeit

und Radikalität) previously unknown to the young reader. His immersion in Dostoevsky is described in spatial terms: *The Possessed* is described as a fluid body into which the narrator "dissolved" himself, and upon "returning" from the book he feared he would fall into "a terrifying abyss" of disappointment. These images of fluid and abyss are supplanted by the image of a path: "The enormity of the Demons had made me strong, had shown me a path, had told me that I was on the right path, the path *out*" (Die Ungeheuerlichkeit der Dämonen hatte mich stark gemacht, einen Weg gezeigt, mir gesagt, daß ich auf dem richtigen Weg sei, *hinaus*) (Thomas Bernhard, *Die Kälte: Eine Isolation* [Salzburg: Residenz, 1981], 141, my translations).

11. Thomas Bernhard, *Frost* (Frankfurt: Suhrkamp, 1972), 20, my translation. Henceforth cited as *F*.

12. Rainer Barbey speaks of a "Bernhard-spezifischen Anarchismus" that is not primarily political but is driven by a "poetics of anarchy that explodes the construct of classical aesthetics along with its normative formal structures" (Poetik der Anarchie, die das Gebäude der klassischen Ästhetik mitsamt ihren normativen formalen Strukturen in die Luft sprengt) (Rainer Barbey, "Spielarten des Anarchismus im Werk Thomas Bernhards," *Literatur für Leser* 30, no. 3 [2007]: 157), my translation.

13. Thomas Bernhard, *Ja* (Frankfurt: Suhrkamp, 1978), 139, my translation.

14. There are four folios in the Thomas Bernhard Archive (NLTB) that contain pages from the *Leichtlebig* novel. Two of them are now in print: W1/1 (available in the 2013 volume *Argumente eines Winterspaziergängers* as "Leichtlebig"); and W1/1a (available in the same volume as "Argumente eines Winterspaziergängers"). Two folios of convolutes (largely disorganized collections of pages mixed in with other drafts of *Frost*) remain entirely unpublished. These are W1/3, which contains roughly seventy pages belonging to the *Leichtlebig* novel, and W1/3a, which contains around eighty pages belonging to that novel. When citing W1/1 and W1/1a, I have included references to the published edition: Thomas Bernhard, "Leichtlebig. Ein Fragment zu 'Frost,'" in *Argumente eines Winterspaziergängers: Zwei Fragmente zu Frost* (Berlin: Suhrkamp, 2013), 45–105; henceforth cited as *LL*.

15. See Raimund Fellinger and Martin Huber, "Editorische Nachbemerkung," in Bernhard, *Argumente eines Winterspaziergängers*, 139–47.

16. Ibid.

17. Hermann Rafetseder, *NS–Zwangsarbeits–Schicksale: Erkenntnisse zu Erscheinungsformen der Oppression und zum NS-Lagersystem aus der Arbeit des Österreichischen Versöhnungsfonds; Eine Dokumentation im Auftrag des Zukunftsfonds der Republik Österreich* (Bremen: Wiener Verlag für Sozialforschung, 2014), 662.

18. See Brigitte Bailer-Galanda and Gerhard Botz, *Widerstand und Verfolgung in Oberösterreich: 1934–1945: Eine Dokumentation*, vol. 1 (Vienna: Österreichischer Bundesverlag, 1982), 84, cited after Timothy Kirk, *Nazism and the Working Class in Austria: Industrial Unrest and Political Dissent in the "National Community"* (Cambridge: Cambridge Univeristy Press, 1996), 163ff., 69.

19. See William Bader, *Austria between East and West, 1945–1955* (Stanford: Stanford University Press, 1966).

20. For more on Lawrence, see Coeli Fitzpatrick, "T. E. Lawrence," in *Orientalist Writers*, ed. Fitzpatrick and Dwayne A. Tunstall (Detroit: Gale, 2012), Web.

21. Jakob Norberg, "On Display: Conditions of Critique in Austria," *Austrian Studies* 46, no. 1 (Spring 2013): 25.

22. Jill Lewis, *Workers and Politics in Occupied Austria, 1945–55* (Manchester: Manchester University Press, 2007), 204.

23. The original German reads: "eine Fülle von unerledigten Preis- und Lohnfragen vor der Kommission" (*LL*, 83).

24. Lewis, *Workers*, 176.

25. Jan Rehmann, *Theories of Ideology* (Chicago: Haymarket, 2013), 140.

26. See Rainer Nick and Anton Pelinka, *Bürgerkrieg--Sozialpartnerschaft: Das politische System Österreichs 1. und 2. Republik: ein Vergleich* (Vienna: Jugend und Volk, 1984).

27. Günter Bischof and Anton Pelinka, introduction to *Austro-Corporatism: Past—Present—Future* (New Brunswick: Transaction, 1996), 10.

28. Oliver Rathkolb, "Die Zweite Republik (seit 1945)," in *Geschichte Österreichs*, ed. Thomas Winkelbauer (Stuttgart: Reclam, 2015), 546.

29. NLTB, W1/3a, 96 .

30. Ibid., W1/3a, 101.

31. Fellinger and Huber, "Nachwort," 143.

32. NLTB, W1/3, 50.

33. NLTB, W1/3, 47.

34. Ibid.

35. Thomas Bernhard, "Argumente eines Winterspaziergängers," in *Argumente eines Winterspaziergängers*, 23. Henceforth cited as AEW.

36. NLTB, W1/3, 47.

37. Ibid., W1/3, 48.

38. Ibid.

39. Richardson, *Unnatural Narrative*, 46.

40. McHale, *Postmodernist Fiction*, 37.

41. Selection from the entry in the Grimms' dictionary: *Gestrüppe, Gestrüpp, n.*, "wirres Dickicht . . . verwachsenes, verwirrtes und verwildertes Gewächs." See entry in the online edition of the Grimms' dictionary (*Deutsches Wörterbuch von Jacob Grimm und Wilhelm Grimm*, http://germazope.uni-trier.de/Projects/DWB).

42. McHale, *Cambridge Introduction to Postmodernism*, 42.

43. NLTB, W1/1a, 48.

44. Ibid.

45. McHale, *Postmodernist Fiction*, 37.

46. NLTB, W1/3, 61.

47. NLTB, W1/3a, 97.

48. Ibid.

49. Ibid., W1/3, 61; W1/3a, 96.

50. NLTB, W1/3, 36–37.

51. Ibid., 47.

52. The Doctor at one point refers to himself as "dieser Niemand" (ibid., 61).

53. Ibid., 37.
54. Ibid., 36.
55. McHale, *Postmodernist Fiction*, 37.
56. Ibid., 36.
57. Ibid., 37.
58. Ibid., 36.
59. See Brigitte Bailer-Galanda and Gerhard Botz, *Widerstand und Verfolgung in Oberösterreich: 1934–1945: Eine Dokumentation*, vol. 1 (Vienna: Österreichischer Bundesverlag, 1982), 84, cited after Timothy Kirk, *Nazism and the Working Class in Austria: Industrial Unrest and Political Dissent in the "National Community"* (Cambridge: Cambridge Univeristy Press, 1996), 163ff., 69.
60. The Doctor speaks of "eine Auflassung des Grundbesitzes überhaupt" and uses the word "Kolchosenwirtschaft" (ibid., 38).
61. Ibid., 64.
62. See Jill Lewis's chapter "The Putsch That Never Was" in *Workers and Politics in Occupied Austria*, 170–93. Lewis shows that claims about a planned communist putsch in 1950 rested on dubious assumptions and little evidence: "Without concrete proof of a plan to seize power, the case remained circumstantial. In a nine-hour debate in the Austrian parliament, also on 12 October, government politicians repeated the putsch claim time and again. To some speakers, the evidence rested on the nature of Communism itself, in the shape of its revolutionary theory which preached the violent overthrow of the bourgeois state" (183).
63. Ibid., 29.
64. McHale, *Cambridge Introduction to Postmodernism*, 42.
65. Nancy, *The Inoperative Community*, 80.

Chapter 5

1. The general thesis of McHale's *Postmodernist Fiction* is that postmodern literature tends to foreground the issue of world-making (ontology), as opposed to modernism, which is concerned with our knowledge of the world (epistemology).
2. McHale, *Postmodernist Fiction*, 120.
3. Ibid., 10.
4. See Jens Loescher, *Mythos, Macht und Kellersprache: Wolfang Hilbigs Prosa im Spiegel der Nachwende* (New York: Rodopi, 2003).
5. Wolfgang Hilbig, "Alte Abdeckerei," in *Werke*, vol. 3 (Frankfurt: Fischer, 2010), 181. Henceforth cited as AA. My translations. For other discussions of how Hilbig's work directly cites Kafka's prose, see Sylvie Marie Bordaux, *Literatur als Subversion: Eine Untersuchung des Prosawerks von Wolfgang Hilbig* (Göttingen: Culliver, 2000), 249–53.
6. For a discussion of the Hilbig's open antipathy toward and implicit affinity to postmodernism, see Paul Cooke, *Speaking the Taboo: A Study of the Work of Wolfgang Hilbig* (Amsterdam: Rodopi, 2000), 10.
7. See Agamben, *The Coming Community*. For a recent discussion of the shared isolation of "the mediatized" as a collective social subject, see Michael Hardt and Antonio Negri, *Declaration* (New York: Argo-Navis, 2012), 14–23.

8. Wolfgang Hilbig, "Literatur ist Monolog," www.deutscheakademie.de/de/auszeichnungen/georg-buechner-preis/wolfgang-hilbig/dankrede.

9. Ibid.

10. Ibid.

11. Ibid.

12. Michele Willson, "Community in the Abstract: A Political and Ethical Dilemma?" in *Virtual Politics: Identity and Community in Cyberspace*, ed. David Holmes, 145–162 (London: Sage, 1997).

13. Ibid., my emphasis.

14. Nancy, *The Inoperative Community*, 76.

15. Ibid.

16. The mysterious workers at the rendering plant Germania II in "Old Rendering Plant" write letters that, when described, prompt the narrator to quote Joyce's *Finnegans Wake*, as if to suggest that Joyce's words actually belong to this underworld: "*ostrygods gaggin fishygods!*" (AA, 177). This phrase, which plays on a struggle of the Ostrogoths against (gegen) the Visigoths, is also the epigraph of Hilbig's novel.

17. László Krasznahorkai, introduction, trans. Ottilie Mulzet, in Wolfgang Hilbig, *The Sleep of the Righteous* (San Francisco: Two Lines, 2015), 4.

18. For more on the general historical discussion of ecological movements after 1970, see Joachim Radkau, *The Age of Ecology: A Global History* (Cambridge: Polity, 2014). For an example of intellectual and literary dissidents' protests against environmental destruction in the GDR, see the recent reprint of the illegal journal published by Sylvia Kabus and Reinhard Bernhof, *Umfeldblätter* 1 (Leipzig: Leipziger Literaturverlag 2009).

19. See Hilbig, "Literatur ist Monolog."

20. Juri Lotman, *Culture and Explosion* (New York: De Gruyter, 2009), 68.

21. Bertolt Brecht, "An die Nachgeborenen," in *Gesammelte Werke* (Frankfurt: Suhrkamp, 1967), 9:723.

22. See, for instance, the poem "Gespräch über Bäume" by Reinhard Bernhof in the Leipzig underground journal *Umfeldblätter* 1 (2009), which contains a parallel critique of Brecht's dictum. For a discussion of literary retorts to Brecht outside of the GDR, see Helmut Heinze, "Natur im politisch-literarischen Zeitgespräch: Einige Tendenzen in der Naturdiskussion der 80er Jahre," in *Pluralismus und Postmoderne: Zur Literatur- und Kulturgeschichte der achtziger Jahre*, ed. Helmut Kreuzer, 26–45 (Frankfurt: Peter Lang, 1991).

23. Ingo Schulze, "Nachwort," in Wolfgang Hilbig, *Werke* (Frankfurt: Fischer, 2010), 3:319.

24. Ibid.

25. See McHale, *Postmodernist Fiction.*

26. Ibid., 83.

27. Wolfgang Hilbig, "Die Kunde von den Bäumen," in *Werke* (Frankfurt: Fischer, 2010), 3:252. Henceforth cited as DKB. My translations.

28. Fyodor Dostoevsky, *Demons*, trans. Richard Pevear and Larissa Volokhonsky (New York: Vintage Classics, 1995), 3.

29. Bernhard, *Die Kälte: Eine Isolation*, 141.

30. See, for instance, Jean-Luc Godard's 1967 film *La Chinoise*, where Dostoevsky's *Demons* is retold as a story of 1960s student revolutionaries. *La Chinoise*, directed by Jean-Luc Godard (1968; Neuilly-sur-Sein, Gaumont vidéo, 2012), DVD.

31. Dostoevsky, *Demons*, 3.

32. Frank, *Dostoevsky: A Writer in His Time*, 792.

33. Walter Benjamin, *Illuminations*, trans. Harry Zohn (New York: Houghton Mifflin Harcourt, 1968), 257.

34. McHale, *Postmodernist Fiction*, 73.

35. Gabriella Nagy, "Towards New Unrealities: An Interview with László Krasznahorkai," *Hungarian Literature Online*, May 2012, www.hlo.hu/news/krasznahorkai_interview.

36. Ibid.

37. Timothy Morton, *Ecology without Nature: Rethinking Environmental Aesthetics* (Cambridge: Harvard University Press, 2009), 185.

38. Ibid., 187.

39. Richardson, *Unnatural Narrative*, xix.

40. Gillian Pye, "Trash and Transformation: The Search for Identity in Wolfgang Hilbig's *Die Kunde von den Bäumen* and *Alte Abdeckerei*," *New German Critique* 39, no. 2 (2012): 95.

41. Dostoevsky, *Demons*, 235.

42. Ibid., 236.

43. McHale, *Postmodernist Fiction*, 141.

44. Georg Schmid, "Proklamation der 'JENSEITS-DES-POINT-OF-NO-RETURN-LITERATUR' in Form eines ternär strukturierten 'wissenschaftlichen Vortrags' und zweier burlekster Entr'actes," *Manuscripte* 82 (1983): 76.

Chapter 6

1. Frieden, *Genius and Monologue*, 7.

2. For a note on Krasznahorkai's affinities to Dostoevsky, see "Anticipate Doom: The Millions Interviews László Krasznahorkai," *The Millions*, May 9, 2012, www.themillions.com/2012/05/anticipate-doom-the-millions-interviews-laszlo-krasznahorkai.html. For one indication of his debt to Kafka, see the epigraph to the novel *Satantango* (László Krasznahorkai, *Satantango* [New York: New Directions, 2012]). For his avowed connections to Bernhard and Hilbig, see Gabriella Nagy, "Towards New Unrealities. An Interview with László Krasznahorkai," *Hungarian Literature Online*, May 2012, www.hlo.hu/news/krasznahorkai_interview.

3. László Krasznahorkai, *Megy a világ* (Budapest: Magveto, 2013). My translation is based on the German edition: László Krasznahorkai, *Die Welt voran*, trans. Heike Flemming (Frankfurt: Fischer, 2015), 273.

4. László Krasznahorkai, *War and War*, trans. George Szirtes (New York: New Directions, 2006), 261.

5. This is Krasznahorkai's summary from the interview "Anticipate Doom," *The Millions*.

6. Krasznahorkai, *War and War*, 257.

7. Ibid., 18.

8. Erlich, "Notes on the Uses of Monologue," 229.

9. See Mauro Javier Cardena, "Conversations with Lászlo Krasznahorkai," *Music and Literature,* December 12, 2013, www.musicandliterature.org/features/2013/12/11/a-conversation-with-lszl-krasznahorkai.

10. Ibid.

11. On the site www.warandwar.com, the following text appears following the error message "Not Found": "Additionally, please be informed that this home page service has been called off due to recurring overdue payment. Attempted mail deliveries to Mr. G. Korin [*sic*] have been returned to sender with a note: address unknown. Consequently, all data have been erased from this home page."

12. László Krasznahorkai, *The Last Wolf and Herman*, trans. George Szirtes (New York: New Directions, 2016), 7.

13. Ibid., 11.

14. Ibid., 12.

15. Ibid., 11.

16. Ibid., 25.

17. Ibid., 12.

18. Ibid., 71.

19. Ibid., 69–70.

20. Ibid., 76.

21. See Krasznahorkai, "Introduction." See also Nagy, "Towards New Unrealities."

22. Erlich, "Notes on the Uses of Monologue," 229.

23. See the chapter "Voice" in Genette, *Narrative Discourse*, 212–16.

24. Ingeborg Bachmann, "Literatur ist Utopie," in *Essays, Reden, vermischte Schriften, Anhang* (Munich: Piper, 1993), 81–102.

25. Ingeborg Bachmann, *Sämtliche Gedichte* (Munich: Piper, 1983). English translation is modified from Ingeborg Bachmann, "Bohemia Lies by the Sea," in *Ingeborg Bachmann: Schreiben gegen den Krieg / Writing Against War*, ed. Hans Höller and Karl Solibakke (Vienna: Löcker, 2008), 98.

26. Ibid.

27. Ibid.

28. Nicole Schumacher, "Faschismus, Destruktion, Utopie: Die Bedeutung von Ingeborg Bachmanns 'Böhmen liegt am Meer' für Thomas Bernhards 'Auslöschung,'" *Zeitschrift für Deutsche Philologie* 118, no. 4 (1999): 588.

29. See Quintilian, *Institutes of Oratory*, 133.

30. See McHale, *Postmodernist Fiction*, 222–27. The final quote is from Monika Fludernik, "Scene Shift, Metalepsis, and the Metaleptic Mode," *Style*. 37, no. 4 (2003): 396. Note that Fludernik is positing this idea of the centrality of metalepsis as a speculation; she ends her article by maintaining that there are good practical reasons for narratologists *not* to overgeneralize the applicability of metalepsis since it would efface the heuristic distinctions between textual layers that make narratology useful in the first place.

31. McHale writes: "Metalepsis, the violation of ontological boundaries, is a model or mirror of love." He goes on to underscore that this form of love conventionally defines literature but has taken on new life in postmodernist fiction:

"That we 'love' the books we read (and write) is of course a mere cliché, a dead metaphor. Postmodernist writers . . . reanimate this cliché" (McHale, *Postmodernist Fiction*, 226–27).

32. *The Book of Franza & Requiem for Fanny Goldmann*, trans. Peter Filkins (Evanston: Northwestern University Press, 1999), 68.

33. Ingeborg Bachmann, *Das Buch Franza. Requiem für Fanny Goldmann. Texte des "Todesarten"-Projekts* (Munich: Piper, 2004), 61.

34. Ibid., 136.

35. Frantz Fanon, *The Wretched of the Earth,* trans. Richard Philcox (New York: Grove, 2005). For discussion of the complex intersection of race, gender, and the history of colonialism in *The Book of Franza*, see Sara Lennox, "Geschlecht, Rasse und Geschichte in 'Der Fall Franza,'" in *text + kritik: Sonderband Ingeborg Bachmann*, ed. Sigrid Weigel, 156–79 (Darmstadt: Wissenschaftliche Buchgesellschaft, 1984).

36. McHale, *Cambridge Introduction to Postmodernism*, 42.

BIBLIOGRAPHY

Primary Sources

Bachmann, Ingeborg. "Bohemia Lies by the Sea." In *Ingeborg Bachmann: Schreiben gegen den Krieg/Writing against War,* edited by Hans Höller and Karl Solibakke, 98–101. Vienna: Löcker, 2008.

———. *The Book of Franza and Requiem for Fanny Goldman.* Translated by Peter Filkins. Evanston: Northwestern University Press, 2010.

———. *Das Buch Franza. Requiem für Fanny Goldmann. Texte des "Todesarten"-Projekts.* Munich: Piper, 2004.

———. *Essays, Reden, vermischte Schriften, Anhang.* Munich: Piper, 1993.

———. *Sämtliche Gedichte.* Munich: Piper, 1983.

Bernhard, Thomas. *Argumente eines Winterspaziergängers: Zwei Fragmente zu Frost.* Berlin: Suhrkamp, 2013.

———. *Frost.* Frankfurt: Suhrkamp, 1972.

———. *Gargoyles.* Translated by Clara Winston. New York: Vintage, 2006.

———. *Ja.* Frankfurt: Suhrkamp, 1978.

———. *Die Kälte: Eine Isolation.* Salzburg: Residenz, 1981.

———. *The Loser.* Translated by Jack Dawson. New York: Vintage International, 1991.

———. *Meine Preise.* Berlin: Suhrkamp, 2010.

———. *Nachlaß Thomas Bernhard.* Thomas Bernhard Archive, Gmunden.

———. *Der Untergeher.* Frankfurt: Suhrkamp, 1988.

———. *Verstörung.* Frankfurt: Suhrkamp, 1969.

Dostoevsky, Fyodor. *The Brothers Karamazov.* Translated by Richard Pevear and Larissa Volokhonsky. New York: Farrar, Straus and Giroux, 2002.

———. *Crime and Punishment: The Coulson Translation, Backgrounds and Sources, Essays in Criticism.* Translated by Jessie Coulson. New York: Norton, 1989.

———. *Demons.* Translated by Richard Pevear and Larissa Volokhonsky. New York: Vintage Classics, 1995.

———. *The Double: Two Versions.* Translated by Evelyn Harden. Ann Arbor: Ardis, 1985.

———. *The Double and the Gambler.* Translated by Richard Pevear and Larissa Volokhonsky. New York: Vintage Classics, 2007.

———. *Notes from Underground.* Translated by Richard Pevear and Larissa Volokhonsky. New York: Vintage Classics, 1994.

Hilbig, Wolfgang. "Literatur ist Monolog." www.deutscheakademie.de/de/auszeichnungen/georg-buechner-preis/wolfgang-hilbig/dankrede.

———. *Das Provisorium*. Frankfurt: Fischer, 2001.

———. *Werke*. Vol. 3, *Die Weiber; Alte Abdeckerei; Die Kunde von den Bäumen*. Frankfurt: Fischer, 2010.

Kafka, Franz. *Beschreibung eines Kampfes und andere Schriften aus dem Nachlaß*. Frankfurt: Fischer, 1994.

———. *Briefe 1902–1924*. Frankfurt: Fischer, 1958.

———. *The Complete Stories*. New York: Schocken, 1971.

———. *Hefte 2. Historisch-kritische Ausgabe sämtlicher Handschriften, Drucke und Typoskripte* Basel: Stroemfeld/Roter Stern, 1995.

———. *I Am a Memory Come Alive: Autobiographical Writings*. New York: Schocken, 1974.

———. *Letters to Milena*. Translated by Philip Boehm. New York: Schocken, 2015.

———. *Der Proceß. Roman in der Fassung der Handschrift*. Frankfurt: Fischer, 1994.

———. *Sämtliche Erzählungen*. Frankfurt: Suhrkamp, 1973.

———. *Tagebücher*. Volume 3, *1914–1923*. Frankfurt: Fischer, 2008.

Krasznahorkai, László. "Anticipate Doom: The Millions Interviews László Krasznahorkai." *The Millions*. May 9, 2012. www.themillions.com/2012/05/anticipate-doom-the- millions-interviews-laszlo-krasznahorkai.html.

———. Introduction. Translated by Ottilie Mulzet. In Wolfgang Hilbig, *The Sleep of the Righteous*, 1–4. San Francisco: Two Lines, 2015.

———. *The Last Wolf and Herman*. Translated by George Szirtes. New York: New Directions, 2016.

———. *Megy a világ*. Budapest: Magveto, 2013.

———. *War and War*. Translated by George Szirtes. New York: New Directions, 2006.

———. *Die Welt voran*. Translated by Heike Flemming. Frankfurt: Fischer, 2015.

Landauer, Gustav. *Erkenntnis und Befreiung: Ausgewählte Reden und Aufsätze*. Frankfurt: Suhrkamp, 1976.

———. *Macht und Mächte: Novellen*. Berlin: Fleischel, 1903.

———. *Signatur: g.l.: Gustav Landauer im "Sozialist," 1892–1899*. Edited by Ruth Link-Salinger. Frankfurt: Suhrkamp, 1986.

———. *Skepsis und Mystik*. Berlin: Fleischel, 2003.

———. *Der Todesprediger*. Cologne: Marcan-Block-Verlag, 1923.

———. *Der Todesprediger*. Lucerne: Edition Libertaire, 1990.

Nietzsche, Friedrich. *Complete Works XIV: The Will to Power I*. Translated by Oscar Levy. New York: Russell and Russell, 1964.

———. *Complete Works XVI: Twilight of the Idols*. Translated by Oscar Levy. New York: Russell and Russell, 1964.

———. *Götzen-Dämmerung*. In *Nietzsche. Werke: Kritische Gesamtausgabe*, pt. 6, vol. 3, edited by Giorgio Colli and Mazzino Montinari, 51–154. Berlin: De Gruyter, 1969.

———. *Human, All Too Human*. Translated by Marion Faber and Stephen Lehmann. London: Penguin Classics, 1994.
———. *On the Genealogy of Morals and Ecce Homo*. Translated by Walter Kaufman. New York: Vintage, 1989.
———. *Thus Spoke Zarathustra*. Translated by R. J. Hollingdale. New York: Penguin Classics, 1961.
———. *The Will to Power*. Translated by Walter Kaufman and R. J. Hollingdale. New York: Vintage, 1968.
Schopenhauer, Arthur. *On the Basis of Morality*. Translated by E. F. J. Payne. Indianapolis: Hackett, 1999.
———. *Parerga und Paralipomena*. Vol. 2. Berlin: A. W. Hayn, 1851.
———. *Die Welt als Wille und Vorstellung I*. Frankfurt: Suhrkamp, 1986.
———. *Die Welt als Wille und Vorstellung II*. Frankfurt: Suhrkamp, 1986.
———. *The World as Will and Representation*. Vol. 1. Translated by E. F. J. Payne. Mineola, NY: Dover, 1966.
———. *The World as Will and Representation*. Vol. 2. Translated by E. F. J. Payne. Mineola, NY: Dover, 1966.

Secondary Sources

Agamben, Giorgio. *The Coming Community*. Translated by Michael Hardt. Minneapolis: University of Minnesota Press, 1991.
Al-Kassim, Dina. *On Pain of Speech: Fantasies of the First Order and the Literary Rant*. Berkeley: University of California Press, 2010.
Allen, Emily. "The Victorian Novel and Theater." In *The Oxford Handbook of the Victorian Novel*, 571–88. Oxford: Oxford University Press, 2013: 571–88.
Anders, Günther. *Franz Kafka*. London: Bowes and Bowes, 1960.
Anderson, Benedict. *Imagined Communities*. New York: Verso, 2006.
Anderson, Mark. *Kafka's Clothes: Ornament and Aestheticism in the Habsburg Fin de Siècle*. Oxford: Clarendon, 1992.
Arendt, Dieter. *Nihilismus: Die Anfänge von Jacobi bis Nietzsche*. Cologne: Hegner-Bücherei, 1970.
Asher, J. A. "Turning Points in Kafka's Stories." *Modern Language Review* 57, no. 1 (1962): 47–59.
Bader, William. *Austria between East and West, 1945–1955*. Stanford: Stanford University Press, 1966.
Bailer-Galanda, Brigitte, and Gerhard Botz. *Widerstand und Verfolgung in Oberösterreich: 1934–1945; Eine Dokumentation* Vol. 1. Vienna: Österreichischer Bundesverlag, 1982.
Bakhtin, Mikhail. "The Hero's Monologic Discourse and Narrational Discourse in Dostoevsky's Early Novels." In *Modern Critical Views: Fyodor Dostoevsky*. Edited by Harold Bloom. New York: Chelsea House, 1989: 9–34.
———. *Problems of Dostoevsky's Poetics*. Minneapolis: University of Minnesota Press, 1984.

Bal, Mieke. *Narratology: Introduction to the Theory of Narrative*. Toronto: University of Toronto Press, 1997.
Barbey, Rainer. "Spielarten des Anarchismus im Werk Thomas Bernhards." *Literatur für Leser* 30, no. 3 (2007): 147–57.
Barthes, Roland. "Myth Today." In *A Barthes Reader*, edited by Susan Sontag, 93–149. New York: Hill and Wang, 1983.
Ben-Merre, David. "Time Travels: Metalepsis and Modern Poetry." PhD diss., Brown University, 2008.
Benjamin, Walter. *Illuminations*. Translated by Harry Zohn. New York: Houghton Mifflin Harcourt, 1968.
Bernstein, Eduard. "Etwas Erzählungsliteratur." In *Die Neue Zeit: Revue des geistigen und öffentlichen Lebens* 11, no. 2 (1893): 260–70.
Bischof, Günter, and Anton Pelinka, eds. *Austro-Corporatism: Past–Present–Future*. New Brunswick: Transaction, 1996.
Blackbourn, David, and Geoff Eley. *The Peculiarities of German History: Bourgeois Society and Politics in Nineteenth-Century Germany*. Oxford: Oxford University Press, 1984.
Bookchin, Murray. *The Spanish Anarchists: The Heroic Years, 1868–1936*. New York: Free Life Editions, 1977.
Bordaux, Sylvie Marie. *Literatur als Subversion: Eine Untersuchung des Prosawerks von Wolfgang Hilbig*. Göttingen: Culliver, 2000.
Brecht, Bertolt. "An die Nachgeborenen." In *Gesammelte Werke*, 9:723. Frankfurt: Suhrkamp, 1967.
Bridgwater, Patrick. *Kafka, Gothic and Fairytale*. Amsterdam: Rodopi, 2003.
Broch, Hermann. *Die Schlafwandler: Eine Romantrilogie*. Frankfurt: Suhrkamp, 1978.
Brod, Max. *Über Franz Kafka*. Frankfurt: Fischer, 1974.
Bull, Malcolm. *Anti-Nietzsche*. London: Verso, 2011.
Burssow, B. "Dostojewski und der Modernismus." *Sowjetwissenschaft: Kunst und Literatur* 14 (1966): 155–74.
Butzer, Günter. *Soliloquium: Theorie und Geschichte des Selbstgesprächs in der europäischen Literatur*. Munich: Fink, 2008.
Cardena, Mauro Javier. "Conversations with Lászlo Krasznahorkai." *Music and Literature*. December 12, 2013. www.musicandliterature.org/features/2013/12/11/a-conversation-with-lszl-krasznahorkai.
Carr, Reg. *Anarchism in France: The Case of Octave Mirbeau*. Manchester: Manchester University Press, 1977.
Cersowsky, Peter. *"Mein ganzes Wesen ist auf Literatur gerichtet": Franz Kafka im Kontext der literarischen Dekadenz*. Würzburg: Königshausen and Neumann, 1983.
Cladis, Mark. "Beyond Solidarity? Durkheim and Twenty-First Century Democracy in a Global Age." In *The Cambridge Companion to Companion to Durkheim*, edited by Jeffrey Alexander and Philip Smith. Cambridge: Cambridge University Press, 2005.
Conway, Daniel. "Whither the 'Good Europeans'? Nietzsche's New World Order." *South Central Review* 66, no. 3 (2009): 40–60.

Cooke, Paul. *Speaking the Taboo: A Study of the Work of Wolfgang Hilbig.* Amsterdam: Rodopi, 2000.

Cottom, Daniel. "Futurism, Nietzsche, and the Misanthropy of Art," *Common Knowledge* 13, no. 1 (2007): 87–97.

Coupeau, Steeve. *The History of Haiti.* Westport, CT: Greenwood, 2007.

Culler, Jonathan. *The Literary in Theory.* Stanford: Stanford University Press, 2007.

Davis, Whitney. "Schopenhauer's Ontology of Art." *Qui Parle* 15, no. 1 (2004): 63–80.

Despoix, Philippe. "Toward a German-Jewish Construct: Landauer's Arnold Himmelheber." In *Gustav Landauer: Anarchist and Jew*, 121–31. Berlin: De Gruyter, 2015.

Dodd, William J. *Kafka and Dostoevsky.* New York: St. Martin's, 1992.

Dolezel, Lubomir. *Heterocosmica: Fiction and Possible Worlds.* Baltimore: Johns Hopkins University Press, 1998.

Dowden, Stephen. *Sympathy for the Abyss: A Study in the Novel of German Modernism: Kafka, Broch, Musil, and Thomas Mann.* Tübingen: Niemeyer, 1986.

Driscoll, Kári. "Copia Nostri: Echoes of a Poetic Self in Kafka's 'Der Ausflug ins Gebirge.'" *German Quarterly* 84, no. 3 (2011): 275–91.

Durkheim, Émile. *On Suicide.* Translated by Robin Buss. London: Penguin Classics, 2007.

———. *Professional Ethics and Civic Morals.* Translated by Cornelia Brookfield. Glencoe: Free Press, 1958.

Eikhenbaum, Boris. "Leskov and Contemporary Prose." *Russian Literature Triquarterly* 11 (1975): 211–24.

Ellison, Ralph. *Invisible Man.* New York: Vintage, 1995.

Engel, Manfred, and Bernd Auerochs. *Kafka-Handbuch: Leben–Werk–Wirkung.* Stuttgart: Metzler, 2010.

Engels, Friedrich. *The Origin of the Family, Private Property, and the State.* New York: Penguin Classics, 2010.

Erlich, Victor. "Notes on the Uses of Monologue in Artistic Prose." *International Journal of Slavic Linguistics and Poetics* 1–2 (1959): 223–31.

———. "Two Concepts of the Dostoevsky Novel," *International Journal of Slavic Linguistics and Poetics* 25–26 (1982): 127–36.

Esposito, Roberto. *Terms of the Political.* Translated by Rhiannon Noel Welch. New York: Fordham University Press, 2012.

Fanon, Frantz. *The Wretched of the Earth.* Translated by Richard Philcox. New York: Grove, 2005.

Fitzpatrick, Coeli. "T. E. Lawrence." In *Orientalist Writers*, edited by Fitzpatrick and Dwayne A. Tunstall. Detroit: Gale, 2012. Web.

Fludernik, Monika. "Scene Shift, Metalepsis, and the Metaleptic Mode." *Style* 37, no. 4 (2003): 382–400.

Földenyi, László. *Dostojewskij liest in Sibirien Hegel und bricht in Tränen aus.* Translated by Hans Skirecki. Berlin: Matthes and Seitz, 2008.

Fortmann, Patrick. "Kafka's Literary Communities." *Modern Language Review* 104 (2009): 1038–62.

Frank, Joseph. *Dostoevsky: A Writer in His Time*. Princeton: Princeton University Press, 2009.

———. "Nihilism and 'Notes from the Underground.'" *Sewanee Review* 69, no. 1 (1961): 1–33.

Frieden, Ken. *Genius and Monologue*. Ithaca, NY: Cornell University Press, 1985.

Gamper, Herbert. "Ordnung, Gewohnheit, Anarchie: Thomas Bernhard und Paul Landsberg." In *Thomas Bernhard: Traditionen und Trabanten*, 61–67. Würzburg: Königshausen und Neumann, 2009.

Gelber, Mark. *Kafka, Zionism, and Beyond*. Tübingen: Niemeyer, 2004.

Genette, Gérard. *Narrative Discourse: An Essay in Method*. Translated by Jane Lewin. Ithaca, NY: Cornell University Press, 1980.

Gillespie, Michael Allen. *Nihilism before Nietzsche*. Chicago: University of Chicago Press, 1994.

Girard, René. *Resurrection from the Underground: Feodor Dostoevsky*. Translated by James Williams. East Lansing: Michigan State University Press, 2012.

Goethe, Johann Wolfgang von. *Sämtliche Werke, Briefe, Tagebücher und Gespräche*. Vol. 1. Frankfurt: Deutscher Klassiker-Verlag, 1987.

Grimm, Jacob, and Wilhelm Grimm et al. *Deutsches Wörterbuch von Jacob Grimm und Wilhelm Grimm*. Leipzig: Hirzel. http://germazope.uni-trier.de/Projects/DWB.

Hardt, Michael, and Negri, Antonio. *Declaration* (New York: Argo-Navis, 2012).

Haushofer, Marlen. *Die Wand*. Munich: DTV, 1991.

Heidegger, Martin. *Sein und Zeit*. Tübingen: Niemeyer, 2006.

Heinze, Helmut. "Natur im politisch-literarischen Zeitgespräch: Einige Tendenzen in der Naturdiskussion der 80er Jahre." In *Pluralismus und Postmoderne: Zur Literatur- und Kulturgeschichte der achtziger Jahre*, edited by Helmut Kreuzer, 26–45. Frankfurt: Peter Lang, 1991.

Helms, Hans. *Die Ideologie der anonymen Gesellschaft*. Cologne: Verlag M. DuMont Schauberg, 1967.

Herman, David. "Toward a Formal Description of Narrative Metalepsis." *Journal of Literary Semantics* 6, no. 2 (1997): 132–52.

Hinterhäuser, Hans. *Fin de siècle: Gestalten und Mythen*. Munich: Fink, 1977.

Hobbes, Thomas. *Leviathan*. New York: Penguin Classics, 1982.

Ignatov, Assen. "Demon and the Übermensch: The Anticipation of Totalitarianism in Dostoevsky and Nietzsche." *Philosophical Alternatives Journal* 20 (2011): 147–61.

Ingenkamp, Heinz Gerd. "Gefühlsfalle oder Intertext? Kritisches zu Schopenhauers Lehren über Leid und Mitleid." In *Schopenhauer im Kontext: Deutsch-polnisches Schopenhauer-Symposium 2000*, 23–42. Würzburg: Königshausen und Neumann, 2002.

Jacobsen, Eric Paul. *From Cosmology to Ecology: The Monist World-View in Germany from 1770 to 1930*. New York: Peter Lang, 2005.

James, Ian. "Naming the Nothing: Nancy and Blanchot on Community." *Culture, Theory and Critique* 51, no. 2 (2010): 171–87.

Janouch, Gustav. *Conversations with Kafka*. Translated by Goronwy Rees. New York: New Directions, 1971.

Jünger, Ernst. *Der Waldgang*. Frankfurt: Vittorio Klostermann, 1952.

Kabus, Sylvia, and Reinhard Bernhof. *Umfeldblätter* 1 (2009). Leipziger Literaturverlag.

Kaiser, Corinna. *Gustav Landauer als Schriftsteller*. Berlin: De Gruyter, 2014.

Kant, Immanuel. *Critique of Judgement*. Translated by James Creed Meredith. Oxford: Oxford University Press, 2008.

Kauffeldt, Rolf. "'Rückkehr in die Großstadt': Bemerkungen zu einem frühexpressionistischen Text Gustav Landauers." In *Literarische Fundstücke: Wiederentdeckungen und Neuentdeckungen: Festschrift für Manfred Windfuhr*, edited by Manfred Windfuhr, Ariane Neuhaus-Koch, and Gertrude Cepl-Kaufmann, 224–35. Heidelberg: Winter, 2002.

Kelemen, János. *The Rationalism of Georg Lukács*. New York: Palgrave Macmillan, 2014.

Kirk, Timothy. *Nazism and the Working Class in Austria: Industrial Unrest and Political Dissent in the "National Community."* Cambridge: Cambridge Univeristy Press, 1996.

Koelb, Clayton. *Kafka's Rhetoric: The Passion of Reading*. Ithaca, NY: Cornell University Press, 1989.

Kracauer, Siegfried. *The Mass Ornament: Weimar Essays*. Translated by Thomas Y. Levin. Cambridge: Harvard University Press, 1995.

Kristeva, Julia. *Revolution in Poetic Language*. Translated Leon Roudiez. New York: Columbia University Press, 1984.

Kuhn, Axel. *Die deutsche Arbeiterbewegung*. Stuttgart: Reclam, 2004.

La Chinoise. Directed by Jean-Luc Godard (1968). DVD/ Neuilly-sur-Sein, Gaumont vidéo, 2012.

Lantz, K. A., ed. *The Dostoevsky Encyclopedia*. Westport, CT: Greenwood, 2004.

Lennox, Sara. "Geschlecht, Rasse und Geschichte in 'Der Fall Franza.'" In *text + kritik: Sonderband Ingeborg Bachmann*, edited by Sigrid Weigel, 156–79. Darmstadt: Wissenschaftliche Buchgesellschaft, 1984.

Lethen, Helmut. *Verhaltenslehre der Kälte*. Frankfurt: Suhrkamp, 1994.

Levi, Mijal. *Kafka and Anarchism*. New York: Revisionist, 1972.

Levine, Caroline. *Forms: Whole, Rhythm, Hierarchy, Network*. Princeton: Princeton University Press, 2015.

Lewis, Jill. *Workers and Politics in Occupied Austria, 1945–55*. Manchester: Manchester University Press, 2007.

Liska, Vivian. *When Kafka Says We: Uncommon Communities in German-Jewish Literature*. Bloomington: Indiana University Press, 2009.

Loescher, Jens. *Mythos, Macht und Kellersprache: Wolfang Hilbigs Prosa im Spiegel der Nachwende*. New York: Rodopi, 2003.

Lotman, Juri. *Culture and Explosion*. Translated by Wilma Clark. New York: De Gruyter, 2009.

Löwy, Michael. "Franz Kafka and Libertarian Socialism." *New Politics* 6, no. 3 (1997): 120–74.

———. *Redemption and Utopia: Jewish Libertarian Thought in Central Europe. A Study in Elective Affinity*. Stanford: Stanford University Press, 1992.

Lukács, Georg. *The Destruction of Reason*. Translated by Peter Palmer. Atlantic Highlands: Humanities Press, 1981.

Lunn, Eugene. *Prophet of Community: The Romantic Socialism of Gustav Landauer*. Berkeley: University of California Press, 1973.

Luxemburg, Rosa. *The Essential Rosa Luxemburg*. Edited by Helen Scott. Chicago: Haymarket, 2008.

Malchow, Timothy. "Thomas Bernhard's *Frost* and Adalbert Stifter: Literature, Legacy, and National Identity in the Early Austrian Second Republic." *German Studies Review* 28, no. 1 (2005): 65–84.

Mann, Thomas. *Doktor Faustus. Das Leben des deutschen Tonsetzers Adrian Leverkühn, erzählt von einem Freunde*. Edited by Ruprecht Wimmer and Stephan Stachorski. Frankfurt: Fischer, 2007.

Marx, Karl. *Grundrisse: Foundations of the Critique of Political Economy*. Translated by Martin Nicolaus. New York: Penguin, 1993.

Marx, Karl, and Frederick Engels. *The Marx-Engels Reader*, edited by Robert Tucker. New York: Norton, 1978.

———. *Selected Correspondence*. Moscow: Foreign Languages Publishing House, 1953.

McHale, Brian. *The Cambridge Introduction to Postmodernism*. New York: Cambridge University Press, 2015.

———. *Postmodernist Fiction*. London: Routledge, 1989.

Mendes-Flohr, Paul. *From Mysticism to Dialogue: Martin Buber's Transformation of German Social Thought*. Detroit: Wayne State University Press, 1989.

Morton, Timothy. *Ecology without Nature: Rethinking Environmental Aesthetics*. Cambridge: Harvard University Press, 2009.

Mukařovský, Jan. *The Word and Verbal Art: Selected Essays by Jan Mukařovský*. Translated by John Burband. New Haven: Yale University Press, 1977.

Nägele, Rainer. *Literarische Vexierbilder: Drei Versuche zu einer Figur*. Eggingen: Edition Isele, 2001.

Nagy, Gabriella. "Towards New Unrealities: An Interview with László Krasznahorkai." *Hungarian Literature Online*. May 2012. www.hlo.hu/news/krasznahorkai_interview.

Nancy, Jean-Luc. *The Inoperative Community*. Translated by Peter Connor. Minneapolis: University of Minnesota Press, 1991.

Nick, Rainer, and Anton Pelinka. *Bürgerkrieg–Sozialpartnerschaft: Das politische System Österreichs 1. und 2. Republik: Ein Vergleich*. Vienna: Jugend und Volk, 1984.

Norberg, Jakob. "On Display: Conditions of Critique in Austria." *Austrian Studies* 46, no. 1 (Spring 2013): 23–45.

Nordau, Max. *Degeneration*. New York: H. Fertig, 1968.

———. *Entartung*. Berlin: Duncker, 1896.

Novalis, *Philosophical Writings*. Translated by Margaret Mahony Stoljar. Albany: State University of New York Press, 1997.

Pawel, Ernst. *The Nightmare of Reason: A Life of Franz Kafka*. New York: Farrar, Straus and Giroux, 1984.

Petru, Marta. *An Infamous Past: E. M. Cioran and the Rise of Fascism in Romania*. Chicago: Ivan R. Dee, 2005.

Plessner, Helmuth. *The Limits of Community: A Critique of Social Radicalism*. Translated by Andrew Wallace. New York: Humanity Books, 1999.

Pribic, Rado. *Bonaventura's "Nachtwachen" and Dostoevsky's "Notes from the Underground": Comparison in Nihilism*. Munich: Sagner, 1974.

Pye, Gillian. "Trash and Transformation: The Search for Identity in Wolfgang Hilbig's *Die Kunde von den Bäumen* and *Alte Abdeckerei*." *New German Critique* 39, no. 2 (2012): 87–102.

Quintilian. *Quintilian's Institutes of Oratory; Or, Education of an Orator*. Translated by. J. S Watson. London: Bell, 1875.

Radkau, Joachim. *The Age of Ecology: A Global History*. Translated by Patrick Camiller. Cambridge: Polity, 2014.

Rafetseder, Hermann. *NS-Zwangsarbeits-Schicksale: Erkenntnisse zu Erscheinungsformen der Oppression und zum NS-Lagersystem aus der Arbeit des Österreichischen Versöhnungsfonds; Eine Dokumentation im Auftrag des Zukunftsfonds der Republik Österreich*. Bremen: Wiener Verlag für Sozialforschung, 2014.

Rathkolb, Oliver. "Die Zweite Republik (seit 1945)." In *Geschichte Österreichs*, edited by Thomas Winkelbauer, 525–94. Stuttgart: Reclam, 2015.

Rehmann, Jan. *Theories of Ideology*. Chicago: Haymarket, 2013.

Richardson, Brian. *Unnatural Narrative: Theory, History, and Practice*. Columbus: Ohio State University Press, 2015.

———. *Unnatural Voices: Extreme Narration in Modern and Contemporary Fiction*. Columbus: Ohio State University Press, 2006.

Richter, Gerhard. "Siegfried Kracauer and the Folds of Friendship." *German Quarterly* 70, no. 3 (1997): 233–46.

Riesman, David. *The Lonely Crowd: A Study of the Changing American Character*. New Haven: Yale University Press, 1950.

Rothenberg, Molly Anne. *The Excessive Subject*. Boston: Polity, 2010.

Rousseau, Jean-Jacques. *Discourse on the Origin of Inequality*. Translated by Donald Cress. Indianapolis: Hackett, 1992.

———. *Reveries of a Solitary Walker*. Translated by Russell Goulbourne. Oxford: Oxford University Press, 2011.

Schillemeit, Jost. "Kafkas *Beschreibung eines Kampfes:* Ein Beitrag zum Textverständnis und zur Geschichte von Kafkas Schreiben." In *Der junge Kafka*, edited by Gerhard Kurz, 102–32. Frankfurt: Suhrkamp, 1984.

Schmid, Georg. "Proklamation der 'JENSEITS-DES-POINT-OF-NO-RETURN-LITERATUR' in Form eines ternär strukturierten 'wissenschaftlichen Vortrags' und zweier burlekster Entr'actes." *Manuscripte* 82 (1983): 76–86.

Schmid, Wolf. *Der Textaufbau in den Erzählungen Dostoevskijs*. Munich: Wilhelm Fink, 1973.

Schmidt, Arno. *Brand's Haide: zwei Erzählungen*. Hamburg: Rohwolt, 1951.

Schulze, Ingo. "Nachwort." In Wolfgang Hilbig, *Werke*, 3:283–346. Frankfurt: Fischer, 2010.

Schumacher, Nicole. "Faschismus, Destruktion, Utopie: Die Bedeutung von Ingeborg Bachmanns 'Böhmen liegt am Meer' für Thomas Bernhards 'Auslöschung.'" *Zeitschrift für Deutsche Philologie* 118, no. 4 (1999): 572–91.

Schwartz, Yossef. "Martin Buber and Gustav Landauer: The Politicization of the Mystical." In *Martin Buber: Neue Perspektiven/New Perspectives*, edited by M. Zank, 209–22. Tübingen: Mohr Siebeck, 2006.

Sebald, W. G. *The Rings of Saturn*. Translated by Michael Hulse. New York: New Directions, 1998.

Shaftesbury, Antony Earl of. "Soliloquy; or, Advice to an Author." In *Characteristics of Men, Manners, Opinions, Times, with a Collection of Letters*, 1:131–312. Basil: Tourneisen, 1790.

Shah, Nayan. *Contagious Divides: Epidemics and Race in San Francisco's Chinatown*. Berkeley: University of California Press, 2001.

———. *Stranger Intimacy: Contesting Race, Sexuality, and the Law in the North American West*. Berkeley: University of California Press, 2011.

Sieg, Ulrich. *Jüdische Intellektuelle im Ersten Weltkrieg: Kriegserfahrungen, weltanschauliche Debatten und kulturelle Neuenwürfe*. Berlin: Akademie, 2001.

Sloane, T. O. "From Elocution to New Criticism: An Episode in the History of Rhetoric." *Rhetorica: Journal of the History of Rhetoric* 31, no. 3 (2013): 297–330.

Smith, David. "Nietzsche's Hinduism, Nietzsche's India: Another Look." *Journal of Nietzsche Studies* 28 (2004): 37–56.

Sokel, Walter. "Kafka's Beginnings: Narcissism, Magic, and the Function of Narration in 'Description of a Struggle.'" In *The Myth of Power and the Self: Essays on Franz Kafka*, 166–80. Detroit: Wayne State University Press, 2002.

Stach, Reiner. *Kafka: Die frühen Jahre*. Frankfurt: Fischer, 2014.

Stellino, Paolo. *Nietzsche and Dostoevsky: On the Verge of Nihilism*. New York: Peter Lang, 2015.

Stern, Fritz. *The Politics of Cultural Despair: A Study in the Rise of the Germanic Ideology*. Berkeley: University of California Press, 1961.

Stirner, Max. *The Ego and His Own: The Case of the Individual against Authority*. Translated by James Joseph Martin. London: Verso, 2014.

Stock, Brian. *Augustine's Inner Dialogue*. Cambridge: Cambridge University Press, 2010.

Sulzer, Johann Georg. *Allgemeine Theorie der schönen Künste: In einzelnen, nach alphabetischer Ordnung der Kunstwörter aufeinanderfolgenden, Artikeln abgehandelt, IV*. Hildesheim: Olms, 1967.

Suskind, Richard. *By Bullet, Bomb, and Dagger: The Story of Anarchism*. London: Macmillan, 1971.

Tönnies, Ferdinand, *Community and Civil Society*. Translated by Margaret Hollis. Cambridge: Cambridge University Press, 2001.

Trojanow, Ilija. "Freiheit, Skepsis, Totenkopf: Eine kurze Reise durch die glorreiche Vielfalt anarchistischen Denkens und Wirkens." In *Anarchistische Welten*. Hamburg: Edition Nautilus, 2012. Kindle eBook.

Verhoeven, Claudia. *The Odd Man Karakozov: Imperial Russia, Modernity, and the Birth of Terrorism*. Ithaca, NY: Cornell University Press, 2009.

Vidler, Anthony. *Warped Space: Art, Architecture, and Anxiety in Modern Culture*. Cambridge: MIT Press, 2001.

Vogl, Joseph. *Ort der Gewalt: Kafkas literarische Ethik*. Munich: Fink, 1990.

Volosinov, Valentin. *Marxism and the Philosophy of Language*. Translated by Ladislav Matejka and I. R. Titunik. New York: Seminar Press, 1973.

Walser, Robert. *The Robber*. Translated by Susan Bernofsky. Lincoln: University of Nebraska Press, 1986.

Wellbery, David. *Schopenhauers Bedeutung für die moderne Literatur*. Munich: Carl Friedrich von Siemens Stiftung, 1998.

Weller, Christine. "'Die Praktizierung des Gehirns': Zur Logik des psychotischen Sprechens am Beispiel Thomas Bernhards." *seminar* 43, no. 3 (2007): 499–507.

Wertheimer, Jürgen. *Der Güter Gefährlichstes, die Sprache: Zur Krise des Dialogs zwischen Aufklärung und Romantik*. Munich: Fink, 1990.

Willson, Michele. "Community in the Abstract: A Political and Ethical Dilemma?" In *Virtual Politics: Identity and Community in Cyberspace*, edited by David Holmes, 145–62. London: Sage, 1997.

Woodcock, George. *Anarchism*. Toronto: University of Toronto Press, 2004.

Zupancic, Alenka. *The Shortest Shadow: Nietzsche's Philosophy of the Two*. Boston: MIT Press, 2003.

INDEX